W9-AVT-091

SUICIDE BOMBERS
IN IRAQ

THE STRATEGY AND IDEOLOGY OF MARTYRDOM

SUICIDE BOMBERS IN IRAQ

THE STRATEGY AND IDEOLOGY OF MARTYRDOM

MOHAMMED M. HAFEZ

UNITED STATES INSTITUTE OF PEACE PRESS
Washington, D.C.

The views expressed in this book are those of the author alone. They do not necessarily reflect views of the United States Institute of Peace.

UNITED STATES INSTITUTE OF PEACE

1200 17th Street NW, Suite 200
Washington, DC 20036-3011

First published 2007

Printed in the United States of America

The paper used in this publication meets the minimum requirements of American National Standards for Information Science—Permanence of Paper for Printed Library Materials, AN SI Z39.48-1984.

Library of Congress Cataloging-in-Publication Data

Hafez, Mohammed M., 1970–
  Suicide bombers in Iraq : the strategy and ideology of martyrdom /
    Mohammed M. Hafez. p. cm.
  Includes bibliographical references and index.
  ISBN-13: 978-1-60127-004-7 (pbk. : alk. paper)
  ISBN-10: 1-60127-004-6 (pbk. : alk. paper)
1. Suicide bombers—Iraq. 2. Suicide bombings—Iraq. 3. Terrorism—Iraq.
4. Insurgency—Iraq. 5. Martyrdom—Islam. I. United States Institute of Peace.
II. Title.
  HV6433.I72H34 2007
  956.7044'3—dc22
                    2007014114

For peace in the land of the two rivers

CONTENTS

Suicide bombings in Iraq are among today's most pressing and puzzling issues. The number of attacks is extraordinarily high: Although hard to pinpoint, the total is certainly greater than all such incidents in other conflicts, including Israel-Palestine and Sri Lanka, combined. The attacks, most of which are by car bombs, are primarily directed by violent Islamists against fellow Muslims, and civilians are the targets of choice. The bombers are mostly foreign, not Iraqi, although we still do not know who is behind most attacks (the identity of 58 percent of the perpetrators is unknown). Clearly suicide bombing in Iraq is largely an imported phenomenon.

Although suicide bombings constitute only a part of the broad-based insurgency—whether or not it is a civil war—they are a critical part of the dilemma the U.S. government faces. The bombings both represent and provoke sectarian violence that has disrupted Iraq's state-building process and spread fear and insecurity. Approximately half of all suicide bombings occur in and around Baghdad, the center of power. Ironically, both the major group organizing them, al Qaeda in Iraq, and the U.S. government agree that the war in Iraq is an integral part of a global struggle and that what happens there will affect the future of Islamism and terrorism worldwide.

The author of *Manufacturing Human Bombs: The Making of Palestinian Suicide Bombers*, Mohammed Hafez has extensive experience as both a scholarly researcher and an expert adviser to many organizations and government agencies. *Suicide Bombers in Iraq* reflects his impressive knowledge and research. His extensive use of texts in Arabic is indispensable to the persuasiveness and authenticity of a carefully presented and documented argument. The phenomenon of suicide bombing has attracted immense attention, but his is the first in-depth study of the Iraqi experience. It is a particularly timely contribution to our understanding of contemporary political violence.

Hafez uses a social movement approach to explain in convincing detail the dynamics and complexities of the mobilization process behind suicide bombings. He emphasizes the way suicide attacks have been framed as martyrdom operations and how the sponsoring organizations have relied on existing social networks to recruit volunteers in the region and in Europe. He shows that although all the Sunni insurgent groups use the language of Islam, only two (al Qaeda in Iraq and Ansar al-Sunna) make suicide bombings the hallmark of their campaigns. The ideological basis of both groups is jihadi Salafism, not Iraqi nationalism, and these organizations are not rooted in Iraq's Sunni community. They seek state collapse in order to establish an Islamic regime that will replace the safe haven they lost in Afghanistan after 2001. Thus suicide attacks do not occur at random but follow a pattern; they are timed to coincide with both military and political initiatives by coalition forces and the Iraqi government.

The study reveals the heavy weight of the past, something those unfamiliar with history have not always appreciated. The legacy of Afghanistan in the 1980s and 1990s, for example, is still very much with us. The foreign networks on which al Qaeda in Iraq and Ansar al-Sunna depend—indeed the groups outside the country from which they sprang—grew out of the dispersion of the al Qaeda organization in Afghanistan. Without these contacts, few suicide bombers would have gone to Iraq. The strength of the jihadi Salafist movement in Iraq and elsewhere also results from the historical deficiencies of Middle Eastern Muslim regimes that have failed to provide effective or legitimate governing structures and, in the eyes of Islamists, failed to defend Muslims against Western encroachments. By suppressing dissent at home rather than trying to solve the problems that lay behind it, they drove radical Islamists abroad—a displacement of discontent that they did not discourage. Furthermore, suicide terrorism in Palestine provided an important basis for the legitimization of the tactic in Iraq. The practice of "martyrdom" had become normalized and accepted by many Muslims in the Middle East, facilitating its adoption under different circumstances in Iraq.

Another significant contribution of Hafez's analysis is its emphasis on the emotional as well as the ideological justifications of violence. What he calls the mythology of martyrdom historically has been associated with Shia, rather than Sunni, Islam. But in Iraq the jihadists have managed to develop a compelling narrative that justifies and venerates both self-sacrifice and the killing of civilians in the name of religion. They tell a story of humiliation and redemption through the heroic acts of a small band of defenders of the faith. Moreover, the religious story is grafted onto traditional values in Iraqi society, such as defense of honor and masculinity. Hafez shows how hatred of the Shia, regarded by jihadi Salafists as apostates, heretics, and collaborators since the very beginning of Islam, can justify violence that seems inexplicably cruel to outsiders.

Obviously the abuses at Abu Ghraib played directly into the hands of the jihadists. Disseminated via satellite television and the Internet, their videos appeal to susceptible audiences across the globe. The images they convey are a powerful recruiting tool.

This study's prognosis is a sober one. However well-intentioned U.S. actions might have been in 2003, by intervening in Iraq the United States has made the "near" and "far" enemies of Islamism into one. Mohammed Hafez ably explains how and why suicide terrorism has contributed to the "slide toward chaos" observed by the Iraq Study Group in 2006.

Martha Crenshaw
John E. Andrus Professor of Government
Wesleyan University

ACKNOWLEDGMENTS

This book would not have seen the light of day without the generous support of the United States Institute of Peace. In 2003 the Institute awarded me a two-year grant to study the tragic phenomenon of suicide bombers in the Palestinian-Israeli conflict. As I was beginning that research, war broke out in Iraq and suicide bombers exploded, literally and figuratively, onto the scene. This book tries to make sense of the appalling violence in Iraq since 2003. I am indebted to Steven Riskin, Kay Hechler, Linda Rabben, and other Institute staff for helping bring this volume to the public in a timely fashion.

This book also benefited tremendously from individuals who contributed resources, access, and insights. First and foremost, I wish to express my sincerest gratitude to Ami Pedahzur for inviting me to present my research at two conferences on suicide terrorism at the University of Texas at Austin in 2005 and 2006. More significantly, Dr. Pedahzur shared with me valuable data that would have taken me months to collect, even with the help of several research assistants. I also wish to extend my appreciation to Ryan Alsabagh for working with me on creating relevant charts of the quantitative data. He was most obliging and efficient. I owe him a special acknowledgment for his hard work. Three anonymous reviewers significantly enriched the content of this book with their valuable feedback.

I want to thank Nicole Argo and John Tirman at the Massachusetts Institute of Technology for inviting me to present my research on Iraq at the "Transnational Violence in the Persian Gulf" workshop at MIT's Center for International Studies on April 20–21, 2006; Payam Foroughi, Hakan Yavuz, and the Hinckley Institute at the University of Utah for inviting me to give the plenary address on Iraq for the Middle East and Central Asia Politics, Economics, and Society Conference, September 7–9, 2006; and Professor Bruce Hoffman of Georgetown University for providing valuable feedback on chapter 3.

I am indebted to staff and personnel at Fort Leavenworth, Kansas, for giving me access to resources and U.S. servicemen who came back from Iraq. Finally, I am privileged to have come to know and befriend Thuy, Quintan, Rich, Guy, and Jonathan. Their unrelenting support and encouragement extended far beyond this book.

As any writer who is married with children would confess, such a labor of love can put a strain on relations with those whose love truly matters the most. I am fortunate to have an understanding wife, Abby, who contained her frustration at the seemingly endless hours I spent reading, writing, and "zoning out" at the dinner table. She gave me the time and space to do what I am passionate about; to her I owe a debt of gratitude that can never be repaid fully.

To my two boys Omar and Kareem: I have been away too much from your playtime. You are too young to read this book and too innocent to contemplate its content. I hope one day you will understand.

1920 RB	1920 Revolution Brigades of the Islamic Resistance Movement
AI	Ansar al-Islam
AQI	Al Qaeda in Iraq
ASG	Ansar al-Sunna Group
CA	Conqueror Army (also known as Conquest Army [*Jaysh al-Fatihin*])
COIN	Counterinsurgency
CPA	Coalition Provisional Authority
DST	Territorial Surveillance Directorate
FS	Fedayeen Saddam
GCMAF	General Command of the Mujahidin of the Armed Forces (Baathists)
GIA	Armed Islamic Group
GICM	Moroccan Islamic Combatants Group
IAI	Islamic Army of Iraq
IED	Improvised explosive device
JCB	Joint Coordination Bureau for Jihad Groups
LTTE	Liberation Tigers of Tamil Eelam (also known as Tamil Tigers)
MA	Muhammad's Army
MAI	Mujahidin Army in Iraq
MCC	Mujahidin Central Command (Baathists)
MENA	Middle East and North Africa
MSC	Mujahidin Shura Council
OSC	Open Source Center
PFLP	Popular Front for the Liberation of Palestine
PKK	Kurdistan Workers Party
RA	Al Rashidin Army
SCIRI	Supreme Council for the Islamic Revolution in Iraq
SDAB	Salah al-Din al-Ayoubi Brigades of the Islamic Front for Iraqi Resistance
SVBIED	Suicide vehicle-borne improvised explosive device
TWJ	Al Tawhid wal-Jihad (Monotheism and Jihad, later AQI)

I finished writing this book in October 2006. However, data collection for the majority of charts that appear in chapter 3 ended in February 2006. As a result, some developments that occurred after February 2006 are not reflected in these charts. This limitation is unfortunate, but it is also inevitable. Sorting through press reports and other source materials to update charts with reliable data would have delayed publication by several months, during which time events in Iraq would have necessitated further data collection and, thus, further delays. I have tried to compensate for this shortcoming by including some of the most recent data from other sources in the main text.

The data in the descriptive charts are based on open-source information and papers of record. These resources include the Open Source Center (OSC, previously Foreign Broadcast Information Service, FBIS), which can be located at www.opensource.gov. However, this is a password-protected Web site and requires U.S. government permission for access. Other sources include the *New York Times*, the *Washington Post*, and other news agencies accessible through the LexisNexis Academic search engine. Chart 2 draws from data in the Brookings Institution Iraq Index (www.brookings.edu/iraqindex).

I checked each data point for accuracy by seeking specific information on the date and location of an attack, as well as the casualty rate and group claiming responsibility. A news report that did not include at least the date and location of the attack was left out of the data. This selection process undoubtedly will raise objections that this book underestimates the number of suicide attacks in Iraq. That may be the case, but the procedure was necessary to ensure the reliability of the data.

This book refers to many documents and videos produced by insurgents in Iraq. They were downloaded from their Web sites or the sites of their supporters. Unfortunately, many of these sites regularly disappear and reappear under different Web addresses. Therefore, it is very likely that some of the Web sites in the notes cannot be accessed. I have downloaded all the insurgent video clips referred to in chapters 4 and 5, as well as all the Arabic documents from the *Tawhid wal Jihad* Web site referred to repeatedly in chapters 4 and 5. This Web site is frequently down. Readers interested in a specific document for research purposes may send an e-mail request to me at hafezm@umkc.edu.

The source data for appendix 2, which contains the names of 102 known suicide bombers in Iraq, came from insurgent materials such as al Qaeda in Iraq's *Biographies of Eminent Martyrs*, an online publication distributed through jihadi forums; video clips of suicide operations distributed by insurgent groups; and a 157-page document entitled *Martyrs in Iraq*, featuring the names of 394 volunteers (mostly Arabs) who perished in that country. The document was distributed on the Majdah Forum (www.majdah.com/vb).

I transliterated Arabic words phonetically so that the reader may pronounce them as an Arabic speaker does. As a result, I did not always adhere to the *International Journal of Middle Eastern Studies* transliteration system customarily used by specialists on the Middle East. I also did not use diacritic marks to denote the Arabic letter `*ayn* (`a, `u, or `i) except in rare instances when it might be confused with the letter *alif*. Finally, specialists usually distinguish the collective noun *Shia* from the singular or adjectival *Shii* (for example, "the Shia in Najaf attended a Shii shrine"), but I use Shia throughout to avoid confusing nonspecialists.

SUICIDE BOMBERS IN IRAQ

SUICIDE BOMBERS IN HISTORICAL AND THEORETICAL PERSPECTIVE

H ardly a day passes without bad news coming out of Iraq. By now we are accustomed to the daily headlines: "String of bombings kills Shia civilians in Baghdad," "Suicide bombers target police recruitment center," "Five U.S. soldiers killed by roadside bomb." However, nothing is more mind-boggling to observers of this conflict than the pace of suicide attacks in Iraq. From March 22, 2003, to August 18, 2006, approximately 514 suicide attacks took place there.

Even though suicide attacks account for a very small percentage of overall insurgent violence in Iraq, which includes the use of improvised explosive devices (IEDs), rockets, snipers, and hit-and-run-operations, the rate of suicide attacks in the Iraqi insurgency has surpassed the number of suicide operations by all previous insurgent groups combined, including those by Hezbollah in Lebanon, the Tamil Tigers in Sri Lanka, and Hamas in Israel.[1] More important, despite their relatively small number in the overall insurgency, suicide attacks have a disproportionate impact on political developments in Iraq because of their targets, lethality, and psychological potency.

It should not have turned out this way. Those who planned the war on Iraq assumed it would be relatively easy to topple the regime and rebuild its institutions. The war was presumed to be a solid stepping-stone to major political restructuring in the Middle East, the likes of which had not been seen since the formation of modern Arab states following World War I. The regime was fragile, unpopular, defeated on the battlefield time and again. Remove the leadership of the defunct Baathist party and the people would applaud, welcome the coalition with open arms, and accept its plans unquestioningly. Iraq is not like Afghanistan, U.S. officials repeatedly said. It is rich in oil, steeped in secularism, and has intellectual and technocratic elites capable of taking the helm and administering the state. Above all, it had a developed opposition in exile that had been working with the United States and other Western governments to prepare for the new order in Iraq. Things seemed to be in place for a swift victory, one that might have shocked and awed even the coalition by exceeding all its expectations. By May 2003, nearly two months into the invasion, things seemed to be on track. "Mission accomplished," the banner read. The coalition did not see them coming—the insurgents, the suicide bombers.

Since the invasion of Iraq in March 2003, more than 3,100 American soldiers have been killed and 23,000 wounded.[2] Estimates of Iraqi deaths since the invasion in March 2003 range from as low as 57,000 to as high as 650,000; the actual toll of Iraqi deaths, injuries, displaced, and disappeared may never be known.[3] Instead of becoming a flourishing democracy in the U.S. camp, Iraq has plunged into anarchy and ethnosectarian political strife that is tearing the country asunder.

Rather than deliver a clear message to terrorists around the world that the United States would not brook an attack on its homeland and stand idly by in the face of murderous terrorism, the occupation of Iraq has delivered the opposite message: Islamic resistance and martyrdom can defeat a superpower, just as jihadists did against the Soviet Union in Afghanistan during the 1980s. Involvement in Iraq has not strengthened the United States and made it more secure in the face of extremism; instead Iraq has turned into an inviting war zone for jihadists seeking a place to call home after the fall of Afghanistan's Taliban regime in late 2001. Today Iraq has entered a civil war whose duration, scope, and magnitude have yet to crystallize. Talk has faded of a pluralist democracy that could serve as a guiding light to other authoritarian regimes in the region. Iraqis just want an end to the bloodshed and the insecurity. Many in the United States just want to get out.

What went wrong? Who are these insurgents? Where did they come from? What do they want? Why are they deploying suicide bombers? Why are they killing their own people? What will it take to stop them? Is it too late? Answers to these questions are central to salvaging the situation in Iraq and ending the bloodshed. This book delves deep into the Iraqi insurgency to map its political and strategic divides and explain the patterns of suicide violence therein. We cannot answer all these questions yet, but the broad outlines of the insurgency and the suicide bombings within it are becoming clearer as time passes.

Suicide attacks in Iraq arose after a U.S.-led invasion of the country and a subsequent occupation by multinational forces. Yet the overwhelming majority of suicide attacks in Iraq has targeted Iraqi security forces and Shia civilians, not coalition forces. The perpetrators of these suicide bombings appear to be mainly non-Iraqis who volunteered to fight and die in Iraq. Many came from Saudi Arabia, but substantial numbers have come from Europe; neighboring Arab states such as Syria, Kuwait, and Jordan; and North Africa. Most of the bombers appear to be connected to transnational networks associated with "second-generation" jihadists who trained in Afghanistan during the 1990s or militants fleeing arrest in their home or host countries. These suicide bombers have dragged Iraq into civil war because their attacks overwhelmingly target Shia police and civilians. They are also foiling U.S. plans to stabilize the country and turn it into a democratic regime and a solid ally in a sea of religious radicalism, entrenched authoritarianism, and hostile states with nuclear ambitions. Understanding this phenomenon, therefore, is vitally important for U.S. national security, foreign policy in the Muslim world, and the war on terrorism.

In previous suicide bombing campaigns, observers asked what motivated ordinary men and women to strap explosives around their bodies, walk into crowded public places, and blow themselves up to kill themselves and others around them. In Iraq the questions have become much more complex: What motivates non-Iraqis to make their way to Iraq to kill fellow Muslims? Why are Saudis flocking to die in Iraq? What motivates a Tunisian living in Italy and a female Muslim convert living in Belgium to go to Iraq to kill people they have never met or from whom they have not felt direct oppression? How could a country like Iraq, which never experienced suicide terrorism before 2003, produce the largest arsenal of "martyrs" ever seen in a comparatively short time? Why are the Shia and Iraqi security forces the main targets of the suicide bombers? The vexing questions seem endless.

In this study I try to answer some of these questions, drawing extensively on national and international, open-source intelligence and papers of record; primary sources from insurgent groups, such as their online documents and videos; and some interviews with U.S. service personnel who are currently in or have returned from Iraq. It is too early to make definitive statements about the identities of the suicide bombers, where they come from, what motivates them to fight and die in Iraq, and why recruiters have successfully mobilized such a large number of them in a relatively short time. Therefore, the findings of this book must be seen as preliminary and subject to further research. However, it is possible to broadly sketch the phenomenon of suicide bombings in Iraq from the limited information available. This study may serve as one of many that fill the gaps in our knowledge about the insurgency in Iraq and suicide terrorism in general.

HISTORICAL PERSPECTIVE ON SUICIDE BOMBINGS

Since the early 1980s many insurgent and terrorist groups, including secular nationalists, Marxists, and religious fundamentalists, have adopted the tactic of suicide attacks to coerce governments into making concessions, changing policies, abandoning territory, or desisting from negotiations.[4] I use the terms *suicide attacks*, *suicide bombings*, and *suicide terrorism* interchangeably. Despite some controversy as to what to label or how to define this phenomenon, I view suicide terrorism as a premeditated attack by an individual who willingly uses his or her body to carry or deliver explosives to attack, kill, or maim others.[5] These attacks usually target civilians, but they could accompany conventional battlefield attacks against soldiers. Key to this definition is the requirement of self-immolation to execute an operation—the death of the bomber is a necessary part of carrying out an attack. This is different from a high-risk operation, where the death of the attacker is likely but not inevitable in the execution of an assault.

Moreover, suicide bombings are different from operations in which the attackers fight to the end in the hope of achieving martyrdom. In the latter, although the intent is still to die, the death of the individual is not necessary for the operation to take place. This narrow definition of suicide terrorism focuses mainly on the bombers known to have killed themselves in Iraq, not all the transnational volunteers in the Iraqi insurgency.

The introduction of suicide bombings in the modern world is most commonly associated with the Japanese kamikaze pilots of World War II. The imperial government of Japan organized and sanctioned kamikazes against the U.S. naval fleet in the Pacific in a last-ditch effort to forestall the allied invasion of the Japanese mainland. Although there can be no doubt that some kamikazes volunteered wittingly for their mission, others were ambivalent about what they had been compelled to undertake.[6] The kamikazes did not fit neatly into the category of suicide terrorists because they were military men who attacked military targets, not civilians. However, as the phenomenon of suicide attacks has evolved since the 1980s, discrimination between military and civilian targets has all but withered away.

Suicide attacks were reintroduced during the 1980s, beginning in Lebanon. The most dramatic were the suicide bombings of the U.S. embassy and U.S. and French peacekeeping forces in Beirut in 1983. Their significance stems not only from the high casualty rate they produced—a total of 299 killed and hundreds wounded—but also from their demonstration effect. The subsequent withdrawal of multinational forces from Lebanon sent the message that suicide attacks were an effective tactic. This form of violence continued during the 1990s, mainly by Hezbollah against Israeli targets in southern Lebanon.[7] During the 1990s, Palestinian groups deployed thirty-three bombers in twenty-six separate attacks against Israeli targets. However, the pace of attacks increased many times during the second Palestinian uprising known as al Aqsa intifada. From October 2000 to February 2005, approximately 116 suicide attacks took place.[8]

Suicide missions are not limited to the Middle East or to Islamic groups. The Liberation Tigers of Tamil Eelam (LTTE) in Sri Lanka have perfected sophisticated suicide missions, which succeeded in killing the former prime minister of India and the president of Sri Lanka. According to Gunaratna, since July 5, 1987, the date of its first suicide operation, LTTE has carried out at least 250 suicide attacks. The Tamil Tigers set a new precedent by training children for and deploying women in suicide operations.[9] The Marxist Kurdistan Workers Party (PKK) in Turkey and ethnonationalist and Islamist Chechens in Russia also used suicide terrorism. In both places female bombers played a major role in the attacks.[10]

Since the 1980s suicide attacks have spread to Afghanistan, Bangladesh, Britain, Egypt, India, Indonesia, Iran, Iraq, Israel, Jordan, Kenya, Kuwait, Lebanon, Morocco, Pakistan, Palestinian territories, Qatar, Russia, Saudi Arabia, Sri Lanka, Tanzania, Tunisia, Turkey, the United States, Uzbekistan, and Yemen. The question is why.

THEORETICAL PERSPECTIVES ON SUICIDE BOMBINGS

Studies of suicide terrorism around the world have produced a number of plausible explanations. Some argue that oppression, injustice, and personal trauma produce a dual desire for escapism and revenge, leading those physically and psychologically injured to volunteer for suicide missions.[11] Others point to the strategic logic of suicide attacks in the context of occupation and asymmetry in power between occupier and occupied.[12] Still others explain this phenomenon by referring to factional competition between groups and the dynamic of "outbidding," whereby one group adopts deadlier measures against a hated enemy to outdo its competitors and, consequently, garner greater public support, financing, and recruits.[13] Some cite religious fanaticism and the cult of martyrdom produced by fundamentalist groups and worldviews.[14] Still others contend that the explanation of suicide terrorism lies in the interaction among individual motivations, organizational strategies, and societal conflicts.[15] All these explanations are reasonable, and therefore I will evaluate them in the conclusion in light of the evidence from Iraq.

What makes suicide terrorism an intriguing puzzle is the inability of experts to identify a common socioeconomic, religious, or psychological profile of the bombers. Although some of the suicide bombers are poor, others come from middle-class or affluent families; some come from impoverished societies (such as Egypt, Syria, or Pakistan), while others come from relatively well-developed countries (such as England, Italy, or Saudi Arabia). Many of the suicide bombers are Muslims, but before the second Palestinian uprising and the invasion of Iraq in the first decade of the new millennium, most suicide bombers came from non-Muslim countries or were secular nationalists, not religious fundamentalists. Both men and women carry out suicide attacks. Educated and uneducated individuals volunteer to be martyrs. The majority of the bombers have been in their teens and twenties, but more than a few were in their middle or senior years. Many of the bombers had previous histories of violent activism, but equally prevalent were bombers who carried out only one violent political act in their life: a suicide attack. Some were traumatized by ongoing conflicts, but others seem to have identified with the suffering of coreligionists or compatriots, even though they did not endure direct personal suffering at the hands of their victims. The only thing experts seem to agree on is that suicide bombers are normal individuals; they are not "crazy" or born with a psychopathology that predisposes them to violent activism. This finding, of course, is of limited value and does not aid in identifying, let alone combating, suicide terrorists.

Profiling suicide bombers may not be possible, but researchers have identified four critical advantages to suicide terrorism that explain its appeal across militant groups:

- Tactical effectiveness in comparison to conventional terrorism;
- Ability to communicate strategic messages to target audiences;
- Potent psychological impact on targeted countries;
- Ability to enhance the legitimacy of insurgent organizations among their constituent publics.

Suicide bombings in Iraq have introduced a fifth element: destroying an emerging democratic government and sparking a sectarian civil war.

TACTICAL ADVANTAGES OF SUICIDE BOMBINGS

Suicide terrorism is one of the means for weak groups to coerce strong opponents into making concessions or changing their policies. Observers point out four tactical advantages to this strategy.

Kill Ratio. Suicide terrorism on average kills and injures more people with a single attack than does any other form of terrorism. According to one estimate, conventional terrorist attacks since the early 1980s have killed on average less than one person per incident, whereas suicide attacks during the same period have killed on average twelve people per incident. Through suicide terrorism those seeking to coerce opponents can impose unacceptable human and material losses, on average twelve times deadlier than conventional terrorism, on the targeted countries.[16]

Smart Bombs. Suicide terrorists are "smart bombs" that can pinpoint their targets, walk into highly secure areas, make last-minute adjustments in their plans, and choose the time of detonation to inflict the greatest damage. In Israel, in at least two incidents bombers changed their targets minutes before their operations because they noticed extra security presence near their original targets. In one recent incident in Iraq, the suicide bomber waited for crowds to gather before setting off his explosives, killing scores of civilians. This tactical flexibility is rare in conventional terrorist attacks or even with the most expensive and technologically advanced weaponry.

Cost-effectiveness. Suicide bombing is an attractive option for terrorist groups seeking a cost-effective way to inflict the greatest possible damage on their opponents with the least number of cadres. In highly repressive environments where recruitment is difficult, terrorist groups become conscious of the need to cause the greatest damage without sacrificing many valued assets. Suicide terrorism allows them to inflict mass casualties with one or a few bombers. If we assume that a suicide attack kills at least three times as many people as a conventional terrorist attack, it would require three separate attacks to achieve what one suicide bomber could achieve in a single mission. Also, suicide operations do not require complicated escape plans that put other organizational personnel at risk of capture.

Some may question the assertion that suicide attacks are cost-effective. A more efficient use of resources demands that groups protect the lives of their members so they can attack more than once. This is especially important if recruitment is difficult and insurgents are waging a war of attrition against a powerful foe that cannot be defeated through a few mass-casualty attacks.[17] A suicide bomber can strike only once; a living militant can attack again and again. This criticism, however, assumes that terrorists are operating in security environments where they can attack and then evade arrest or death for an extended period. In some conflict areas this may be the case, but in places such as Israel or Saudi Arabia vigilant security services often can capture and punish militants after they have acted once or twice. For example, Palestinian militants have learned through experience that attacking a military post in the West Bank through conventional hit-and-run operations probably will result in their capture or death, because Israel has a long history of protecting its personnel in danger zones. Less risky tactics, such as firing homemade rockets or exploding roadside bombs, rarely kill their targets, making them less effective as coercive tactics.[18] In these circumstances it might be more effective to engage in mass-casualty attacks and lose one bomber than to engage in conventional, low-casualty attacks and assume the risk of protecting a wanted terrorist. Given the substantial difference between the kill rate of a suicide attack and that of a conventional operation, some groups might deem it more cost-effective to lose one member in a mass-casualty suicide operation than to send several militants on operations repeatedly to achieve the same kill rate.

In addition, every organization, even informal groups, engages in a division of labor in which the most experienced and skilled members are protected to maintain the organization, while those with fewer skills can be sacrificed for the cause without loss of organizational continuity.[19] Finally, not all violent groups are pursuing a strategy of attrition. Some pursue a strategy of sabotaging peace, as some Palestinian groups tried to do during the Oslo peace process from 1993 to 2000.[20] Others follow a strategy of agitation, in which the goal is to induce the state to overreact by excessively repressing a category of people such as workers, Muslims, or Sunnis. Such repression can turn these people into supporters of terrorists. Many of the anarchists and other left-wing terrorists in Europe and Latin America adopted this strategy in the past. The attacks of September 11, 2001, could arguably be seen as a form of agitation in the Muslim world. In such instances, the desire to succeed in producing mass casualties (or destroying hard targets) can override the need to protect valuable personnel. In Iraq suicide attacks are not about waging a war of attrition or "death by a thousand cuts," but producing sectarian polarization that can mobilize Sunnis behind the most extreme and marginal faction in the insurgency.

Group Security. Suicide terrorists are less likely to be captured and forced to reveal their recruiters' modus operandi. Even if the mission fails to kill or injure anyone besides the suicide terrorist, the recruiters of the terrorist remain undetected, able to recruit others for future operations.

SUICIDE TERRORISM AS STRATEGIC COMMUNICATION

Suicide terrorism is intended not only to kill; it also is an effective form of strategic communication with the targeted countries, as well as the international community and the terrorists' own constituency.[21] Observers of this phenomenon point out at least five strategic messages that suicide terrorists seek to communicate.

Determination. Suicide attackers send the message to the targeted country that they are so determined to achieve their goals that they are willing to die for their cause. Suicide terrorists' willingness to sacrifice their lives voluntarily is often interpreted as the ultimate testimony to the righteousness of the cause. This extraordinary commitment cannot be deterred easily by the threat of counterterrorism. The targeted country, therefore, is coerced into addressing the terrorists' underlying demands.

Commitment to Escalate. Suicide attacks heighten expectations of future attacks in three ways. First, suicide terrorists often issue prerecorded statements that they are part of an ever-growing pool of "living martyrs" awaiting the opportunity to serve their cause. Second, by breaching societal taboos and international norms on the use of violence, they make threats of escalation appear credible. If they did it once, surely they are likely to do it again. Third, groups that send suicide bombers are under internal organizational pressure to continue such attacks, so that the deaths of the initial "martyrs" are not in vain. Failure to continue on this path without achieving the organization's major objectives could demoralize the organization's members.

Deterrence of Neutral Observers. The extraordinarily destructive nature of suicide terrorism sends a message to uncommitted allies to stay on the sidelines lest they become targets of mass-casualty attacks. For example, the suicide attacks in Britain on July 7, 2005—clearly intended to coerce Britain to abandon its support of the United States in Iraq and Afghanistan—also included a message to other governments, including Italy and Denmark, to reconsider their current alliance with the United States.

Shaming the Enemy. Suicide attacks send the message that oppression by the targeted country has reached such unbearable levels that ordinary men and women are willing to kill themselves to end it. In reaction to conventional terrorism against civilians, the natural tendency of neutral observers is to sympathize with the victims of terrorism. However, suicide terrorism, generally speaking, shifts sympathy toward the perpetrators of violence because they are seen as victims of intolerable oppression; otherwise they would not have taken such extraordinary measures for their cause. However, there are limits to this aspect of suicide terrorism. Suicide attacks can result in a public backlash if the attackers appear to be unrestrained in their killing of noncombatants, especially civilians in their constituent group. Suicide bombings in Saudi Arabia that killed innocent Muslims resulted in a public outcry against the terrorists. Similarly, the massacre of schoolchildren in Beslan, Russia, resulted in worldwide condemnations of Chechen terrorists.[22]

As in the case of public backlash, international support is likely to decline after the initial wave of sympathy for the suicide terrorists. International backlash emerges when suicide terrorism is no longer localized within conflict zones but instead diffuses worldwide. In Europe, for example, sympathy for Palestinian suicide bombers waned as suicide attacks spread to America on September 11 and subsequently to countries around the world. This decline in international support stems partly from international diplomacy to counter suicide bombings, as more and more countries feel the effects of this form of terrorism.

Solicitation of Recruits. Suicide attacks serve as a wake-up call to the terrorists' constituent publics, asking them to make similar sacrifices for the cause. Suicide terrorists try to achieve this goal in four ways. First, suicide terrorists are likely to capture national and international media attention because of the extraordinary nature of their mission. Suicide terrorism is shocking and seemingly incomprehensible, attracting worldwide media attention. Media coverage helps terrorists publicize their grievances and solicit support in the form of financing, political support, and volunteers. Their prerecorded statements contain messages to the supporting public to join the struggle; otherwise the sacrifices of the "heroic martyrs" will be in vain. This is especially the case with female suicide bombers, who send the implicit message that women have risen to the challenge, so it is men's turn to do the same. Second, suicide terrorists send the message that their target enemies are vulnerable to attack; they are not invincible. In other words, suicide attackers try to empower weaker parties by showing them the way to inflict maximum pain on their enemies. Third, suicide terrorists foster a culture of martyrdom by highlighting the "heroism" and sacrifice of their members. Groups such as Hamas in the Palestinian territories, the Tamil Tigers in Sri Lanka, and al Qaeda honor their suicide bombers with video montages, poems, commemorative books, songs, posters, or monuments. The veneration of suicide terrorists reduces public inhibitions against suicide and killing civilians.

PSYCHOLOGICAL IMPACT

Suicide bombing, like other tactics of terrorism, is a form of psychological warfare. It is intended not only to kill and demonstrate commitment to a cause, but also to demoralize the public of the targeted country. Demoralization of the general public is intended to weaken its resolve in the face of adversity and induce it to pressure its government to compromise or change policies. Suicide attacks are more potent than conventional terrorism in their psychological impact. Two elements of suicide terrorism make it a powerful tool of psychological warfare.

Intimate Killers. Suicide attacks rarely distinguish between combatants and civilians. In this respect, they are not different from other forms of terrorism. However, unlike conventional bombs, which often cannot distinguish between the old and the young, men and women, soldiers and civilians, human bombs can make these distinctions because they walk among their victims, hear their voices, and look into their faces. The intimate nature of suicide terrorism is psychologically damaging because the killers appear to be callous and exceptionally cruel. Furthermore, suicide attacks are carried out by individuals who often appear undistinguishable from their victims, heightening the sense of insecurity among the general public. One cannot profile suicide terrorists because they purposely disguise themselves during their missions to look like their victims.

Unprecedented and Incomprehensible Threat. Suicide attacks are not new in history, but the general public views them as an unprecedented threat to its security because of their relatively recent revival. The public's unfamiliarity with this tactic, at least initially, naturally raises its anxiety and apprehension about this "new" form of terrorism. Moreover, suicide terrorism is not easily comprehensible; indeed, it appears illogical or downright crazy to the general public. After all, would rational persons kill themselves to kill others? Terrorist groups often seek to make suicide attacks appear motivated solely by the "love of martyrdom," while their enemies are motivated solely by the "love of life."

The apparent illogic of suicide attacks is disconcerting because it implies that the terrorists are not people with whom one could reason. Moreover, their willingness to die implies that they cannot be deterred. However, the psychological impact of suicide terrorism lessens over time through the process of normalization; its shock value diminishes as the tactic becomes overused. So there are limits to the psychological potency of suicide attacks. For example, in Israel the general public has become resilient in the face of such attacks. Suicide bombings are seen as tragic but not unprecedented or incomprehensible. People have become accustomed to them. Normalization is also achieved through government efforts that quickly repair the scene of the attack and restore it to its original condition, encouraging the public to proceed as it did before the attack.

ENHANCING ORGANIZATIONAL LEGITIMACY

Suicide terrorism is directed not only against the targeted country. It is also oriented toward enhancing the legitimacy and appeal of the terrorist group for its constituent public. Suicide terrorism might increase the legitimacy of terrorist groups among their societies in two ways.

Factional Competition. Groups that deploy suicide attacks appear the most daring, heroic, and sacrificing. These qualities naturally raise their legitimacy among the public in the context of conflict with outside groups. For example, in the case of Israel, suicide bombings by Hamas during the Oslo peace process years did not raise the appeal of the organization because the public was supporting the peace process. However, when the second Palestinian uprising broke out in late 2000, Hamas's use of suicide bombings increased its appeal tremendously because the public saw the attacks as just retribution against a powerful enemy that was unwilling to compromise peacefully. Other groups, such as the secular Al Aqsa Martyrs Brigades, felt forced to emulate Hamas by using suicide terrorism. Similarly, the Lebanese Hezbollah was a new actor on the political scene when it first deployed suicide attacks in 1983 against U.S. and French targets. The success of those attacks resulted in its meteoric rise in popularity among the Shia population in southern Lebanon, marginalizing its Shia competitor, Amal. Today Hezbollah is a premier Islamic organization because of its perceived sacrifices for the cause of liberating southern Lebanon from Israel's presence.[23]

Induce Repression. Suicide terrorism naturally induces an initial strong response from the targeted country. Repression is generally undesirable for terrorist groups because it forces them to divert their human and material resources away from the struggle. However, when the terrorist group lacks general appeal or a hospitable environment, indiscriminate repression following suicide attacks can create anger toward the repressive regime and sympathy for the terrorists. Historically, several terrorist groups sought to provoke their governments into taking extremely repressive measures against the population to compel a passive public to take action on the side of the terrorists. Some have argued that al Qaeda's 9/11 attacks were intended to induce a strong American response in the Muslim world, which al Qaeda assumed would compel Muslims to take its side.

Many of the elements present in previous campaigns of suicide terrorism also can be found in the Iraqi insurgency. Insurgent groups that utilize this tactic do so in the name of tactical effectiveness, strategic necessity, and psychological effect. They also use their attacks to show that they are legitimate actors willing to pay the ultimate price to liberate the land and purge it of foreign impositions and local collaborators. However, several aspects of suicide bombings in Iraq are unique in the contemporary history of suicide terrorism. While researching this book, I concluded that current researchers on suicide terrorism would have to refocus their analytical lenses to describe, let alone explain, the rise of suicide bombings in the Iraqi insurgency.

A SOCIAL MOVEMENT FRAMEWORK OF ANALYSIS

One of the most puzzling aspects of suicide attacks in Iraq is the transnational character of many of the bombers. These suicidal militants were not homegrown but came from as far away as Europe and North Africa. Even those from neighboring countries such as Saudi Arabia, Syria, and Jordan assumed tremendous risk in making their way into Iraq and paid the ultimate price once they got there. Moreover, these transnational "martyrs" were mobilized by informal networks, not states or formal organizations that could provide them with money, airline tickets, or a consolation package for their surviving families. Finally, these willing "martyrs" killed fellow Muslims; more Iraqis than non-Muslim foreign occupiers have died at the hands of suicide bombers.

In this study I apply a social movement approach to solve the puzzle of the transnational "martyrs" in Iraq. Such an approach explains how groups outside state structures mobilize collective action to make demands for reform or revolution. Mobilizing collective action consists of more than calling on people to rise up or take to the streets; it involves framing social ills as threats and opportunities for action, networking among activists and their constituencies, building formal and informal organizations, forging collective identities and alliances, making claims against opponents and states, and motivating individuals to assume personal costs when the benefits of success are not readily apparent.

In other words, the dynamics of mobilization in social movements are not too different from the dynamics of transnational terrorism. Specifically, suicide terrorism by transnational activists in Iraq and social movements both involve actors "in conflictual relations with clearly identified opponents; ... linked by dense informal networks; [and sharing] a distinct collective identity." [24]

Social movement approaches have a distinct advantage over purely political, psychological, or cultural approaches because they are interdisciplinary and multipronged. They analyze relationships among political environments, organizational dynamics, and cultural frameworks. [25] Above all, they seek to explain collective action at three levels of analysis: individual involvement, organizational strategies, and sociopolitical facilitators of activism.

These three levels of analysis—individual, organizational, and societal—are necessary to understand suicide terrorism in Iraq. Consider the following scenario. A Tunisian Muslim living in Europe is angry about what is going on in Iraq and is highly motivated to "do something." Despite his high motivations, this would-be insurgent cannot act on his own, generally speaking, unless he knows other individuals in groups willing to indulge his desire to fight in Iraq. Immediately, we begin to see the interaction between individual motivations and preexisting organizational ties or networks.

But why would groups make the effort of helping would-be insurgents and take the associated risk if they did not deem it advantageous in some way to do so? If this Tunisian arrived in Iraq looking to carry out a "martyrdom operation," the groups that would equip him with the explosives would do so not because they wanted to fulfill his death wish, but because they saw some benefit coming out of his impending mission. Without a clear purpose, or a strategy perhaps, the group would not undertake this effort—not on a consistent basis, anyway. Therefore, individual motivations must align with the group's strategy or objectives. Without this symbiosis, suicide terrorism would not get off the ground.

But what shapes the group's strategy and objectives? Do groups merely make up objectives and strategies independent of their surroundings and the mix of opportunities and constraints confronting them? The answer is clearly no. Also, how are these groups able to recruit so many bombers and operate with the frequency seen in Iraq? Do they merely have excellent organizational skills and persuasive leadership, or are the political and security environments facilitating their activities? If the latter is true, as is often the case, then we can see how organizational strategies interact with societal conflicts and the broader political and security contexts. In short, there is no escaping the interdependence of individual motivations, organizational objectives, and societal conflicts in the making of suicide terrorism.

The social movement approach is not a unitary theory that makes law-like propositions concerning collective action. Rather it is an analytical approach that yields a number of concepts or mechanisms that could be used to understand different forms of collective action or contentious politics.[26] The following social movement concepts are helpful in explaining suicide terrorism in Iraq: *political opportunity structures, strategic framing, mobilization structures and networks, and repertoires of action, modularity, and diffusion.* These concepts comprise an explanatory schema that is not necessarily generalizable beyond Iraq; but it is not clear that a generalizable theory of suicide terrorism is currently attainable.

POLITICAL OPPORTUNITY STRUCTURES

Political opportunity structures refer to political environments, systems, or alignments that create opportunities for collective action that previously did not exist.[27] Political contenders operate in environments that shape opportunities for and constraints on collective action. Some political environments make collective action nearly impossible. For example, highly repressive regimes that suppress any form of extra-institutional mobilization make it difficult for political contenders to call for marches and protests. Other contexts, however, combine constraints and opportunities, or threats and incentives, making collective action thinkable.

For example, in their study of transnational advocacy networks, Keck and Sikkink highlight how domestic political blockage in authoritarian states, combined with the availability of international support networks, creates opportunities for national advocacy groups to engage in transnational activism to put international pressure on their own governments (the "boomerang" strategy).[28] Similarly, a number of social movement theorists have shown that globalization and the rise of regional and international governmental organizations guided by neoliberal economic doctrines created new threats to organized labor and environmental advocates as well as opportunities for social movement cooperation across borders.[29] These examples suggest that the political context shapes both the rise and strategies of collective action.

Social movement theorists and political scientists point to a number of factors that could generate or constrain opportunities for collective mobilization, including whether or not the system is partially or completely open to political contestation; availability or absence of influential allies, as well as elite unity or fragmentation; the strength and nature of state repression; differential policing strategies; transition from authoritarianism to democracy; and new threats to organizational survival.[30]

The concept of political opportunity structures as applied to suicide terrorism in Iraq shows how shifts in the post-9/11 security environment around the world and the toppling of the authoritarian Baathist regime in Iraq created new threats and opportunities for global jihadists to mobilize Muslims for martyrdom in Iraq. The rise and pace of suicide attacks in Iraq are intimately linked, on the one hand to the sense of siege radical Islamists felt as they lost hospitable havens in Afghanistan, Pakistan, and Europe, and on the other hand to the opportunities generated by the unpopularity of the Iraq war in the Muslim world, the legitimacy crisis of official Muslim leaders that stemmed from their failure to halt the invasion of Iraq, and the rise of a nationalist insurgency in Iraq. This mix of threats and opportunities made Iraq a "field of dreams" for the new global insurgents.

STRATEGIC FRAMING

Humans are not robots or laboratory rats that respond automatically to external commands or stimuli. Mobilization involves framing a problem, attributing blame for it, suggesting solutions, and motivating collective action with material and moral incentives.[31] All these mobilization tasks are intricately connected to issues of identity. Social movement theorists recognize the complexity of identity formation and have contributed greatly to understanding how collective identity emerges.[32]

One of the most important concepts to emerge from social movement theory is cultural framing, which refers to "conscious strategic efforts by groups of people to fashion shared understandings of the world and of themselves that legitimate and motivate collective action."[33] A frame is an "interpretive schemata that simplifies and condenses the 'world out there' by selectively punctuating and encoding objects, situations, events, experiences, and sequences of action within one's present and past environment."[34]

Frames also can be thought of as "condensed symbols" that situate contemporary actors and their experiences within historical narratives that are intelligible, meaningful, and suggestive of certain courses of action.[35] The symbols are "condensed"—that is, they express a series of ideas and retrieve a number of familiar images that are mythically, if not logically, coherent. Liberation theology, for example, sought to reframe the ubiquitous and familiar notions of sin and salvation to enable activists to contest existing power structures in Latin America. Sin was no longer defined as personal impiety or wrongdoing, but rather as structural sin, generated by economic and political arrangements that oppress people and produce flagrant inequalities. Salvation was disconnected from its transcendental origins and framed as worldly historical salvation that demands activism to produce social justice on earth.[36]

The term strategic framing connotes the use of discourse and symbolism for political aims. Framing is strategic because it selectively draws from shared identities, histories, revered symbols, rituals, and narratives to mobilize people for action. It is not an objective process; it is replete with subjectivity and strategic choices from the "tool kit" of tradition.[37] Insurgents choose some symbols, texts, and narratives while they downplay or entirely ignore others that may contravene their strategic aims. Movement activists celebrate certain identities while suppressing others, depending on their objectives.[38]

The concept of strategic framing is helpful in explaining how global jihadists marshal ideological, theological, and emotional claims to appeal to potential recruits, legitimize themselves in the insurgency, justify violence against Iraqis, deactivate self-inhibiting norms against killing fellow Muslims, and counter the claims of established authorities. Above all, jihadists forge the myth of heroic martyrdom to motivate militants and newcomers to jihad to sacrifice themselves for heavenly rewards and to erase the shame of humiliation.

The ability of transnational jihadists to frame self-sacrifice as martyrdom was connected to earlier public support for martyrdom in Palestine and Lebanon. The normative context in which Muslim publics gave suicide operations privileged legitimacy made the mobilizing tasks of global jihadists easy; they were able to marshal the same texts, arguments, and rituals to justify suicide attacks. To the extent that additional arguments were necessary to justify attacks on fellow Muslims, the transnational jihadists managed to extend the framing of suicidal violence as martyrdom by drawing on cultural and political beliefs concerning humiliation inflicted by foreigners, the illegitimacy of collaboration with occupiers, and threats to female honor by strangers.

MOBILIZATION STRUCTURES AND NETWORKS

Mobilization structures are the formal and informal organizational vehicles through which people mobilize for and engage in collective action. They range from informal, decentralized networks to formal, centralized professional associations and social movement organizations. Social movement theorists recognize that opportunities and frames alone are not sufficient to persuade people to challenge authorities. Collective action requires preexisting social ties and organizational settings from which to draw recruits, resources, and leaders.[39]

The concept of networks in social movement theory has, oddly enough, remained undefined. However, the concept often refers to private and public ties, whether direct or indirect, among individuals, clusters of individuals (such as social clubs or tribes), groups, and organizations (all of which are often referred to as nodes). These links could include friends and family, coworkers and colleagues, acquaintances and neighbors in social or religious organizations, activists across a number of political organizations or even borders, and so on.[40]

One of the strongest findings in social movement theory is that network ties greatly facilitate collective action, insurgency, and terrorism.[41] Formal mobilization structures are rarely the starting point for social movement activism, especially in the context of repressive political systems in which vigilant authorities heavily monitor or suppress formal organizing.

Networks facilitate mobilization in five ways. First, they often link individuals who are already committed to a cause or a social category, creating a "catnet" (category x network) or, more simply, a "collective we."[42] It is much easier to mobilize people with a shared sense of identity than to struggle to forge a new one. In addition, networks reduce the cost of information transmission between individuals, allowing for repeated political exchanges between the nodes in the network. Virtual networks, where access to a computer and an online connection is sufficient to replace more costly leaflets, pamphlets, and audiocassettes, are especially useful.

Second, when mobilization involves high-risk activism, including participation in violence, social ties become a prerequisite for trust and commitment. Trust and solidarity are embedded in social networks. Recruiters for risky activism first dip into the pool of family, friends, and like-minded activists because trust is already established and the risk of talking to the "wrong people" is minimal. Potential recruits are more willing to entertain radical ideas when they have shared experiences and bonds of friendship with their interlocutors. In her study of high-risk collective action for human rights in Chile, Uruguay, and Argentina, Loveman found that "face-to-face networks permit a high degree of trust that helps to counteract the selective disincentives to participate posed by threats of state persecution." She added, "Dense interpersonal networks tend to insulate activists, which contributes to their intensified commitment and willingness to act despite risks of horrific repercussions." [43]

In her study of left-wing terrorism in Italy, della Porta found that 843 of 1,214 members of a clandestine organization joined while they had at least one friend already involved in that organization. In 74 percent of these cases, the participant had more than one friend involved.[44] In a study of the civil rights movement in the United States, Morris showed how the networks of black churches served as the institutional center of the movement by providing activists with a preexisting mass base, leadership, an institutionalized financial base, meeting places, and cultural solidarity.[45]

Third, and related to the second point, network ties create social incentives and reputational concerns that discourage individuals from "free-riding." Free-riders are individuals who choose to forgo participation in a collective action that, if successful, could bring them and others a benefit such as higher pay for striking workers, an end to racial inequality for an oppressed minority, the right to vote for disenfranchised citizens, or freedom from foreign domination for an occupied people. If others act and succeed, the free-riders still benefit because the public good produced by the collective action is not limited to those who participated.[46] Staying on the sidelines is a common behavior when social struggles are raging, but being part of a tight-knit activist network could discourage people from free-riding. As Chong illustrated with regard to the U.S. civil rights movement, personal ties within the black churches made it difficult for individuals or groups to stay behind as others were mobilizing for the collective good. Those who did risked sullying their reputations and losing valued friendships.[47] Expectations of valued peers were also noted by Gibson, who maintained that participants in the mass protests against the 1991 coup in the former Soviet Union mobilized out of a need to satisfy "expectations of friends to do something." [48] In her interviews with left-wing militants in Italy, della Porta pointed out that many terrorists did not want to leave the movement because of a sense of commitment to their jailed comrades.[49]

Fourth, networks facilitate the act of collective attribution, whereby an activist can define a problem, attribute blame to culprits, and suggest solutions. Social movement theorists recognize that individual mobilization depends partly on new ways of seeing the world or aspects of it. Therefore, mobilizing agents must produce "injustice frames," "cognitive liberation," or "insurgent consciousness" to induce ordinary people to break their daily routines and engage in high-risk activism.[50] But individuals often do not make complex decisions or label events as "risks" and "opportunities" in isolation from valued others. Passy noted, "Once individuals have been integrated into formal and informal networks, they find themselves in an interactive structure that enables them to define and redefine their interpretive frames, facilitates the process of identity-building and identity-strengthening, and creates or solidifies political consciousness towards a given protest issue."[51]

Finally, networks present mobilizing agents with a pool of potential militants who can be activated through "bloc recruitment," which involves group commitments that are self-reinforcing.[52] Once a few individuals make a commitment to a cause, it is difficult for those around them to stay behind. Bloc recruitment may be facilitated by a number of psychological mechanisms, including peer pressure, concern for reputation, or "power in numbers."

In the case of Iraq, I show that preexisting transnational networks played an important role in mobilizing volunteers, including suicide bombers. Both experienced activists and new jihadists were linked by activist networks in a number of countries. Those activists, in turn, constituted a transnational network of second-generation jihadists with ties to the Afghan-Pakistani training camps during the 1990s or to jihads in Bosnia, Chechnya, or their home countries. Without these preexisting networks, jihadists could not have mobilized so many volunteers.

REPERTOIRES OF ACTION, MODULARITY, AND DIFFUSION

Social movement activism usually involves familiar and tried repertoires of action. Organizers of collective action do not choose tactics randomly but draw on past experiences, history, and societal norms and habits.

"Protest makers do not have to reinvent the wheel at each place and in each conflict.... They often find inspiration elsewhere in the ideas and tactics espoused by other activists."[53] The values and goals of the movement, as well as the political context in which it operates, also shape repertoires of contention.[54] They are not static, however. Social movement theorists recognize that organizers of collective action are strategic and learning actors who can adopt new tactics and mobilization forms, especially if these appear successful. Tactics produced in some contexts can become "modular" and be "diffused" to other contexts.[55]

Strategic and tactical diffusion may occur through relational and nonrelational ties.[56] Relational diffusion involves the transfer of innovative tactics through established lines of interpersonal interactions within networks of activists with high levels of trust. In the case of terrorism, this type of diffusion involves secret meetings, selective training camps, or password-protected Web sites.

Innovation is not shared widely with the public. Left-wing terrorist groups in Western Europe during the 1970s adopted airline hijacking and other tactics they had learned through close ties to operatives in the Popular Front for the Liberation of Palestine and their training camps in Lebanon and South Yemen.[57] Chechen rebels learned about suicide attacks in the second Chechen war in 2000 from Arab fighters led by the Saudi Samir al-Suwail, better known as Ibn al-Khattab.[58] The Indonesian group Jemaah Islamiah learned to use suicide attacks in al Qaeda training camps in Afghanistan and from operatives who used Southeast Asia as an enabling region (or "administrative back office") for its global operations.[59]

Nonrelational diffusion involves the transfer of innovative tactics through the media, writings, and the Internet. In those instances, activists who see cultural or structural similarities between their movement and another diffuse tactics from one context to another, even when concrete ties between the two movements are lacking. In other words, "perceptions of common circumstances" enable activists to adopt strategies and tactics from different countries or regions because they see a "functional equivalence" between the transmitters and adopters of innovation.[60] A common example is the diffusion of nonviolent protest from India during the time of Mahatma Gandhi to the American civil rights movement led by Dr. Martin Luther King Jr. These were two movements separated by time and space, yet the civil rights leadership emulated the strategy of the anticolonial struggle in India, partly because of its perceived successes, but also because admirers of Gandhi in the United States publicized it.[61]

We cannot understand the rapid spread of suicide attacks in Iraq without referring to the concepts of repertoires of action, modularity, and diffusion. Much of the Muslim world saw suicide attacks in Lebanon and Israel as part of a legitimate and desirable repertoire of resistance. The tactic became modular, but its uses in Iraq differed radically from its uses in Lebanon and Israel. In these two countries, Hezbollah and Hamas used this tactic mainly against foreign occupations; in Iraq insurgents use it against fellow Iraqis labeled "apostates" and "collaborators." The diffusion of the tactic took place through relational ties; individuals with links to jihadi training camps were the ones to deploy this tactic the most.

Diffusion also takes place through nonrelational ties. Insurgent literature and online productions framed the occupation in Iraq as functionally equivalent to the occupation of Palestine and Lebanon. Some insurgent groups venerated martyrdom in their media to encourage the use of the tactic in Iraq and around the world.

ORGANIZATION OF THE BOOK

This book is divided into three parts: Part I deals with the insurgents in Iraq and their objectives, strategies, and ideological orientations. It argues that there are two insurgencies in Iraq, not one. The first is led by Islamic nationalists who deploy Islam as the vocabulary of resistance to oust the coalition forces and reintegrate Sunnis in a new political process that is not dominated by hostile sectarian interests. The second is led by ideological Baathists and Sunni extremists known as jihadi Salafis. Both factions are also interested in ending foreign presence in Iraq, but they are pursuing the additional goal of system collapse. They seek to create a failed state in Iraq because only then will they be able to survive and possibly ascend to power.

Chapter 1 addresses the Islamic nationalists and ideological Baathists; chapter 2 describes jihadi Salafi insurgents, the most extreme faction in the insurgency and the one that deploys most suicide attacks. Chapter 3 presents the data on suicide bombings in Iraq and tries to make sense of the trends related to the timing, targeting, and geography of violence.

Part II deals with the ideology, theology, and mythology of suicide bombers in Iraq. Chapter 4 addresses the ideological and theological justifications jihadi Salafis make to legitimize their extreme tactics against fellow Iraqis and especially the Shia. Chapter 5 examines how organizers of suicide attacks deploy media productions to construct narratives that mythologize martyrs and frame terrorism as heroic martyrdom.

Part III addresses the jihadi networks that have been instrumental in sending militants and suicide bombers to fight and die in Iraq. Chapters 6 and 7 discuss the networks in Jordan, Saudi Arabia, Kuwait, Syria, Lebanon, and Europe. These networks linked the second-generation jihadists who trained in Afghanistan during the 1990s with the emerging third-generation jihadists who have been driven to action by the new security environment in the war on terrorism and by images of Muslim suffering in Iraq.

Finally, the conclusion revisits the theoretical claims laid out in the introduction and assesses the applicability of these claims to Iraq. It concludes with a discussion of the limitations of counterinsurgency in dealing with suicide attacks in Iraq.

NOTES

1. Since January 2005 insurgents in Iraq have carried out an average of forty-five to 100 attacks per day, only a few of which are suicide attacks—usually one or two, but in rare instances as many as eleven. For the rate of suicide attacks by all the other groups outside Iraq, see data in the appendices in Robert Pape, *Dying to Win: The Strategic Logic of Suicide Terrorism* (New York: Random House, 2005), and Ami Pedahzur, *Suicide Terrorism* (Cambridge, U.K.: Polity, 2005).

2. These figures reflect reporting on the Iraqi Coalition Casualty Count Web site (http://icasualties.org/oif/) as of March 5, 2007. The Brookings Institution Iraq Index (www.brookings.edu/iraqindex) reported similar numbers as of March 4, 2007.

3. As of October 31, 2006, www.brookings.edu/iraqindex estimated up to 70,100 Iraqis had been killed following the period of major combat operations; Iraq Body Count Web site (www.iraqbodycount.net/database/) put the figure at between 57,805 and 63,573 as of February 7, 2007; the high estimate of more than 650,000 deaths comes from Gilbert Burnham, Riyadh Lafta, Shannon Doocy, and Les Roberts, "Mortality after the 2003 Invasion of Iraq: A Cross-Sectional Cluster Sample Survey," *Lancet* 368 (October 2006): 1421–28.

4. Christoph Reuter, *My Life Is a Weapon: A Modern History of Suicide Bombing* (Princeton, N.J.: Princeton University Press, 2004); Diego Gambetta, ed., *Making Sense of Suicide Missions* (New York: Oxford University Press, 2006);

Ami Pedahzur, ed., *Root Causes of Suicide Terrorism: The Globalization of Martyrdom* (London: Routledge, 2006).

5. For a discussion on definitional controversies, see Assaf Moghadam, "Defining Suicide Terrorism," in Pedahzur, ed., *Root Causes,* 13–24.

6. Rikihei Inoguchi and Tadashi Nakajima, *The Divine Wind: Japan's Kamikaze Force in World War II* (Annapolis, Md.: Naval Institute Press, 1958); Albert Axell and Hideaki Kase, *Kamikaze: Japan's Suicide Gods* (New York: Longman, 2002); Emiko Ohnuki-Tierney, *Kamikaze Diaries: Reflections of Japanese Student Soldiers* (Chicago: University of Chicago Press, 2006).

7. Not all, or even the majority of, suicide attacks during the 1980s were carried out by Hezbollah. Secular nationalists linked to Syria emulated the Shia fundamentalists by undertaking suicide attacks, including with female bombers. Ariel Merari, "The Readiness to Kill and Die: Suicidal Terrorism in the Middle East," in *Origins of Terrorism: Psychologies, Ideologies, Theologies, States of Mind,* Walter Reich, ed. (Washington, D.C.: Woodrow Wilson Center Press, 1990), 192–210; Hala Jaber, *Hezbollah* (New York: Columbia University Press, 1997).

8. Mohammed M. Hafez, *Manufacturing Human Bombs: The Making of Palestinian Suicide Bombers* (Washington, D.C.: United States Institute of Peace Press, 2006).

9. Rohan Gunaratna, "Suicide Terrorism: A Global Threat," *Jane's Intelligence Review,* April 12, 2000: 52–55.

10. Pedahzur, *Suicide Terrorism;* Yoram Schweitzer, ed., *Female Suicide Bombers: Dying for Equality?* (Tel Aviv: Jaffee Center for Strategic Studies, 2006).

11. Eyad El-Sarraj, "Suicide Bombers: Dignity, Despair, and the Need of Hope," *Journal of Palestine Studies* 4 (2002): 71–76; Anne Speckhard, Nadejda Tarabrina, Valery Krasnov, and Khapta Akhmedova, "Research Note: Observations of Suicidal Terrorist in Action," *Terrorism and Political Violence* 16, no. 2 (Summer 2004): 305–27; Anne Speckhard and Khapta Akhmedova, "The Making of a Martyr: Chechen Suicide Terrorism," *Studies in Conflict and Terrorism* 29, no. 5 (July–August 2006): 429–92.

12. Pape, *Dying to Win.*

13. Mia Bloom, "Palestinian Suicide Bombing: Public Support, Market Share and Outbidding," *Political Science Quarterly* 119 (Spring 2004): 61–88; Mia Bloom, *Dying to Kill: The Allure of Suicide Terror* (New York: Columbia University Press, 2005).

14. Raphael Israeli, *Islamikaze: Manifestations of Islamic Martyrology* (London: Frank Cass, 2003); Shaul Shay, *The Shahids: Islam and Suicide Attacks* (Somerset, N.J.: Transaction, 2004); Mary Habeck, *Knowing the Enemy: Jihadist Ideology and the War on Terror* (New Haven, Conn.: Yale University Press, 2006).

15. Assaf Moghadam, "Palestinian Suicide Terrorism in the Second Intifada: Motivations and Organizational Aspects," *Studies in Conflict and Terrorism* 26, no. 2 (March–April 2003): 65–92; Mohammed M. Hafez, "Rationality, Culture, and Structure in the Making of Suicide Bombers: A Preliminary Theoretical Synthesis and Illustrative Case Study," *Studies in Conflict and Terrorism* 29, no. 2 (March 2006): 165–85.

16. Robert Pape, "The Strategic Logic of Suicide Terrorism," *American Political Science Review* 97 (2003): 343–61.

17. George Michael and Joseph Scolnick, "The Strategic Limits of Suicide Terrorism in Iraq," *Small Wars and Insurgencies* 17, no. 2 (June 2006): 113–25.

18. Hafez, *Manufacturing Human Bombs.*

19. Ami Pedahzur and Arie Perliger, "The Changing Nature of Suicide Attacks: A Social Network Perspective," *Social Forces* 84, no. 4 (2006): 1987–2008.

20. Andrew Kydd and Barbara F. Walter, "Sabotaging the Peace: The Politics of Extremist Violence," *International Organization* 56, no. 2 (Spring 2002): 263–96.

21. Bruce Hoffman and Gordon McCormick, "Terrorism, Signaling, and Suicide Attack," *Studies in Conflict and Terrorism* 27, no. 4 (July–August 2004): 243–81.

22. Although the children in the Beslan hostage crisis did not die in a suicide attack, the hostage takers wore explosive belts and made declarations concerning their willingness to die as martyrs.

23. It is not clear if the July–August 2006 war between Hezbollah and Israel has dampened support for the Shia organization. It is certain, however, that Hezbollah's core constituency in southern Lebanon still venerates the radical organization despite bearing the brunt of Israeli shelling and air strikes during the war. Moreover, support for Hezbollah among the Arab public has increased substantially, despite condemnations of the group by the governments of Saudi Arabia, Jordan, and Egypt.

24. Donatella della Porta and Mario Diani, *Social Movements: An Introduction* (Malden, Mass.: Blackwell, 2006), 20.

25. Donatella della Porta, *Social Movements, Political Violence, and the State: A Comparative Analysis of Italy and Germany* (New York: Cambridge University Press, 1995); Doug McAdam, John McCarthy, and Mayer Zald, eds., *Comparative Perspective on Social Movements: Political Opportunities, Mobilization Structures, and Cultural Framing* (New York: Cambridge University Press, 1996); Sidney Tarrow, *Power in Movement: Social Movements, Collective Action and Politics* (New York: Cambridge University Press, 1998).

26. Doug McAdam, Sidney Tarrow, and Charles Tilly, *Dynamics of Contention* (New York: Cambridge University Press, 2001).

27. Doug McAdam, *Political Process and the Development of Black Insurgency: 1930–1970* (Chicago: University of Chicago Press, 1982); Tarrow, *Power in Movement.*

28. Margaret E. Keck and Kathryn Sikkink, *Activists beyond Borders: Advocacy Networks in International Politics* (Ithaca, N.Y.: Cornell University Press, 1998).

29. Jackie Smith, Charles Chatfield, and Ron Pagnucco, *Transnational Social Movements and Global Politics: Solidarity beyond the State* (New York: Syracuse University Press, 1997); Jackie Smith, "Globalization and Transnational Social Movement Organizations," in *Social Movements and Organization Theory*, Gerald F. Davis, Doug McAdam, W. Richard Scott, and Mayer N. Zald, eds. (New York: Cambridge University Press, 2005); Donatella della Porta, Massimiliano Andretta, Lorenzo Mosca, and Herbert Reiter, *Globalization from Below: Transnational Activists and Protest Networks* (Minneapolis: University of Minnesota Press, 2006).

30. Peter Eisinger, "The Conditions of Protest Behavior in American Cities." *American Political Science Review* 67 (1973): 11–28; William Gamson, *The Strategy of Social Protest*, 2nd edition (Belmont, Calif.: Wadsworth, 1990); Charles D. Brockett, "The Structure of Political Opportunities and Peasant Mobilization in Central America," *Comparative Politics* 23, no. 3 (1991): 253–47; Tarrow, *Power in Movement*; Charles Tilly, *From Mobilization to Revolution* (Reading, Mass.: Addison-Wesley, 1978); Vincent Boudreau, "State Repression and Democracy Protest in Three Southeast Asian Countries," in *Social Movements: Identity, Culture, and the State,* David S. Meyer, Nancy Whittier, and Belinda Robnett, eds. (New York: Oxford University Press, 2002), 28–46; Mohammed M. Hafez, *Why Muslims Rebel: Repression and Resistance in the Islamic World* (Boulder, Colo.: Lynne Rienner, 2003); della Porta, *Social Movements, Political Violence, and the State*; William Crotty, ed., *Democratic Development and Political Terrorism: The Global Perspective* (Boston: Northeastern University Press, 2005); Ely Karmon, *Coalitions between Terrorist Organizations: Revolutionaries, Nationalists and Islamists* (Leiden, Netherlands: Brill, 2005).

31. Scott A. Hunt, Robert Benford, and David Snow, "Identity Fields: Framing Processes and the Social Construction of Movement Identities," in *New Social Movements: From Ideology to Identity*, Enrique Laraña, Hank Johnston, and Joseph R. Gusfield, eds. (Philadelphia: Temple University Press, 1994), 185–208.

32. James M. Jasper, *The Art of Moral Protest: Culture, Biography and Creativity in Social Movements* (Chicago: University of Chicago Press, 1997); Francesca Polletta and James M. Jasper, "Collective Identity and Social Movements," *Annual Review of Sociology* 27 (2001): 283–305; Meyer, Whittier, and Robnett, eds., *Social Movements.*

33. McAdam, McCarthy, and Zald, *Comparative Perspective on Social Movements*, 6. The concept of frames made its way into social movement studies through the works of Snow and his colleagues: David Snow, Burke Rochford, Steven Worden, and Robert Benford, "Frame Alignment Processes, Micromobilization, and Movement Participation," *American Sociological Review* 51 (1986): 464–81; David Snow and Robert Benford, "Ideology, Frame Resonance, and Participant Mobilization," *International Social Movement Research* 1 (1988): 197–217; Robert Benford and David Snow, "Framing Processes and Social Movements," *Annual Review of Sociology* 26 (2000): 611–39.

34. David Snow and Robert Benford, "Master Frames and Cycles of Protest," in *Frontiers in Social Movement Theory*, Aldon Morris and Carol Mueller, eds. (New Haven: Yale University Press, 1992), 137.

35. David Moss, "Politics, Violence, Writing: The Rituals of 'Armed Struggle' in Italy," in *The Legitimization of Violence*, David E. Apter, ed. (New York: United Nations Research Institute for Social Development, 1997).

36. Sharon E. Nepstad, "Popular Religion, Protest, and Revolt: The Emergence of Political Insurgency in the Nicaraguan and Salvadoran Churches of the 1960s–80s," in *Disruptive Religion: The Force of Faith in Social Movement Activism*, Christian Smith, ed. (London: Routledge, 1996). For similar analysis on Catholic martyrdom in El Salvador, see Anna L. Peterson, *Martyrdom and the Politics of Religion: Progressive Catholicism in El Salvador's Civil War* (Albany: State University of New York, 1997).

37. Ann Swidler, "Culture in Action: Symbols and Strategies," *American Sociological Review* 5, no. 2 (1986): 273–86.

38. Mary Bernstein, "Celebration and Suppression: The Strategic Uses of Identity by the Lesbian and Gay Movement," *American Journal of Sociology* 103, no. 3 (November 1997): 531–65.

39. John McCarthy and Mayer Zald, "Resource Mobilization and Social Movements: A Partial Theory," *American Journal of Sociology* 82 (1977): 1212–41; Christian Smith, "Correcting a Curious Neglect, or Bringing Religion Back In," in Smith, ed., *Disruptive Religion*, 1–25.

40. Mario Diani, "Introduction: Social Movements, Contentious Actions, and Social Networks: 'From Metaphor to Substance?'" in *Social Movements and Networks: Relational Approaches to Collective Action*, Mario Diani and Doug McAdam, eds. (New York: Oxford University Press, 2003), 7.

41. Luther Gerlach and Virginia Hine, *People, Power, Change: Movements of Social Transformation* (Indianapolis: Bobbs-Merrill, 1970); Jo Freeman, "The Origins of the Women's Liberation Movement," *American Journal of Sociology* 78 (1973): 792–811; Doug McAdam, "Recruitment to High Risk Activism: The Case of Freedom Summer," *American Journal of Sociology* 92 (1986): 64–90; Doug McAdam and Ronnelle Paulsen, "Specifying the Relationship between

Social Ties and Activism," *American Journal of Sociology* 99 (1993): 640–67; Karl-Dieter Opp and Christiane Gern, "Dissident Groups, Personal Networks, and the East German Revolution of 1989," *American Sociological Review* 58 (1993): 659–80; Marc Sageman, *Understanding Terror Networks* (Philadelphia: University of Pennsylvania Press, 2004).

42. Tilly, *From Mobilization to Revolution,* 62–64; della Porta and Diani, *Social Movements,* 118–19.

43. Mara Loveman, "High-Risk Collective Action: Defending Human Rights in Chile, Uruguay, and Argentina," *American Journal of Sociology* 104, no. 2 (September 1998): 517.

44. Donatella della Porta, "Recruitment Processes in Clandestine Political Organizations: Italian Left-Wing Terrorism," *International Social Movement Research* 1 (1988): 158.

45. Aldon Morris, *The Origins of the Civil Rights Movement: Black Communities Organizing for Change* (New York: The Free Press, 1984).

46. Mancur Olson, *The Logic of Collective Action* (Cambridge, Mass.: Harvard University Press, 1965).

47. Dennis Chong, *Collective Action and the Civil Rights Movement* (Chicago: University of Chicago Press, 1991).

48. James L. Gibson, "Mass Opposition to the Soviet Putsch of August 1991: Collective Action, Rational Choice, and Democratic Values in the Former Soviet Union," *American Political Science Review* 91, no. 3 (September 1997): 680.

49. Donatella della Porta, "Left-Wing Terrorism in Italy," in *Terrorism in Context,* 2nd edition, Martha Crenshaw, ed. (College Park: Pennsylvania State University Press, 2001), 144–53.

50. William Gamson, Bruce Fireman, and Steven Rytina, *Encounters with Unjust Authority* (Homewood, Ill.: Dorsey Press, 1982); Doug McAdam, *Political Process and the Development of Black Insurgency*; Christian Smith, *The Emergence of Liberation Theology: Radical Religion and Social Movement Theory* (Chicago: University of Chicago Press, 1991).

51. Florence Passy, "Social Networks Matter. But How?" in *Social Movements and Networks: Relational Approaches to Collective Action,* Mario Diani and Doug McAdam, eds. (New York: Oxford University Press, 2003), 24.

52. Anthony Oberschall, *Social Conflict and Social Movements* (Englewood Cliffs, N.J.: Prentice-Hall, 1973).

53. Doug McAdam and Dieter Rucht, "Cross-national Diffusion of Movement Ideas," *Annals of the American Academy of the Political and Social Sciences* 528 (1993): 58.

54. Tilly, *From Mobilization to Revolution.*

55. Tarrow, *Power in Movement*; della Porta and Diani, *Social Movements.*

56. Sidney Tarrow, *The New Transnational Activism* (New York: Cambridge University Press, 2005), chapter 6. Tarrow adds a third category of "mediated diffusion," which he defines as diffusion through *brokers* who link two separate sites or clusters of activists through nonmovement institutions. In this book I treat relational and mediated diffusion as the same.

57. Karmon, *Coalitions between Terrorist Organizations.*

58. Speckhard and Akhmedova, "The Making of a Martyr."

59. Zachary Abuza, *Militant Islam in Southeast Asia: Crucible of Terror* (Boulder, Colo.: Lynne Rienner, 2003).

60. Della Porta and Diani, *Social Movements*, 187.

61. Tarrow, *The New Transnational Activism*, 108.

PART I

INSURGENTS AND THEIR STRATEGIES

NATIONALISTS AND BAATHISTS

The rapid demise of one of the most oppressive regimes in the world created new political grievances and opportunities in Iraq. Rapid political changes often weaken the vigilance of security authorities, make room for new political alignments, and unleash mobilization by groups that previously would have been repressed. Ironically, the Iraqi insurgency developed not when the political system was at its most repressive, but when many, if not most, Iraqis felt a new sense of openness in society.

The insurgency emerged as Iraqis were forming political parties and mobilizing constituencies for political contestation or supremacy. The proliferation of mass demonstrations, public meetings, and unofficial newspapers and independent television channels was not unusual. Parties suppressed under the former regime, such as the Communists, raised their flags once again and reestablished their headquarters. Shia groups such as the Dawa Party, the Mahdi Army, and the Supreme Council for the Islamic Revolution in Iraq (SCIRI), and Sunni organizations such as the Iraqi Islamic Party and the Association of Muslim Scholars emerged and consolidated their bases of support before or at the height of the insurgency.

To be sure, these freedoms came about during war and occupation, which also created feelings of humiliation; public chaos, looting, and insecurity; and disenfranchisement for many Iraqis, especially those who had served the former regime. Put simply, the invasion of Iraq and the subsequent occupation of its territory created a mix of opportunities and threats for Sunnis who were blamed for the sins of Saddam Hussein. This mixture of relaxed repression and a sense of loss or relative deprivation was ideal for insurgent recruitment and rebellion.

Although I repeatedly speak of the "Iraqi insurgency," it is more accurate to speak of two insurgencies. Most insurgents could be categorized as

Islamic nationalists fighting to oust the coalition forces from their country and overturn the political arrangements that have given ascendancy to Shia and Kurdish communities at the expense of Sunnis. Although these insurgents have Islamic worldviews and adopt Islamic symbolism, their main objective—at least when they first mobilized—has been to reverse political developments imposed by foreigners and collaborators through occupation. They use Islam as the vocabulary of resistance against foreign occupation, not as a vehicle to wage a global jihad against the West. Their ultimate goal is to reintegrate Sunnis and nominal Baathists in a political process that does not give disproportionate power to the Shia and Kurds on the basis of narrow communal interests or federalism.

Jihadi Salafis and ideological Baathists lead the second insurgency. They are interested not merely in ousting the occupation but in collapsing the political system and sparking sectarian civil war. The jihadi Salafis, an extremist Sunni movement, are ideologically committed to establishing an Islamic state based on the model of the Prophet and his righteous followers *(al-Salaf al-Salih)*; they cannot tolerate a quasi-secular government dominated by the "heretical" Shia. The foreign jihadists among the Salafis hope to create a base for regional and global jihad to compensate for the one they lost in Afghanistan after the collapse of the Taliban regime in 2001. Both Salafis and Baathists have deployed suicide bombers (Salafis much more than Baathists); the nationalist insurgents rarely use suicide attackers.

THE ISLAMIC NATIONALISTS: SYSTEM REINTEGRATION STRATEGY

The insurgency in Iraq began with localized and decentralized efforts by nationalists, disenfranchised Baathists, disgruntled soldiers, Saddam loyalists, local Islamists, and foreign jihadists. As a result, hundreds of small brigades appeared on the scene—some repeatedly, others only once or twice. (For the names of groups that have participated in the insurgency, see appendix 1.) Over time, the majority of insurgents have converged around the Islamic nationalists.[1] These Islamic nationalists are pursuing a system reintegration strategy; they are interested in restructuring the political process in Iraq to guarantee that Sunni Arabs and nominal Baathists (not Saddam loyalists) are not marginalized by sectarian political arrangements that privilege the combined majority of Sunni Kurds and Shia Arabs at their expense. System reintegration also entails rejecting regional federalism that might give the Kurds and Shia a disproportionate share of political, economic, and military power in the new Iraq.

It is widely recognized that the bulk of active support for the insurgency comes from displaced Iraqi officers, soldiers, and security services personnel dismissed from their jobs without compensation or a pension, or as a result of the "de-Baathification" measures of the Coalition Provisional Authority (CPA, April 2003–June 2004). The armed groups that best represent this category are those with Islamist and nationalist tendencies: the Islamic Army in Iraq (IAI), 1920 Revolution Brigades of the Islamic and National Resistance Movement (1920 RB), Mujahidin Army in Iraq (MAI), and Salah al-Din al-Ayoubi Brigades of the Islamic Front for Iraqi Resistance (SDAB).

The IAI first appeared in July 2004. It did not issue a political statement but instead claimed responsibility for several attacks and kidnappings and warned that it would target transport companies working for the coalition occupation forces. It is responsible for a wave of kidnappings of civilian foreign nationals, including Italians, Australians, and Filipinos, whose countries have a military presence in Iraq. Its videos usually depict attacks on U.S. forces, not Iraqi security forces.

Sunni clerics associated with the Association of Muslim Scholars formed the 1920 RB in June or July 2003. These clerics are tied to specific mosques associated with the Committee for Preaching, Guidance, and Religious Rulings, headed by Sheikh Mahdi al-Sumaydi (currently under arrest). The name 1920 RB reflects a nationalist, anticolonial tendency that harks back to the Iraqi anti-British struggle after World War I. According to its published manifesto, it is a "nationalist jihadist movement."[2]

The MAI appeared sometime in early 2005. It is composed of former military personnel from tribal areas and Salafi religious figures. Its leader is Abu Jandal al-Shamri, who defines the group as a Salafi one that adopts the "middle" road between the secularists and the *takfiris* (Muslim radicals who declare other Muslims to be apostates who may be targeted and killed). Although its goal is to establish an Islamic caliphate, it also reaches out to the Baathists to repent and join its ranks.

The SDAB officially formed May 30, 2004, although the name of its brigade appeared as early as July 19, 1993. In its first communiqué, it declared, "We are not opposed to participating in national politics with the honorable in the political arena, as long as they make opposition to the occupation their priority."[3]

These four groups issue political statements together through the Joint Coordination Bureau for Jihad Groups (JCB). Their immediate aims are to be acknowledged as a legitimate resistance movement that controls the situation on the ground and to gain recognition as the "real" representative of the Iraqi people. They demand that any negotiations to end the occupation and restore stability to the country go through them, and only through them.[4] They use the language of jihad and Salafism, but their ultimate aim is to expel the coalition forces from Iraq to improve their bargaining power vis-à-vis the Shia- and Kurdish-dominated state.

These groups' members are not Saddam loyalists, nor are they ideological Baathists committed to reinstating the Baath party under new leadership. First and foremost, they believe that any nation occupied against its will has a right to resist the occupier. As one insurgent put it, "When we see U.S. soldiers in our cities with guns, it is a challenge to us. America wants to show its power, to be a cowboy.... I don't know a lot about political relations in the world, but if you look at history—Vietnam, Iraq itself, Egypt, Algeria—countries always rebel against occupation.... Even if Saddam Hussein dies we will continue to fight to throw out the American forces. We take our power from our history, not from one person."[5]

The Sunni Sheikh Muayad, the head of the Abu Hanifa mosque in Baghdad's Adhamiyah neighborhood, expressed similar sentiments: "All good people and citizens of the world reject occupation whether they are Muslims or not ... and this is the same thing that America did before against British imperialism, so why do they deny for other people the right to do what they did before?"[6]

Sunni Islam and Arab nationalism are sources of legitimacy in the face of Shia dominance and Kurdish autonomy. Generally speaking, they limit their violence to coalition forces, Iraqi security services fighting the insurgency, foreign contractors, and Shia militias associated with the interior ministry, the Mahdi Army of Muqtada al-Sadr, and the Badr Corps of SCIRI. By attacking coalition forces, they hope to raise the cost of the coalition's presence in Iraq and coerce its members into leaving the country. By attacking Iraqi security forces, they intend to deter others from joining these forces and prevent the new Iraqi regime from establishing a monopoly on the use of force in the country. By attacking foreign contractors, they want to prevent the coalition forces from establishing stability.

By attacking Shia and Kurdish militias associated with the interior ministry and sectarian political parties, they want to prevent the new power brokers in Iraq from imposing security through extra-institutional organs and from engaging in reprisal attacks on Sunnis.

The Islamic nationalists avoid direct attacks on Shia and Kurdish civilians, and they rarely advocate or use suicide attacks, unlike al Qaeda in Iraq (AQI) or Ansar al-Sunna Group (ASG, previously Ansar al-Sunna Army).[7] It is interesting to note that the video clips of the IAI, SDAB, and the 1920 RB rarely, if ever, show any suicide attacks, while those of AQI repeatedly show "martyrdom operations," as well as video statements by suicide bombers.

These insurgents are motivated by events that followed the toppling of the old regime, not just the overthrow of the Baathist state. Instead of being treated as equal victims of Saddam's wars and being rewarded for not fighting to the death during the 2003 invasion of Iraq, they were associated with the crimes of the old regime, despite the fact that many Sunnis attempted coups during the Saddam era and, consequently, bore the brunt of Saddam's brutal purges in the officer corps.

In an interview an unidentified IAI leader states: "It is known by all Iraqis that not all ex-Iraqi army leaders or security officers of the ex-regime are Baathists. There was a group of them who opposed the bad policies adopted by the ex-regime; some of them were arrested and jailed because of their honorable positions, and moreover, some of them were killed [executed] because of their courageous positions."[8]

The Baathist state did not just gas the Kurds in the north and violently suppress Shia rebellions in the south; its circles of violence extended to all segments of society and even to its own members. Purges took place within the Sunni tribes, military, police, party, and state bureaucracies.[9] Some of the major Sunni tribes in Al Anbar province, such as the Jubburis, Ubaydis, and Dulaymis, tried to assassinate Saddam and other Baathists during the mid-1990s and led a revolt in Ramadi.[10]

Instead of being called upon to help restore order and security in Iraq, nominal Baathists were dismissed en masse as bungling, incompetent, and oppressive forces. These Sunnis fear the new security services dominated by Shia and Kurds who harbor animosity toward the old regime and have sought to settle scores through the interior ministry and the other branches of the security forces. Moreover, many of these Sunnis have fought and sacrificed for Iraq in wars with Iran during the 1980s and the

United States in the early 1990s. They feel entitled to be represented as much as (if not more than) Shia and Kurdish parties that lived in exile or "betrayed" their country through close association with Iran.

At least six specific developments or galvanizing events catapulted these Sunnis into action. First, the disbanding of the Iraqi armed forces without salaries or pensions generated mass marginalization and unemployment. Those who lost their positions in government or the security services did not see the new regime welcoming them back or compensating them. One estimate puts the number of dismissed soldiers at 400,000, many of whom undoubtedly have dependents who rely on their salaries. These are trained and equipped soldiers with previous war experience.[11]

In a joint communiqué the IAI, MAI, 1920 RB, and SDAB declare that "the formation of the armed forces and police should be based primarily on a national and professional principle that has nothing to do [with] a sect or a party, and should never be utilized in a confrontation with the citizens of this country...."[12] These nationalists argue that the occupying forces purposely planned the dismissal of the Iraqi army to encourage sectarianism. The IAI, for example, says in one of its publications that the United States planned the rise of the militias and has negotiated with them to bring them into the security forces. So the United States cannot be trusted when it says it is trying to stop civil war and control the Shia militias. Its aim all along has been to give rise to pro-Iranian Shia militias. The first step was to dismantle the Iraqi national army; the second was to allow the Badr Corps to take over the interior ministry; the third was to let the Kurdish Peshmerga take over Mosul, Kirkuk, and Diyala provinces. Finally, it negotiated with the Mahdi Army to keep it in one piece and incorporate its cadres and members of the Shia Dawa Party into the police and military. The United States will never dismantle the militias because it needs them, and it cannot simply send them back to Qom or Tehran (both in Iran).[13]

Second, purging the state and society of Baathist officials and functionaries further alienated a large segment of society. The Higher National Committee for the De-Baathification of Society, headed by Ahmad al-Chalabi, issued two decrees in 2003. The first, on May 15, 2003, declared that "any civil servant who held the rank of division member or a higher rank in the dissolved Baath Party is hereby dismissed from public posts of all grades and must leave his post immediately." Decree No. 2, issued September 14, 2003, declared that the following categories of people were to be "banned from holding special positions or undertaking responsibilities in public posts, political activities, civil society institutions, the press, or the media": whoever held the rank of division member or a higher rank in the dissolved Baath Party; whoever held the post of general manager or higher, district manager or higher, or their equivalent posts involving advisers and experts under the former regime; and individuals affiliated with the repressive agencies of the authority (Special Security, National Security, Presidential Special Protection, Military Intelligence, Saddam's Fedayeen, Public Security, and Intelligence).

Some attribute the policy of de-Baathification to Paul Bremer III, who was in charge of the CPA from May 2003 to June 2004. Bremer is said to have ignored intelligence and other warnings that the dual policy of de-Baathification and dismantling the armed forces might give rise to insurgency.[14] However, there is evidence that de-Baathification was part of prewar planning. U.S. administration advisers saw it as one way to reduce the influence of Sunnis in the state bureaucracy and make room for "fresh faces" from the Shia and Kurds.[15] In any case, de-Baathification was humiliating to many Iraqis, especially since it did not include compensation in the form of a pension or alternative employment. Many of those dismissed were members of the Baath party out of expediency or necessity, not ideological commitment. It is widely known in Iraq that membership in the Baath party was often necessary to gain entry or promotion in public-sector employment, including positions in the military, security services, public administration, universities, professional associations, or industry. Membership in the Baath party also was part of the survival strategy of ordinary Iraqis seeking to evade the omnipresent eye of the state *mukhabarat* (secret police). Joining was a way of feigning loyalty to the regime and gaining access to networks of intermediaries *(wasta)* in case one's family or relatives needed a job or an "insider" who could bail them out of trouble should they ever be suspected of activities against the regime.

The rapid ascendancy of the Shia and Kurds to positions of power, combined with de-Baathification, led to feelings of humiliation among many Sunnis at this reversal of fortune. The security services and Baathist officials are now ridiculed and hunted by the people who once feared them.[16] Peterson described this dynamic of resentment in Eastern Europe's ethnic conflicts that emerged during the 1990s and found it to be the best explanation of why ethnic communities turn against each other in the context of structural changes and state collapse. He wrote, "Resentment stems from the perception that one's group is located in an unwarranted subordinate position on a status hierarchy." He added, "Status reversal creates the highest intensity of resentment and produces the highest likelihood of violent conflict. Status reversal results when a more regionally powerful group in an established hierarchy is dislodged from its position and placed below a less powerful group."[17] The reversal of fortunes might have been alleviated had the new power brokers in Iraq avoided humiliating policies such as the dismissal of the armed forces and de-Baathification. Unfortunately, this did not happen following the collapse of Saddam's regime.

Third, many Sunnis felt physically threatened by the Shia- and Kurdish-dominated security services. After decades of repression, the Shia and Kurds were seeking retribution against former regime functionaries and supporters. The interior ministry, which has been infiltrated by the Shia Badr Corps, has been engaging in secret abductions, torture, and extrajudicial killings.[18] Abu Musab al-Zarqawi, the now-deceased leader of AQI, often justified his indiscriminate violence against the Shia by referring to the transgressions of the Badr Corps. He even formed a distinct militia, known as the Umar Brigades, which specialized in hunting down members of the Badr Corps. In the previously mentioned joint communiqué, the four Islamist and nationalist groups explicitly blame the Shia militias "as one of the main causes behind the deterioration of security in the country" and demand that they "should be dismantled and disallowed to become a part of any armed or security forces."

Fourth, growing insecurity in Iraqi towns and cities, as well as the lack of electricity, fuel, and basic social services, created daily personal grievances. Iraqis felt the diminution in their living standards through daily hardships such as long lines at gas stations, power outages, lack of access to propane fuel, and hyperinflation. Above all, ordinary Iraqis became victims of criminal gangs that kidnapped people for ransom or turned them over to insurgent groups or death squads for a fee.[19]

Deteriorating security and the difficulties in obtaining basic necessities in one of the largest oil-producing countries confirmed suspicions among ordinary Iraqis that their country was not "liberated" to bring democracy and freedom, but rather to plunder its wealth and resources.[20] For example, the IAI claims in a document describing its "creed and methodology" that "Iraq is the wealthiest country in the world, but ... its citizens continue to live in dire misery and unemployment." If Iraq's economic resources and brilliant intellectuals "were ruled by a loyal government that would utilize its incredible wealth and employ its great intellect, in a short time it will be transformed into a world power."[21]

A common theme in the discourse of the nationalist insurgents is that the West seeks to divide Iraq into three states so it can rule through puppet regimes that will depend on the West for their security and provide it with cheap oil as compensation for its protection. They insist that the United States is continuing the British and French colonial legacy of "divide and conquer" following World War I. The previously mentioned communiqué of the four Islamic and nationalist groups addresses this issue directly: "We, as elements of the resistance, realize that our nation is comprised of a variety of spectrums.... Each one of these spectra should enjoy the wealth and amenities of our loving country, according to the established principles, which we should uphold and honor and not deviate away from, some of these principles are the unity and independence of this country and guaranteeing the human rights."

Fifth, the end of the old regime's patronage system deprived tribes and members of the security services of their privileges. Many disgruntled insurgents harbor little sympathy for Saddam; however, they are enraged by the loss of status and privileges they acquired under the Baathist regime. Saddam Hussein, like many dictators in the region, relied on patronage to shore up his base of support in the military and win over the Sunni tribes in central Iraq and Al Anbar province. This was particularly the case during the 1990s, when the state's legitimacy came under stress following the military debacles with Iran (1980–88) and Kuwait (1990–91). The old regime gave privileges to Sunni tribes through land reform, contracts, military bases, and employment in Baathist institutions and security services. The latter, in particular, were paid generously compared to ordinary Iraqis and received a number of fringe benefits that supplemented their relatively high salaries. For example, many in the security services received a free plot of land, inexpensive construction loans that sometimes turned into grants, access to low-priced merchandise in government warehouses and special supermarkets, and free health care in top-of-the-line military hospitals.

Saddam also handsomely rewarded some of the tribes in the Sunni regions to enhance his legitimacy. He paid homage to tribal traditions in public ceremonies, and high-level Baathists paid their respects during funerals of tribal leaders. The tribes loyal to Saddam received financial and developmental support, their members were recruited into Saddam's elite forces and personal guards, and they were permitted to control the lucrative smuggling trade that flourished during the years of sanctions.[22] These tribes do not care for democracy or major social change, but they do not mind it as long as they retain some of the privileges bestowed on them by the former regime. Talk of federalism and regional autonomy invariably implies depriving them of the oil-rich regions of Iraq and control over the patronage through employment and corruption that characterizes many developing economies in the Middle East.

The sixth development contributing to protracted insurgency relates to the prosecution of the initial phase of counterinsurgency in late 2003 and early 2004. The occupation forces engaged in indiscriminate and culturally insensitive tactics that alienated many Iraqis; convinced them that coalition forces were occupiers, not liberators; and drove many ordinary citizens to seek vengeance against the coalition.[23] Mass arrests, night searches, heavy-handed interrogations, and the attitude of U.S. forces toward Iraqi drivers on dangerous roads have built a psychological wall between the coalition and the people.[24]

Personal humiliation is a theme that insurgents capitalize on repeatedly in their videos and literature (as we shall see in chapter 5). Many of the statements on jihadi Web sites stress the importance of taking revenge for the transgressions in Abu Ghraib prison or even for insults to the honor of Islam. Following major incursions by coalition forces into rebellious regions, the insurgents execute major bombing operations in revenge. Arrests and ill treatment at the hands of foreigners, violation of the honor of the household during searches, or loss of friends or relatives in accidental or intentional attacks by coalition forces foster personal rage and incentives to join or at least support insurgent groups.

In Arab tribal society, revenge killing *(thar)* is intricately connected with three values necessary for tribal unity and survival: *sharaf* (nobleness), `*ird* (honor), and *muruah* (chivalry or manliness). If a tribal member is killed, it becomes a matter of individual honor and responsibility to avenge the killing. Failure to take vengeance raises questions about one's nobility and sense of manhood. If the killer cannot be found, it is permissible to kill his close relative. The only honorable way out of revenge is to pay *diya* (blood money). Tribal feuds historically have been a major source of instability because cycles of revenge could go on for decades, if not longer.

The old regime did not attempt to dismantle the clan system in the Sunni Triangle; on the contrary, Saddam Hussein's charisma was based partly on this heritage of tribal chivalry. Consequently counterinsurgency in the Sunni Triangle has combined with the seemingly anachronistic tradition of tribal revenge killing. Many of those fighting point to actual and alleged excesses of coalition forces, including soldiers searching homes without permission, stepping on detainees with their boots, frisking women, and using dogs during home searches. (Practicing Muslims consider dogs to be unclean animals, and they are not allowed to pray in areas dogs have sniffed until the areas are thoroughly cleansed.)

The story of Marwan Abu Ubeida is instructive in this context. Abu Ubeida was a twenty-year-old suicide bomber from a privileged family in Fallujah. He was Sunni and deeply religious. The event that pushed him into the insurgency was the killing of twelve demonstrators by U.S. soldiers near a school in Fallujah in April 2003. Abu Ubeida was among the protestors, but he was not harmed. However, the apparent excessiveness of the shootings caused him to join others in small-scale operations against coalition forces.

Abu Ubeida's initial participation quickly turned into a deeper commitment to the insurgency. He severed ties with his family and former friends. He immersed himself in jihadi tapes, literature, and discussions. He also relinquished all logistical and leadership decisions to his handlers. More important, he made a promise to a friend who blew himself up in early 2005: "We made a pact that we would meet in heaven."[25]

The six developments described above precipitated the grievances of insurgents and produced relative deprivation or a sense of material and status loss in relation to the rising Shia and Kurdish communities. However, grievances alone were not sufficient to produce insurgency. The political instability generated by the rise of leaders who had yet to consolidate their legitimacy in Iraq created an opportunity for newly marginalized actors to seek power through mass mobilization and violence. Resistance became a source of legitimacy in Iraq, especially as the U.S. project faltered through catastrophic mistakes and lack of sufficient postwar planning.[26] Iraq was flooded with guns and ammunition, and the alienated security forces had skills and experience in warfare. Thus potential insurgents possessed the resources necessary for mobilization.

In an interview an unidentified IAI leader points out that the insurgents benefited from policies of the old regime that "forced every youth in

Iraq to join the army and serve for a certain period.... Therefore, all Iraqis are trained to use weapons and many of the arts of war...." He adds that "many Iraqis were involved in fierce international battles, and they gained experience and became used to war.... The previous regime spent most of its ruling time in wars armed and spent large amounts of money buying and producing weapons; this was in the best interests of the holy warriors."[27]

The mix of threats produced by Shia–Kurdish ascendancy, de-Baathification, and physical insecurity combined with political instability, inadequate security forces, and abundance of military arsenals and experienced cadres to produce an insurgency and give it deadly force. As shown below, the nationalist insurgents were augmented by ideological Baathists and jihadi Salafis who had their own reasons to fight.

THE DWINDLING BAATHISTS: SYSTEM-COLLAPSE STRATEGY

The ideological Baathists are individuals who joined the Baath party out of loyalty to the former regime or who attained high positions of power under Saddam Hussein. They are different from the vast majority of nominal Baathists who joined the party out of necessity or expediency. Like the jihadi Salafis (discussed in chapter 2), the ideological Baathists are pursuing a system-collapse strategy: the complete dismantlement of public order, governing political and economic institutions, and state security forces. System collapse leads to a failed state in which power resides with substate paramilitary groups, and public loyalties go to specific political patrons (warlords) or ethnosectarian communities, not the state. Politically marginal factions that can never hope to compete in a democratic political order are pursuing this strategy in Iraq.

The ideological Baathists target coalition forces, economic infrastructure, Iraqi security services, government officials, foreign contractors, Shia and Kurdish parties and civilians, voters, and Sunnis willing to work with the new order.[28] The Baathists are associated with the General Command of the Mujahidin of the Armed Forces, which consists of several regional brigades, and the Mujahidin Central Command. Their cadres consist of former army personnel, members of the security services, and high-ranking officials and intellectuals of the deposed Baathist Party. Many are supported by Saddam Hussein's extended family, which has fled to neighboring countries. Although the Baathists have not used suicide attacks as much as the jihadi Salafis have, they were the first to use this tactic in Iraq during the invasion phase, deploying two female suicide bombers. They have formed the Fedayeen Saddam (FS) and the Faruq Brigades to carry out suicide missions.[29]

Baathists loyal to the former regime naturally took the lead in resisting the invasion and occupation of Iraq. Saddam Hussein did not plan for an insurgency; he never believed the United States would drive its forces all the way to Baghdad. However, according to captured Iraqi leaders and military generals, Saddam anticipated a U.S. strategy of internal subversion, not a complete invasion and occupation. The United States, Saddam thought, would wage a massive aerial bombardment campaign to weaken the internal security structures of the Baathist regime. The Shia, in turn, would be encouraged to rebel in the south, as happened in 1991 following the first Gulf War to liberate Kuwait.

Accordingly, Saddam dispersed the FS paramilitary forces throughout Iraq and deposited weapons caches in schools, mosques, homes, and military bases to repress any possible uprising.[30] In their search for weapons of mass destruction, U.S. forces came across many of these caches but did not clear them out because they did not have the mandate or personnel to destroy small-arms depots.[31] As a result, valuable resources were left behind for Iraqi insurgents. The role of the FS was to contain any uprising until the elite Revolutionary Guards arrived to suppress the rebellion. The FS were trained to employ basic small-arms fire, rocket-propelled grenades (RPGs), and explosives.

In an ominous move, Saddam put his cousin Ali Hassan al-Majeed ("Chemical Ali") in charge of the Shia-populated south. Al-Majeed is best known for killing thousands of Kurds in the town of Halabja during the 1988 Anfal campaign, which featured the indiscriminate use of chemical weapons.[32] The former regime's calculations and preparations suggest that the ideological Baathists have no moral qualms about attacking their own Shia population to maintain power, which helps explain their tacit alliance with the extreme Salafis who have virulently negative views of Shia Islam.

The ideological Baathists insist that Iraq is part of the Arab nation and the cradle of one of the greatest Arab and Islamic civilizations, the Abbasid Empire. The violation of its sovereignty without justification rekindled memories of earlier waves of British and French imperialism in the region, which divided the Arab nation in accordance with imperial designs and without the approval of its people. Many Iraqis see the coalition forces in Iraq as a continuation of the imperialist tradition that seeks to divide Arabs and give ascendancy to non-Arab Kurds and pro-Iranian Shia. They also see the invasion as part of a conspiracy to weaken resistance against Israel and topple other Arab nationalist regimes, including Syria, that are the remaining stalwart opponents of Zionism in the region.[33]

The ideological Baathists have declared their commitment to reinstalling an Iraqi nationalist regime opposed to Iranian influence in Iraq through Shia dominance. This rhetoric, however, masks their real aim, which is to regain their lost privileges under the old regime. To this end, they made a tacit marriage of convenience with indigenous and foreign Salafis who want to install an Islamic state based on the model of the pious ancestors (al-Salaf al-Salih) of Islam. The two are ideologically opposed, and their ultimate objectives radically diverge; but both are working toward the same immediate goal: overthrowing the new regime through a strategy of public insecurity, economic collapse, and a war of attrition, or "death by a thousand cuts." One of the Baathist groups has outlined the steps necessary to cause the collapse of the system in Iraq:

- "Eliminating the Persians, their consulate, their intelligence, and those who cooperate with them, especially the Iraqis who carry out sectarian genocide";
- "Stopping the oil exports from the south";
- "[Forcing] the occupiers to import gasoline and diesel from abroad to embroil them financially and increase the cost of the occupation";
- "[Punishing] the foreign companies and their contractors that support the occupation ... as well as the companies that intend on building an oil refinery"; and
- "[Protecting] our people's lives ... from the treachery of the police gangs and the Persians by any available means, including [an eye for an eye]."[34]

Underlying the Islamic and nationalist rhetoric of the ideological Baathists is a desire to reestablish the dominance of their deposed party. Baathist ideology never really garnered the support of the masses in Iraq. Instead, the party created a "republic of fear," in which the ubiquitous state secret police penetrated all spheres of political, religious, and civil life.[35] The Baathists did attempt to foster an Iraqi nationalism that might overcome ethnosectarian divisions in society and give the Sunni elite legitimacy. This Iraqi nationalism harked back to Iraq's Mesopotamian heritage in an effort to undercut potential Kurdish and Shia objections to Sunni hegemony.[36] However, the war with Iran, genocidal repression of the Kurds for their rebellious demands for autonomy and independence, the war with the United States following Iraq's invasion of Kuwait, and Shia rebellions in the south resulted in a shift during the 1990s toward a mixed (or even contradictory) discourse of anti-Western pan-Arabism, tribalism, and Islamism.[37] The totalitarian nature of the regime, the disasters brought on Iraq by the Baathist state, and its ever-changing ideological facade further reduced its appeal among the masses.

Yet despite its unpopularity, the Baath party was a mobilizing agent with organizational, surveillance, and fighting skills. The party had experienced tribulations in the past and survived. In a 2005 interview, Muhammad Abdullah al-Shahwani, director of the Iraqi National Intelligence Agency, asserted that former Baathists inside and outside Iraq are a dominant force in the insurgency. The Baathist Party had 2 million members, he argued, and "if 20 percent of them remain, that is still a substantial number to lead the insurgency."[38]

Former regime elements that sponsored the insurgency include Izzet al-Duri (former vice president), Mohammed Younis al-Ahmed (a regional commander of the Baath Party), Ibrahim al-Hassan al-Tikriti (Saddam Hussein's half-brother), Yasser Sab`awi al-Tikriti (a nephew of Saddam Hussein), and Major General Rashid Muhammad (head of the FS), to name a few.[39] The first two formations to carry out insurgent activities were (1) Baathists in the Leaders of the Resistance and Liberation and (2) Muhammad's Army (MA). The latter, according to Dr. Muthanna Harith al-Dari, spokesman for the Iraqi Association of Muslim Scholars, is mostly dominated by Baathists who were officers in the Iraqi army.[40] Insurgents from MA confirm the role of the Baathists in this formation, including Staff Colonel Muayyad Yasin Aziz Abd-al-Razzaq al-Nasiri, commander of MA, arrested in late 2004 or early 2005.[41]

According to another account, Baathists were the first to offer resistance in MA. After the fall of Baghdad, they formed a group in Al Anbar province with the help of military officers, FS, and Arab volunteers bewildered by the quick surrender of Baghdad. Baathist leaders funded MA from inside and outside Iraq through money Saddam had given them before the occupation.[42] Although MA has not been on the scene since 2005, the Armed Forces General Command, one of the brigades that made up this formation, continues to operate to this day.

The ideological Baathists are the losers who do not expect any sympathy from the new regime and cannot hope to play any role in a Shia- and Kurd-dominated state. All they can hope for is a failed state in which they can utilize their organizational and military skills to reestablish a party that could take power through a coup, as they did in 1963 and 1968. Their lack of popularity has forced them to melt into other insurgent forces, mainly the indigenous nationalists and jihadi Salafis.[43] Other insurgent groups officially reject Baathism and have made it clear that they will never allow the Baathists to represent them or return to power.

THE VAST POOL OF MERCENARIES

Many of the insurgents in Iraq are not fighting for political programs. According to interviews with U.S. personnel who served in Iraq, many of the initial insurgents were "amateurs paid by professionals."[44] As time passed, these novice insurgents gained expertise, but they have remained mercenaries or, more accurately, opportunists who serve as kidnappers, extortionists, or guns for hire. No specific catapulting events pushed them into action; instead, they are driven by the general state of lawlessness in cities resulting from lack of sufficient police and security forces, their ability to exploit porous borders, and the demand for their services. Some, however, are motivated by the need for income that many skilled personnel from the former military and security forces experienced after being dismissed without a pension or alternative employment.

Preceding the invasion in 2003, Iraq was devastated by two wars (the Iraq-Iran war of 1980–88 and the U.S.-Iraq war of 1990–91) and nearly twelve years of economic sanctions. As a result, the social structure of Iraq was under heavy strain, as many ordinary Iraqis suffered substantial diminution in their salaries and quality of life. During this period, a shadow economy developed in which black marketers, criminal syndicates, and petty criminals played a leading role in providing goods, services, and employment. When the Iraqi regime collapsed in 2003, the situation worsened exponentially. Postwar de-Baathification policies put more stress on an already unsustainable economy. In addition, before the war Saddam

Hussein released many criminals from jail under a general amnesty. It is not clear why he did this, but it might have been an effort to build good-will among their families before the impending war.

The combined effect of economic collapse and the presence of experienced gangs of smugglers, criminals, and black marketers meant that the objective conditions for mercenary recruitment were in place. Ordinary people seeking a form of employment or a supplement to their current meager income engage in apparent resistance activities that are mere opportunities for making money. These mercenaries are probably involved in six relatively low-risk activities:

- Kidnapping foreigners and Iraqi nationals and turning them over to insurgents or death squads for sums of money;
- Lobbing mortars, firing rockets, or placing roadside bombs for US$100–200;
- Smuggling personnel across borders for a fee;
- Stealing supplies from convoys and local merchants under the pretext of funding the resistance;
- Manufacturing improvised devices to be sold to insurgents; and
- Sabotaging oil pipelines and electric stations.

Financing for these opportunists is said to come mainly from criminal activities, such as robbery, kidnapping Iraqis and foreigners for ransom, and intercepting transport vehicles carrying fuel or goods. Money also comes from former regime elements who escaped to Syria and other neighboring countries and from internal financing by disgruntled Sunni tribes and businessmen who feel threatened by the new political and economic realities. These conditions threaten their control over the informal economy that developed during the sanction years or the patronage they were accustomed to receive under the former regime. Money flowing from outside benefactors and charities also facilitates insurgent activities.[45]

U.S. personnel who served in Iraq said in interviews with this author that insurgents in some instances appear to have financed their activities through coalition contract money. The interviewees suspected that some Iraqi contractors take coalition funds for local projects and divert a portion to insurgents as payoffs to allow them to continue working on those contracts. It is difficult to confirm these reports, but in a congressional hearing on insurgent financing, James Roberts, the deputy assistant secretary of defense for special operations and low-intensity conflict, testified that it is common for Iraqi officials or representatives of communities or tribes to cooperate with coalition forces one day and insurgents the next. In the same hearing he and others concluded that insurgents rely on "a relatively robust, diverse and resilient set of funding" from former senior-level regime elements, al Qaeda, and Ansar al-Islam networks in the region and Europe, tribal patrons, sympathetic preachers in mosques, donations from private Saudi individuals and charities, and criminal activities.[46]

Opportunists and mercenaries, however, are working for groups that do have political agendas, if not fully developed political programs. Without these groups, mercenaries would have little incentive to take the risks, as minimal as they may be, to attack coalition forces. Therefore, it would be a mistake to associate the insurgency in Iraq with criminality and opportunism. Mercenaries are working for groups pursuing two overarching strategies: system reintegration and system collapse.

ORGANIZATION AND COORDINATION

Despite their ideological and strategic differences, Islamic nationalists, Baathists, and jihadi Salafis find common ground in their immediate objective of ending the occupation and attacking the Iraqi security forces. The strategic alliance among nationalists, secularists, and religious fundamentalists is not unique to Iraq. Historically such alliances have developed over and over. During the early 1950s the Egyptian secular nationalists known as the "free officers" movement, led by Gamal Abdel Nasser, united with the Muslim Brotherhood to overthrow the British-backed monarchy. During the 1960s General Suharto of Indonesia came to power by inciting Islamic groups to slaughter hundreds of thousands of Communists and ethnic Chinese. During the Iranian revolution Islamists formed alliances with nationalists, leftists, and liberals to overthrow the shah. In each of these episodes, the marriage of convenience ended when one faction repressed the other. In Egypt the Muslim Brothers were jailed, exiled, or executed; in Indonesia the Islamic groups were heavily monitored and co-opted into state institutions; in Iran the Islamists repressed all the other opposition forces as the mullahs established an Islamic theocracy. The marriage of convenience among Iraqi insurgent groups may end as soon as the coalition forces leave the country.

As a result of their marriage of convenience, insurgent factions have coordinated and cooperated on the field of battle. From mid-2003 to early 2005, tens if not hundreds of brigades claimed operations (see appendix 1). However, by 2006 consistent claims of responsibility for operations narrowed substantially to about eight groups: the IAI, Mujahidin Shura Council (which includes AQI), ASG, al-Rashidin Army (RA), 1920 RB, SDAB, MAI, and GCMAF.

Brigades within the major groups continue to operate regionally and on their own turf, despite evidence of some coordination among insurgent groups. Most of the major groups consist of numerous brigades and battalions, reflecting a horizontal rather than a hierarchical structure.[47] The loyalty of these brigades and squadrons to their nominal organizations has yet to be tested. In previous Islamist insurgencies in Algeria and Kashmir, as some groups began to contemplate a peaceful resolution of the conflict they began to splinter.

What explains the convergence of hundreds of brigades under a few major groupings? There are no conclusive answers to this question, but one can come up with four reasonable hypotheses that are not always mutually exclusive. The first involves the initial success of some groups in making a name for themselves in the insurgency. In interviews U.S. personnel who served in Iraq expressed the belief that local brigades latched onto known insurgent groups to appear to be part of a bigger, significant movement. Some of the insurgent groups encouraged local brigades to issue communiqués under the name of the mother group. If this is the case, then insurgent groups most probably are connected by networks of relationships, not ideological bonds or commitment to the larger group.

A second explanation is that insurgent groups in control of large sums of money can entice smaller groups to carry out operations in their name in exchange for continuous funding. The third hypothesis revolves around control over informal economies and criminal activities. Insurgent groups that operate in unison in certain areas can exclude others from their turf, achieving unfettered control over the shadow economy and criminal syndicates while they appear to be engaging in insurgent activities.

The fourth hypothesis is that insurgent groups are thinking in terms of political cooperation and military coordination in light of their initial success in throwing coalition forces off balance and the possibility of dislodging foreign forces from Iraq.[48] Moreover, Iraqis have called for greater transparency as to what the insurgents hope to achieve and whether they can provide an alternative to the existing situation. AQI, for example, felt tremendous pressure from Iraqis because it relied almost exclusively on foreign fighters. As a result of this pressure, Zarqawi surrounded himself with Iraqi leaders and formed a union with the Victorious Sect and several other smaller Iraqi groups in the MSC in January 2006. All the major figures around Zarqawi became Iraqis. His deputy and the head of the Martyrs Brigades was Abu Abdul Rahman al-Iraqi; the head of the military wing was Abu Aseed al-Iraqi; the head of the Islamic legal committee was Abu Hamza al-Baghdadi; and the head of the media wing was Abu Maysara al-Iraqi. Appointing an Iraqi as the leader of the MSC is significant because it shows a degree of political awareness and the need to appeal to a broader public.[49]

It is interesting to note, however, that some of the groups with an ideological affinity for jihadi Salafism did not join Zarqawi's new formation in the MSC. ASG, for example, did not join Zarqawi despite having an almost identical ideology and strategy. Similarly, the IAI, which shares some of the rhetoric of jihadi Salafism, did not join the new formation. This suggests that unity among the jihadists is still incomplete.

Another example of growing coordination among the insurgents is the political position taken by the IAI, MAI, 1920 RB, and SDAB. On several occasions they have issued joint communiqués reflecting a unified voice on some political issues. At one point they issued a political statement under the heading of the JCB.[50] According to Ibrahim al-Shamari, the spokesman of the IAI, insurgent groups are inclined to merge in the field, but security matters necessitate that they work separately for the time being.[51] In another example of coordination, nine groups, including the IAI, MAI, 1920 RB, and ASG, signed a communiqué calling on local police forces in Al Anbar province to return to work to protect citizens from daily insecurity resulting from crime.[52]

Coordination also appears to have taken place on the battlefield. U.S. forces observed that fighters in Fallujah in late 2004 exhibited platoon-like coordination with advanced military training and techniques.[53] In another instance, coalition forces discovered a bunker nearly the size of the Empire State Building's office space filled with arms and ammunition, "suggesting that at least some insurgents are acting like a guerrilla army that has supplies, shelter, food, and arms. The bunker contains a living quarter, showers, and air conditioner. Troops discovered machine guns, mortars, rockets, artillery rounds, ski masks, log books, video camera, night vision goggles, and satellite phones."[54]

Coordination is also apparent in specific operations. For instance, on several occasions ASG has claimed joint responsibility for attacks with the IAI and the MAI.[55] It also claimed joint attacks with AQI at least twice.[56] The IAI claimed responsibility for joint operations with the ASG and MSC.[57] An interview with Abu Umar, an IAI leader residing in Syria, revealed regular contacts with the Islamists: "Often some of these groups ask us for specific help with a target. We recently had discussions about an operation involving a candidate for suicide with whom we actually met. We gave them our information about the intended target and provided maps in our possession as well as specific information about the target's environment."[58]

Insurgents often cooperate to launch coordinated attacks on prisons to free captured insurgents. In February 2004 insurgents in Fallujah attacked a prison, killing more than a dozen police officers and freeing approximately seventy prisoners. In another incident, approximately forty militants attacked the infamous Abu Ghraib prison to free captured insurgents held there. In March 2006 approximately 200 insurgents from several groups attacked a police station prison in Muqdadiya using mortars, grenades, and small-arms fire to free captured insurgents. Before the offensive the insurgents cut telephone lines and placed roadside bombs to block reinforcement troops from reaching the prison.[59] Thus, although insurgent groups are divided by different political and strategic orientations, such divisions have not precluded them from cooperating on the field or in specific operations.

CONCLUSION

Insurgent groups seem united in the objective of expelling coalition forces from Iraq. However, this apparent unity may mask the ideological and strategic divides within the insurgency. As chart 1 illustrates, insurgents diverge along two continua: strategy (system reintegration versus system collapse) and ideology (Islamism versus nationalism). It is important to stress that these strategic and ideological divisions are much more fluid than these representational categories imply. Nonetheless, these appear to be the general ideological and strategic tendencies present in the insurgency.

The indigenous Iraqi Islamic and nationalist rebel groups consisting of disaffected Sunnis and nominal Baathists are pursuing the goal of reintegration of marginalized Sunnis in any future Iraqi regime, on equal

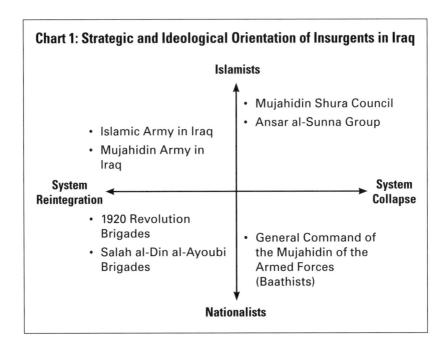

footing with the Shia and Kurds. Although their rhetoric resembles that of the extremists in the jihadi Salafi camp, their use of Islamic discourse is intended to mobilize people for a nationalist project, not for regional or global jihad. They insist on a unified Iraq—as opposed to a federal system based on sectarian divisions—that shares the country's oil wealth, public employment, ministerial positions, and government patronage equally with Sunnis. Above all, they believe existing political arrangements set up by the occupation forces are illegitimate; only when the occupation of Iraq ends will it be possible to begin discussing a new political process.

The second faction, the ideological Baathists, is pursuing a system-collapse strategy that seeks to reinstall a regime thoroughly rejected by Iraqis. Despite their strategic and ideological divisions, these insurgent groups so far have found it advantageous to cooperate politically and coordinate on the battlefield.

NOTES

1. Habib Jaber, "Who Resists in Iraq? What Is Not Said about the Truth of the Iraqi Resistance" (Arabic), *Asharq al-Awsat* (London), August 12, 2004; Zaki Chehab, *Inside the Resistance: The Iraqi Insurgency and the Future of the Middle East* (New York: Nation Books, 2005); Faris Bin Hazam, "The Outsiders Are Not the Majority of al Qaeda's Cadre in Iraq" (Arabic), *Al-Hayat*, February 10, 2006.

2. Open Source Center (OSC), "1920 Revolution Brigades Publishes Jihad Creed; Forum Participant Describes As 'Degradation,'" www.opensource.gov (accessed November 15, 2005).

3. Hassan Khalil Ghraib, *The Iraqi National Resistance: The Decisive Battle against America* (Arabic) (Beirut: Dar al-Taliah, 2004), 218.

4. Dr. Ibrahim al-Shamari, the spokesman of the Islamic Army in Iraq, made it clear in an interview with Al Jazeera television that the "farcical" political process would not end the insurgency. Only direct talks between the resistance and the occupation forces would be acceptable to the insurgents. Genuine negotiations and dialogue to end the crisis must be preceded by official recognition of the resistance as the legitimate representative of the Iraqi people and a direct invitation to the Islamic Army in Iraq to negotiate the withdrawal of multinational forces. The interview aired during the program *Today's Encounter*, hosted by Yasser Abu Hilala, March 24, 2006. This stance was confirmed by the 1920 Revolution Brigades in a communiqué that appeared in *Al-Hayat*, "Iraqi Factions Deny Unification with Al-Qaeda" (Arabic), April 3, 2006.

5. Quoted in Patrick Graham, "Beyond Fallujah: A Year with the Iraqi Resistance." *Harper's*, June 2004, 41.

6. Quoted in Nir Rosen, *In the Belly of the Green Bird: The Triumph of the Martyrs in Iraq* (New York: Free Press, 2006), 61.

7. The Mujahidin Army has claimed two suicide attacks against coalition forces. OSC, "Mujahidin Army Claims Suicide Operation in Al-Fallujah," December 29, 2005; OSC, "Iraq: Armed Group Claims Car Bombing Against US Patrol in Abu Ghurayb," September 26, 2005. The Islamic Army in Iraq declares in its manifesto that it believes suicide attacks are legitimate if they are (1) approved by an Islamic leader, (2) beneficial to Muslims, (3) motivated by the proper beliefs in God, not despair, and (4) the only way to weaken the enemy. It claimed responsibility for only one suicide attack on March 24, 2005, and, along with Ansar al-Sunna and the Mujahidin Army, two other attacks on June 23, 2005. The 1920 RB also claimed one suicide attack. OSC, "1920 Revolution Brigades Claim Suicide Operation against US Officer in Abu-Ghurayb," March 29, 2006. In its published manifesto, the 1920 RB explicitly warns against targeting civilians: "[We stay] away from carrying out jihad operations in markets,

residential areas, and schools because centers and markets belonging to the people are not our battlefields, especially following the latest actions taken by the enemy, with which they intended to mar the pure face of jihad and its people." See OSC, "1920 Revolution Brigades Publishes Jihad Creed; Forum Participant Describes As 'Degradation,'" November 15, 2005.

8. Interview appeared in the ninth issue of the group's online magazine, *al-Fursan* (no date given, but the magazine appeared in August 2006). OSC, "Al-Fursan Magazine Interview with Amir of Islamic Army in Iraq Discusses Strategy, Targets, Cooperation," August 30, 2006.

9. Samir al-Khalil, *Republic of Fear: The Politics of Modern Iraq* (Berkeley: University of California Press, 1989).

10. Amatzia Baram, "Neo-Tribalism in Iraq: Saddam Hussein's Tribal Policies 1991–1996," *International Journal of Middle East Studies* 29, no. 1 (February 1997): 1–31.

11. Edward Cody, "Sunni Resistance to U.S. Presence Hardens," *Washington Post*, July 7, 2004; Hiwa Osman, "What Do the Insurgents Want? Different Visions, Same Bloody Tactics," *Washington Post*, May 8, 2005; Ahmed S. Hashim, *Insurgency and Counter-Insurgency in Iraq* (Ithaca, N.Y.: Cornell University Press, 2006), 27–28.

12. OSC, "Islamic Army in Iraq, 1920 Revolutionary Brigades, Mujahidin Army, Islamic Front Issue Statement," November 21, 2005.

13. OSC, "Islamic Army in Iraq Comments on US Stand on Civil War, Role of Militias," May 30, 2006.

14. Thomas E. Ricks, *Fiasco: The American Military Adventure in Iraq* (New York: Penguin Press, 2006).

15. Michael R. Gordon and Bernard E. Trainor, *COBRA II: The Inside Story of the Invasion and Occupation of Iraq* (New York: Pantheon, 2006), 160–61.

16. Daniel Williams, "In Sunni Triangle, Loss of Privilege Breeds Bitterness," *Washington Post*, January 13, 2004; Robin Wright, "Series of U.S. Fumbles Blamed for Turmoil in Postwar Iraq," *Washington Post*, April 11, 2004; Ricks, *Fiasco*, 158–64.

17. Roger D. Petersen, *Understanding Ethnic Violence: Fear, Hatred, and Resentment in Twentieth-Century Eastern Europe* (New York: Cambridge University Press, 2002), 40, 256.

18. Michael Slackman, "Fearing Revenge: Hussein's Militia Forces Lie Low and Deny Hurtful Role," *Los Angeles Times*, April 16, 2003; Huda Jasim and Niaman al-Haimas, "Iraqi Air Force Officers and Military Doctors Are Suddenly Killed in Their Homes" (Arabic), *Asharq al-Awsat* (London), July 7, 2005; Anthony Shadid and Steve Fainaru, "Militias on the Rise across Iraq: Shiite and Kurdish Groups Seizing Control, Instilling Fear in North and South," *Washington Post*, August 21, 2005; International Crisis Group, "The Next Iraqi War?

Sectarianism and Civil Conflict," *ICG Middle East Report* 52, February 27, 2006.

19. Kirk Semple, "Kidnapped in Iraq: Victim's Tale of Clockwork Death and Ransom," *New York Times*, May 7, 2006.

20. Edward Cody, "To Many, Mission Not Accomplished: Residents Say Occupation's Unkept Promises, Military Tactics Fuel Resistance," *Washington Post*, June 3, 2004.

21. OSC, "Islamic Army in Iraq Posts Creed, 'Methodology,'" August 30, 2005.

22. Slackman, "Fearing Revenge"; Baram, "Neo-Tribalism in Iraq"; Amatzia Baram, "Who Are the Insurgents: Sunni Arab Rebels in Iraq," *United States Institute of Peace Special Report 134* (Washington, D.C.: United States Institute of Peace, April 2005); Hashim, *Insurgency and Counter-Insurgency in Iraq*, 25–26.

23. Jeffery Gettleman, "Anti-U.S. Outrage Unites a Growing Iraqi Resistance," *New York Times*, April 11, 2004; Cody, "To Many, Mission Not Accomplished."

24. Ricks, *Fiasco*, chapters 9 and 11.

25. Aparisim Ghosh, "Inside the Mind of an Iraqi Suicide Bomber," *Time*, July 4, 2005.

26. Gordon and Trainor, *COBRA II*, chapter 8; Ricks, *Fiasco*.

27. See the group's online magazine, *al-Fursan*, issue 9 (no date, but sometime in August 2006). OSC, "Al-Fursan Magazine Interview."

28. For Baathist communiqués justifying attacks on each of these targets, see Ghraib (*The Iraqi National Resistance*, 65–72); OSC, "Mujahidin Central Command Calls for Killing 'Iraqi Pro-Government' Leaders, Targeting Oil Pipes, Foreign Interests," September 22, 2005; OSC, "Mujahidin Central Command Urges Attacks on Financial Resources, Oil," March 8, 2006.

29. For claims of suicide attacks by Baathists, see OSC, "Iraq: Group Claims Responsibility for Attacks on US Troops in Al-Fallujah," June 6, 2003; OSC, "The Sixth Communiqué Issued by the 'Higher Command of the Mujahidin in Iraq–Media Branch,'" June 7, 2003; OSC, "Terrorism: Jihadist Chat Room on 20 Nov–2 Dec Iraqi Resistance," December 12, 2003; OSC, "Jihadist Bulletin Board Reports on 4–10 Dec Iraqi Resistance," December 16, 2003; and list of communiqués by the Leaders of the Iraqi Resistance and Liberation in Ghraib, *The Iraqi National Resistance*, 187–216.

30. Gordon and Trainor, *COBRA II*, 136.

31. Ricks, *Fiasco*.

32. Gordon and Trainor, *COBRA II*, 61–62, 122.

33. For a clear expression of their views, see the Baathist political and strategic program issued September 9, 2003, "The Political and Strategic Program of the Iraqi Resistance under the Leadership of the Arab Socialist Baath Party" (Arabic), *Al-Majd* (Amman), September 15, 2003, 5.

34. OSC, "Mujahidin Central Command Lists Steps to Dismantle Iraqi Government," July 25, 2006.

35. Al-Khalil, *Republic of Fear*.

36. Amatzia Baram, *Culture, History, and Ideology in the Formation of Ba'thist Iraq, 1968-1989* (New York: St. Martin's Press, 1991).

37. Baram, "Neo-Tribalism in Iraq."

38. Interview with Maad Fayadh in *Asharq al-Awsat*, January 5, 2005.

39. Other names mentioned in association with the FS organization are Lt. Gen. Ali Abd Mahmud Ali al-Luhaybi (died under interrogation), Maj. Gen. Abd-al-Ilah Uwayn Jumah al-Tikriti, Maj. Gen. Makki Mustafa Humudat, Maj. Gen. Riyad Taha Abd Ahmad al-Tikriti, Maj. Gen. Humud al-Mahmud, Maj. Gen. Mahmud Hamadi Awdah al-Janabi, Maj. Gen. Jasim Hasan Salih Abd Salih al-Dulaymi, Maj. Gen. Sadr Hashim Hasan Latif al-Rawi, Maj. Gen. Taha Abd Ahmad al-Tikriti, Maj. Gen. Ayiz Nijm Hunaysh al-Marsumi, Maj. Gen. Raed Abd-al-Mahdi Karim al-Juburi, Maj. Gen. Saadi Abd-al-Razzaq Said al-Ani, Maj. Gen. Jabbar Said al-Ani, Lt. Gen. Ali al-Hibi, and Maj. Gen. Said Wahib Salman Jasim al-Ubaydi, and the head of the Baghdad Military Office, Fadil Ibrahim Mahmud al-Mashhadani.

40. OSC, "Iraq's Al-Dari Says Boycott of Elections Final, Discusses 'Resistance' Formation," January 17, 2005.

41. OSC, "Iraqi Channel Airs 'Confessions' of Muhammad's Army Commander on Syria, Iran Links," January 14, 2005; OSC, "UK Reporters Talk to Iraqi Insurgent Commander Coordinating Suicide Bombers," May 9, 2005.

42. Hamam Hassan, "Saddam Was the First to Attract Islamic Organizations and Later Regretted it" (Arabic), *Al-Hayat*, February 25–26, 2006, parts 1 and 2.

43. Sudud al-Salihi, "Iraqi Baath Party Leader Confirms Cooperation with Islamist Sunni Movements" (Arabic), *Al-Hayat* (London), December 31, 2004. Also see interview with General Hussein Ali Kamel, head of Iraq's internal intelligence service (Ministry of Interior) in *Azzaman* (Arabic, London), March 5, 2005.

44. In interviews three U.S. servicemen who have served in Iraq asserted that the consensus in the field was that "many" insurgents were "guns for hire"; January 5, 2006, interview in Fort Leavenworth, Kans., with a company commander in the First Cavalry Division who served in Baghdad and North Babel between February 2004 and March 2005 and e-mail correspondence, February 28, 2006, with a major in the 130th Engineer Brigade serving in Victory Base (Baghdad) and LSA Anaconda (Balad) since October 25, 2005. Both requested anonymity.

Author's interview with Maj. Daniel A. Schmitt at Fort Leavenworth, Kans., May 5, 2006.

45. Adnan Hussein and Amar al-Jundi, "Interview with Huwishar Zaybari, Iraqi Foreign Minister" (Arabic), *Asharq al-Awsat* (London), April 12, 2004; Anne Barnard, "Lethal Alliance Fuels Kidnappings: Iraq's Militants, Criminals Team Up." *Boston Globe*, September 25, 2004; Eric Schmitt and Thom Shanker, "Estimates by U.S. See More Rebels with More Funds," *New York Times*, October 22, 2004; Ghaith Abdul-Ahad, "Outside Iraq but Deep in the Fight: A Smuggler of Insurgents Reveals Syria's Influential, Changing Role," *Washington Post*, June 8, 2005; Sabrina Tavernise, "Unseen Enemy Is at Its Fiercest in a Sunni City," *New York Times*, October 23, 2005.

46. Committee Hearing, "U.S. Representative Jim Saxton (R-N.J.) Holds Hearing on Financing the Iraqi Insurgency," *Congressional Quarterly Transcriptions*, July 28, 2005, 16. See also John F. Burns and Kirk Semple, "U.S. Finds Iraq Insurgency Has Funds to Sustain Itself," *New York Times*, November 26, 2006.

47. Dexter Filkins, "The Struggle for Iraq: Structure of Rebellion; Profusion of Rebel Groups Helps Them Survive in Iraq," *New York Times*, December 2, 2005.

48. International Crisis Group, "In their Own Words: Reading the Iraqi Insurgency," *ICG Middle East Report 50*, February 15, 2006. According to this report, signs of growing centralization and coordination include more consistent claims of responsibility by fewer groups with distinctive logos and publications; creation of specialized brigades within each group for military, intelligence, and communication tasks; and joint declarations by several groups concerning military operations and political positions.

49. Hazam, "The Outsiders Are Not the Majority."

50. OSC, "Islamic Army in Iraq, 1920 Revolutionary Brigades, Mujahidin Army, Islamic Front Issue Second Joint Statement," November 22, 2005.

51. Interview was conducted by Yasser Abu Hilala, host of Al Jazeera program *Today's Encounter*, first aired March 24, 2006.

52. OSC, "Jihadist Groups in Al-Anbar Call for Return of Police Force," April 3, 2005.

53. Peter Mackler, "Iraqi insurgents an evolving force," *Agence France Presse*, April 22, 2004, www.afp.com/english/home/.

54. Edward Wong, "U.S. Uncovers Vast Hide-Out of Iraqi Rebels," *New York Times*, June 5, 2005.

55. OSC, "Ansar al-Sunnah Army Claims Destroying Hummer in Al-Karadah," June 24, 2005; OSC, "Mujahidin Army Claims Attack on Abu-Ghurayb Collective Effort by Insurgent Groups," April 4, 2005; OSC, "Statement by Ansar al-Sunnah, Mujahidin, Islamic Armies Threatens Iraqi Election," December 30, 2004.

56. Ansar al-Sunna Group claimed joint responsibility for attacks with al Qaeda on April 14, 2005, and May 31, 2005.

57. OSC, "Islamic Army in Iraq Claims Operation with Mujahidin Shura Council, Ansar al-Sunnah Army," February 6, 2006.

58. OSC, "Iraqi Sunni Insurgent Leader Describes Cooperation with Jihadists," June 15, 2006.

59. Bryan Bender, "U.S. Military Worried Over Change in Iraq Attacks," *Boston Globe*, April 24, 2005; Jeffery Gettleman, "Insurgents Captured in New Assault on Iraqi Police Station," *New York Times*, March 22, 2006.

CHAPTER 2

THE JIHADI SALAFIS

A casual observer of the Iraqi insurgency might label all the insurgent groups "Islamic" because of their names, rhetoric, and stated objectives. Even Baathists have jumped on the Islamic bandwagon. Known to be secular nationalists with visions of pan-Arab unity, the Baathists are not interested in establishing Islamic states or reviving the Islamic caliphate. Yet three of the main Baathist groups are the General Command of the Mujahidin of the Armed Forces, the Mujahidin Central Command, and Muhammad's Army. All three have Islamic terms in their titles (such as *Mujahidin*, or holy warriors). All three often pepper their communiqués with Islamic verses to give themselves the aura of Islamic rebels. The same could be said of groups such as the Islamic Army in Iraq or the Mujahidin Army in Iraq. Nearly all groups in the insurgency use Islam as the vocabulary of resistance. Their Islamism, however, is motivated by different strategic objectives. It is difficult to differentiate among the various tendencies in the "Islamic" insurgency without careful analysis of what each group is saying and doing on the ground.

At least three types of Islamic insurgents operate in Iraq. Like Hamas in Palestine and Hezbollah in southern Lebanon, the Islamic nationalists seek to harness the discourse of Islam to fight foreign occupiers. They use Islamism to mobilize against actual or perceived colonialists or imperialists, not to establish Islamic states or wage global jihad.

The second type of insurgent advocates revolutionary Islamism to transform the existing political order in a given state or national territory. This ideology resembles the revolutionary Islamism of the 1979 Iranian revolution, when Ayatollah Khomeini inspired the masses to rise up and overthrow the secular shah. In Egypt and Algeria during the 1990s armed Islamic groups rebelled against the state and sought to undermine its economic infrastructure. They targeted the state's security forces, police, government officials, intellectuals, artists, tourists, and ordinary civilians in hopes of collapsing the ruling order and mobilizing a social revolution. In Iraq Ansar al-Sunna Group (ASG) belongs in this category.

The third type of insurgent is the transnational Islamic terrorist, who struggles to replace regional governments and establish a base for permanent jihad. Al Qaeda in Iraq (AQI) falls into this category. Success for the transnational terrorists means not only ousting the foreign presence from Iraq, but also enabling *(tamkeen)* the jihadists to grow and wage the next jihad and the one after that, until Islam prevails on earth and "all religion is exclusively for God."

The revolutionary Islamists and the transnational terrorists often embrace jihadi Salafism, which represents an extreme form of Sunni Islamism that rejects democracy and Shia rule. As of 2006 the two major groups within the jihadi Salafi camp were the Mujahidin Shura Council (MSC) and ASG. The MSC is an umbrella organization consisting of several groups, the most important of which is AQI. The latter helped form the MSC in January 2006 with several other like-minded groups. Both the MSC and ASG have carried out suicide attacks through specific brigades. MSC has the Bara Bin-Malik Battalion (or al-Bara Bin-Malik Martyrdom Brigade) and a Martyrs Brigade (or Martyrdom Brigade). ASG has the Martyrs Brigade of Ansar al-Sunna. Their core cadres are composed of fighters connected to the second-generation jihadists who trained in Afghan camps during the 1990s, after the Soviet Union withdrew from Afghanistan. The most extreme jihadi Salafis are the foreign fighters linked to AQI, formed by the now deceased Abu Musab al-Zarqawi.

WHAT IS (JIHADI) SALAFISM?

Contemporary Salafism[1] is a strand of Islamic revivalism that idealizes and seeks to emulate the virtues, piety, and leadership that characterized the formative period of Islam from 610 CE, when the prophetic mission of Muhammad began in the Arabia Peninsula (modern day Saudi Arabia), until 661 CE, when Ali bin Abi Taleb, the last of the rightly guided successors *(al-Khulafa al-Rashidun)*, was killed. Salafism also refers to the pious companions of the Prophet *(sahaba)* who believed in his monotheistic message and suffered hardships because of their loyalty to him during the emergent phase of Islam. The Prophet, his loyal companions, and scholars who followed closely in their footsteps *(tabiun)* are referred to as *al-Salaf al-Salih* (the righteous predecessors or "founding fathers").

Jihadi Salafism should not be confused with other strands of Salafism such as the *sahwa* (Islamic awakening or political Islamic) movement in Saudi Arabia associated with Salman al-Awda or Safar al-Hawali, or with apolitical and conservative Salafi scholars such as Sheikh Naser al-Din al-Albani, Sheikh Ibn Uthaimin, Sheikh Abdel Aziz bin Baz, and Sheikh Abd al-Aziz al-Shaykh.[2]

Salafism is a modernist concept that initially emerged during the late nineteenth century in response to the decline of the Muslim Ottoman Empire vis-à-vis the West. Reformers such as Jamal al-Din al-Afghani (1838-1897) and Muhammad Abdu (1849-1905) were concerned that the West was advancing in science, commerce, and the art of warfare, while the Muslim world was lagging behind.

Part of the problem, the Salafi reformers argued, is that Muslims have "closed the gates of *ijtihad*," which is to say they have abandoned the spirit of exercising independent interpretation or reasoning based on the original sources of Islam (the Quran and the traditions of the Prophet or Sunna). Instead Muslims have become reliant on religious rulings and laws established by the four Islamic schools of jurisprudence *(madhahib)* between the late seventh and tenth centuries. In light of continuous historical change, excessive reliance on *taqlid* (imitation) results in stagnation in thought and precludes critical judgment necessary for innovation and progress.

These reformers were mainly concerned with circumventing the inherent traditionalism in the legal corpus of classical Islamic jurisprudence. They could not introduce major innovations in education, economics, government, and social relations without first questioning the godlike authority of the traditional jurists and scholars. Their answer to this dilemma was to return to the original sources of Islam and argue that only these sources—not the authority of fallible, albeit venerable, jurists and scholars—could constitute the foundations of Islamic law.

Contemporary fundamentalists adopted the modernist concept of Salafism and imbued it with different meanings.[3] Salafism became equated with traditionalist sects, known as *as-hab al-hadith* (people of the prophetic traditions) or *ahl al-sunna wal jamaah* (adherents of right practice and communal solidarity), that developed in the eighth and ninth centuries.[4] Contemporary Salafism privileges the golden age of the *Salaf al-Salih* over others because in this period the Muslims followed the Quran closely and without accretions of culture, human reason, philosophy, or any other innovations. They could do so because the Prophet Muhammad not only transmitted the Quran, the revealed word of God according to the Islamic tradition, but also interpreted its verses and shed light on its divine meaning. The Prophet Muhammad is touched with divine grace according to the Islamic tradition, so following closely in his footsteps by heeding his sayings and emulating his deeds is the best way to reach for perfection. He preached monotheism for twenty-two years (dying in 632 CE), and his rightly guided companions, both men and women, applied his teachings for almost thirty more years, so their lives provide abundant examples of how they would have acted in different situations and ruled on various issues. What better model to follow than theirs?

Contemporary jihadi Salafism is characterized by five features. First, it places immense emphasis on the concept of *tawhid* (unity of God, or monotheism). This emphasis is warranted because the first pillar of faith in Islam is the confession *la ilaha illa lah, Muhammad Rasul al-lah* (no God but Allah, Muhammad is his messenger). In this respect, jihadi Salafis are on the same page as apolitical Salafi scholars. However, to jihadi Salafis *tawhid* is more than a confession of faith; it is a way of life. It is more than an utterance to gain entry into the community of the faithful; it is sincere devotion and belief in the heart and proper behavior in everyday life. Conservative Salafi scholars also believe this but disagree about how to evaluate behavior when it has crossed the line from piety into apostasy.

Tawhid consists of affirming the unity of God's lordship in the universe *(tawhid al-rububiyyah),* which means that God is the only creator and provider. He has no partners, no intermediaries, and no offspring. He alone giveth and taketh away. *Tawhid* also consists of affirming worship of no one else but God *(tawhid al-uluhiyyah).* In other words, one cannot pray to anyone except God, so those who pray to saints, angels, idols, magicians, or objects such as gravesites are violating the unity of God. Finally, *tawhid* consists of affirming the uniqueness of God's features and attributes described in the Quran *(tawhid al-asma wal sifat).* In other words, although the Quran (explicitly or implicitly) describes God as having eyes, hands, and feet and as being omniscient and omnipresent, his characteristics are not the same as the eyes, hands, and feet of humans. His nominal attributes are not equivalent to the attributes of any human being. God has nothing in common with humans.

The second feature of contemporary jihadi Salafism is its emphasis on God's sovereignty *(hakimiyyat allah)*. As the only lawgiver, only God can define right and wrong, good and evil, permissible and forbidden. Unlike the *mutazila* (rationalist strand in Islam), Salafis do not believe that humans can arrive at the truth or distinguish between right and wrong through reasoning. There are limits to human rationality, and because one can never comprehend God's plan beyond what he has revealed for us, so one just has to follow the word of God as exemplified by the sayings and deeds of his Prophet and the pious ancestors.

God's sovereignty has three aspects. Salafis claim that the Quran is the revealed word of God, and much of its content falls in the category of clear and unequivocal verses *(muhkamat, nusus qatiyyah)*. Well-intentioned scholars may disagree on the meaning of some of the ambiguous verses *(mutashabihat)*, but they cannot disagree regarding the clear verses. The Quranic verses are not a puzzle or an enigma that contains multiple meanings. They are the final revelation from God intended to guide humanity until Judgment Day. Discovering and applying the intended meaning of the Quranic verses, therefore, is the ultimate form of devotion to God. Conversely, altering, ignoring, or nullifying God's revelation is violating God's sovereignty and subverting his will. Salafis also believe the Quran is the comprehensive guidance of God on matters of worship *(ibadat*, how to exhibit faith in God) and social relations *(muamalat*, economics, warfare, marriage, taxes, and so on). Therefore, there is no need for ancillary worldviews or ideologies such as Marxism, liberalism, or humanism. God has said it all. Salafis believe in the universalism of the Quran; it is applicable in all places on earth and at all times *(salih li kul makan wa zaman)*. Therefore, one cannot say that times have changed and we need new rules to live by, at least as far as the *muhkamat* (clear) verses are concerned. Saying so violates God's sovereignty on earth.

The third feature of contemporary Salafism follows closely from the second. It pertains to strict constructionist jurisprudence and rejection of innovations *(bida)*. The Quran is the final revelation of God and it is complete. Therefore, one must read it literally and adhere to a strict construction of its rules. Every innovation is usurping God's role and violating his unity and sovereignty. It creates space for human deviation, desire, and power. On the authority of prophetic tradition, Salafis argue that every innovation is a misguidance, and all misguidance produces damnation.

In practice, when ruling on an issue—say, the permissibility of marrying more than one wife—a Salafi scholar first would refer to the Quranic verses and determine what they had to say about marriage; then he would refer to the authentic traditions of the Prophet and see what he said and did with regard to marrying more than one wife. If the Quran says it is permissible to take more than one wife, as indeed it does, then the issue is virtually closed to discussion. If the prophetic tradition reveals that Muhammad took more than one wife, as indeed he did, then the Quranic revelation is further clarified and affirmed in action. It is not necessary to reason why God has permitted men to take more than one wife, nor is it necessary (although it might be instructive) to inquire as to the circumstances under which the Prophet took more than one wife. These are extracurricular exercises that, at best, increase people's faith in Islam and, at worst, create opportunities to imbue God's revealed word with human desires and deviation.

This example is perhaps a bit of an oversimplification of Salafi jurisprudence, but the point is that Salafis encourage a strict constructionist reading of the Quranic verses and prophetic traditions and downplay the role of human interpretive capacity and extratextual rationality. When reading a religious ruling *(fatwa)*, a Salafi scholar invariably begins by citing a plethora of Quranic verses and then prophetic traditions. To the extent that he calls on other authorities to make a case, he relies on classical scholars hostile to rationalism and philosophical interpretation who uphold a strict constructionist reading of Quranic and prophetic texts.

Contemporary Salafism makes claims concerning the permissibility and necessity of *takfir* (declaring a Muslim to be outside the creed, the equivalent of excommunication in Catholicism). Salafis believe Muslims can be judged to have committed major transgressions that put them outside the Islamic faith. They believe adherence to faith requires *niyyah* (sincere devotion in one's heart), *iqrar* (verbal affirmation of one's belief in the unity of God and his Prophet), and *a'amal* (deeds that show adherence to the pillars of the faith, including praying, fasting, and so on). This triad of the heart, tongue, and action implies the indivisibility of faith.

One cannot, for instance, be considered a Muslim if he or she never says, "There is no God but Allah and Muhammad is his Prophet," even if that person believes in God. Similarly, a person is not considered a Muslim in the eyes of God if he or she verbally affirms the unity of God and upholds his or her religious obligations but does not truly believe in his or her heart. Finally, one may declare belief in God and genuinely believe in his existence but in practice fail to uphold religious obligations, out of idleness or obstinacy. In this case, the person is not a Muslim in the eyes of God because he or she refused to heed God's commands.

The notion of *takfir* in Salafi thought is a complex one that cannot be explained fully here. Suffice it to say, Salafis distinguish themselves from two strands of Muslim thought that emerged in the formative stages of Islam: *Khawarij* and *Murjiah*. The *Khawarij* (those who have seceded from the official ruler) claim that anyone who violates God's word and rules by something other than what God commanded is no longer a Muslim; he is an apostate. The *Murjiah* (those who postpone judgment), which developed in response to *Khawarij* claims, argue that as long as a person publicly declares he or she is a Muslim, no one can declare that person to be otherwise; it is up to God to judge people's faith. (These two original positions, the *Khawarij* and *Murjiah* strands, later developed more nuanced arguments that I do not address here.)

Salafis reject *Khawarij* thought by arguing that there are gradations of impiety. Not every sinner is considered a *kafir* (infidel) on earth, although God may indeed view each sinner as an infidel on Judgment Day. Specifically, short of being a *kafir*, a Muslim may commit transgressions that do not constitute *al-kabair* (major sins) leading to heresy or apostasy. Although Muslims may dislike a person's actions and even condemn his behavior, they cannot declare that person an apostate or infidel. In this respect, Salafis appear to uphold the *Murjiah* line of thought. However, unlike the *Murjiah*, the Salafis say mere declaration of faith is insufficient to keep a Muslim within the community of the faithful. Certain declarations or behaviors require excommunication.

For example, a person may declare he or she is a Muslim but publicly reject the Quran as the word of God. In this instance, the person has exhibited a great unbelief. He or she must repent or face excommunication and its consequences.

Salafis disagree among themselves as to when *takfir* must take place. The jihadi strand argues that a Muslim can be said to have committed an apostasy if he or she exhibits great unbelief *in word or action* and has been warned or given guidance to repent but fails to do so. For example, if a Muslim does not pray and has been told that this is a grave sin that God will not forgive, and if he or she continues to refuse praying, then that person can be called a *kafir*. A second Salafi strand rejects this radical disposition. It argues that if a person commits a great sin but does not publicly justify the sin through words, then he or she is not an infidel. Going back to the example of a person who does not pray, if the person admits he or she is sinning, he or she is considered a *fasiq* (sinner), not a *kafir* (infidel). However, if the person argues he or she does not pray because it is not required or because the Quran is wrong on this point, that person is not merely a sinner; he or she has crossed the threshold of impiety and has become an infidel.

The issue of *takfir* has become relevant because many jihadi Salafis today argue that existing Muslim regimes rule according to secular laws. Thus, because they violate God's sovereignty, they no longer can be considered Muslim. Consequently, it is permissible to reject them and rebel against them until they repent and apply Islamic law or are removed from power. Many jihadi Salafis declare democratic regimes to be un-Islamic because sovereignty is vested in human beings and popular will, not God and his divine will. Salafis have applied *takfir* to the Shia and other sects such as Sufis because of their "innovative" beliefs and practices. In Iraq, the belief in the "heresy" of the Shia is at the core of rationalizing violence against them. *Takfir* also is invoked against any person working for the "apostate" regimes or the occupation, including police and security services, translators, manual workers, and anyone giving aid or comfort to the occupiers.

Another feature of jihadi Salafism is the centrality of jihad in the path of God.[5] Jihadi Salafis believe that jihad is an Islamic obligation against infidel regimes that do not rule according to God's laws. Jihad is an indispensable component of comprehensive Islamic activism, which begins with preaching *(dawa)* and culminates with confronting obstinate unbelievers. This strategy is the only appropriate one because it is how the Prophet Muhammad spread Islam in the Arabian Peninsula in the seventh century CE. Jihad is also an imperative to counter foreign aggression and ultimately regain all the lands that were once in the abode of Islam. Finally, jihad is continuous until all of humanity submits to Islam or the authority of Muslim rule. Jihad for the radicals is therefore an aggressive doctrine, not a defensive concept. It persists until Judgment Day.

THE JIHADI SALAFIS IN IRAQ

The jihadi Salafis are pursuing a system-collapse strategy that seeks to install an Islamic emirate based on Sunni dominance, similar to the

Taliban regime in Afghanistan. This faction uses suicide terrorism to attack targets other than coalition personnel; it targets mainly Iraqi security forces and Shia civilians. It also uses conventional attacks against foreign journalists, "collaborators" such as translators and transport drivers, and the economic and physical infrastructure of Iraq. AQI has gone much further by seeking to spark a sectarian war through provocative attacks on Shia civilians in markets and mosques and at funerals and religious ceremonies.

The jihadi Salafis initially coalesced around an indigenous Kurdish-Iraqi group known as Ansar al-Islam (AI), based in northern Iraq, particularly in the Al-Sulaymaniyah governorate on the border with Iran. Other groups replaced AI as the latter was decimated by U.S. aerial attacks and Peshmerga militia ground attacks in 2003. These groups include ASG (which splintered from AI), the Victorious Sect, Ahl al-Sunna wal-Jamaah Army, and the Conquest Army (CA), among others. A number of observers have made the point that Salafism developed in Iraq during the early 1990s partly in response to the major military defeat and social crises that gripped the country during that decade.[6] ASG is one of the key factions of indigenous Iraqi jihadi Salafis. It officially formed in September 20, 2003, under the leadership of Abu Abdullah al-Hassan Bin Mahmoud. It issues the monthly online magazine *Ansar al-Sunna*.

Jihadi Salafis also include foreign jihadists initially under the Mujahidin Brigade in Muhammad's Army and al-Tawhid wal-Jihad (TWJ, later AQI), headed by Abu Musab al-Zarqawi. It must be made clear that the foreign jihadists comprise a tiny percentage of the overall insurgency. In September 2004 only 130 to 140, around 2 percent, of the 5,500 suspected insurgents detained by the authorities were foreigners. As of March 2006, of the estimated 15,000 to 20,000 insurgents, only 700 to 2,000 (4 to 10 percent) were said to be non-Iraqis.[7] However, these numbers are an unreliable indicator of their destructive potential. Foreign jihadists are the main arsenal of suicide bombers in Iraq; thus they can kill and maim more people in each suicide attack than indigenous insurgents can with conventional tactics. Moreover, because many come with specialized skills in manufacturing explosives and have experience fighting other jihads around the globe, they can serve as commanders and trainers of native insurgents and untrained foreign fighters. As shown below, suicide attacks have been a major precipitating factor in the Shia–Sunni sectarian spiral of violence.

Many of the foreign fighters made their way into northern Iraq (especially the Kurdistan region controlled by AI) in late 2001 and early 2002 via Iran, as they were seeking a safe haven after being driven out of Afghanistan.[8] Others came from a variety of Salafi networks in Jordan, Syria, Lebanon, Saudi Arabia, Kuwait, Yemen, North Africa, and Europe.[9] Israeli analyst Reuven Paz estimates that the majority (61 percent) of these volunteers are Saudi nationals.[10] However, others show the distribution to be relatively the same across countries, with Algerians at 20 percent, Syrians at 18 percent, Yemenis at 17 percent, Sudanese at 15 percent, Egyptians at 13 percent, and Saudis at 12 percent.[11] It is difficult to know who is right, but of the 102 known suicide bombers (see appendix 2), 43 percent came from Saudi Arabia.

What distinguishes the Salafis in AQI and ASG on the one hand from the Islamic and nationalist insurgents on the other is their ideological emphasis and strategic orientation. Although they all share the goal of expelling U.S. forces from Iraq and some Salafi worldviews, the Islamic and nationalist insurgents see the war in Iraq as a defensive one imposed on them by aggressive forces intent on dividing the country, marginalizing the Sunnis by turning power over to the Iranian-backed Shia parties and the U.S.-dependent Kurdish parties, and plundering Iraq's oil wealth. These forces do not stress the Shia-Sunni divide as an inherent schism tearing Iraq apart; rather, they blame the invaders for emphasizing this fault line to divide and conquer.

The jihadi Salafis, on the other hand, see the war in Iraq as an opportunity not only to expel foreign forces, but also to establish a genuine Islamic state based on the model of the Prophet Muhammad and his companions. For example, Zarqawi repeatedly declared, "We are not fighting for illusionary borders drawn by Sykes-Picot. Nor are we fighting to replace a Western tyrant with an Arab tyrant. Our jihad is more honorable than that. We fight to raise God's word on earth."[12]

The commander of ASG made a similar declaration in the first communiqué announcing the formation of the group.[13]

> The task [of jihad] is great and the issue momentous and concerns the fate of a nation and the aim does not end with the expulsion of the occupier and weakening him with inflicted wounds, but with the establishment of Allah's religion and the imposition of Muslim law to govern this Muslim land. For what use is it to shed

the blood of the Muslim holy warriors to repel the occupation forces only to have a secular Iraqi or a renegade agent and lackey of the Americans come to reap the fruit, take over, and implement their programs and therefore take us back to the eras of the agent governments that rule by the laws of unbelief in the name of Islam and are actually run by the Jews and Christians.

In 2005 the Islamic legal committee of AQI, headed by Sheikh Abu Hamza al-Baghdadi, issued a document entitled "Why Do We Fight, and Whom Do We Fight?"[14] In this document AQI outlines its objectives:

1. Restore the rightly guided caliphate *(khilafa)* so that it rules according to God's law, the *Sharia*.
2. Reject rule by the Shia *(al-Rafidah)* who have betrayed Muslims, "the people of the Sunna," in the past and today. They "pose a great threat to the life of the nation of Islam.[15] Only the sharp and cutting sword will be the judge between us and them." The Shia in Iraq, the document continues, "provided [the United States] with an easy path into the land [just as they] supported the Tartars against the Muslims, which was a direct cause of the Abbasid Caliphate's overthrow [in 1258 CE]."[16]
3. Oppose democracy because it is another form of religion opposed to the true religion of Islam. "The crusader democratic West no longer wants to convert the Muslims to the Christian religion, as the early missionaries tried to do.... Now the West wants the Muslims to embrace its new religion, the religion of democracy, because that would bring it more gains and benefits than it had obtained from the church's religion."[17]
4. Counter the falsehoods propagated by the "evil scholars" that divert people away from jihad until Judgment Day. Jihad is an obligation of Muslims in accordance with God's command: "Fight them until there is no more sedition [or disbelief, *fitna*] in the land, and all religion is for God." Muslims must continuously strive until Islam is "the observable and prevailing religion in the entire world." This command is based on the prophetic imperative: "I was commanded to fight the people until they declare there is no God but God and Muhammad is his messenger, perform prayers, and pay alms tax. If they do so, they will safeguard their lives and property from my hand...."[18]

The jihadi Salafis, especially AQI, have visions of a regional jihad to overthrow existing regimes in the area, including Jordan and Saudi Arabia. The former borders on Israel and is the original home of Zarqawi, and the latter is the principal ally of the United States, the richest oil-producing country in the Muslim world, and the original home of bin Laden. Many of the jihadi Salafis had prior experience in Afghanistan.

The vision of these wandering jihadists is to establish a strategic base for the global jihadist movement in the heart of the Arab world, to compensate for the one they lost in Afghanistan in late 2001. A base in Iraq would give global jihadists new strategic depth because it would operate in a country with a substantial geographic area that borders on Saudi Arabia, Jordan, Turkey, Syria, Kuwait, and Iran. Four of these countries are close allies of the United States, and the other two are dominated by "heretical" Shia (Iran) and secular Baathists (Syria). A base in Iraq would be a major achievement for the global jihadists. A monograph linked to AQI, entitled "Jihad in Iraq: Hopes and Dangers," affirms the importance of Iraq for the global jihad.[19]

> [I]f the United States is defeated this time—and this is what we pray will happen—the doors will open wide to the Islamic tide. For the first time in modern history, we will have an advanced foundation for Islamic awakening and jihad close to the land of the two mosques [Saudi Arabia] and Al-Aqsa mosque [Jerusalem]. Such a foundation will extend from the land of solidarity in Al-Sham [the region that includes Syria, Lebanon, Jordan, and Palestine] to bolster the Islamic awakening in the region and the Islamic world.

The Salafis view Iraq as part and parcel of the Islamic *umma* (nation); they do not recognize borders between Muslims. An invasion of Iraq is an invasion against Muslims all over the world. In this situation, jihad is *fard ayn* (an individual obligation) of every Muslim.[20] The U.S.-led invasion of Iraq mirrors the Soviet invasion of Afghanistan more than two decades earlier, when thousands of Arab volunteers mobilized to fight the communist invasion. Fighting in Afghanistan was intended not only to liberate an occupied Muslim land; it also presented an opportunity to gain legitimacy, train a new cadre of militants, acquire valuable skills, and recruit for the wider jihad to overthrow corrupt, secular regimes in the Muslim world.

Moreover, the Salafis do not see Iraq in isolation from other "humiliations," including Palestine, Kashmir, Bosnia, Chechnya, and Afghanistan in 2001; they view these conflicts as connected episodes of a campaign or "crusade" against Islam and Muslims. They see the end of the occupation of Iraq as the beginning of jihad against their governments, not the end of the struggle.

For the Salafis, the ascendancy of the Shia in Iraq is particularly troubling because it is "heresy" and "apostasy" in their view (see chapter 4). The Shia reject the legitimacy of the first three caliphs in Islam (Abu Bakr al-Siddiq, Umar Ibn al-Khattab, and Uthman Bin Afan). However, these three caliphs, along with Ali Bin Abi Talib, the fourth caliph, constitute the core of the pious ancestors for Sunni Islam. Other important theological and ritual divisions between the Shia and Sunna cannot be covered here.[21] Suffice it to say, Shia dominance in Iraq is anathema to Salafis and, thus, an added motivation to overthrow the entire new leadership of Iraq.

Despite its anti-Shia rhetoric, the jihadist struggle in Iraq does not center on a theological dispute. It is more accurate to conclude that given the ascendancy of the Shia in Iraqi politics after decades of exclusion and repression, some Sunnis have harnessed the most rigid interpretations of Islam, represented by Salafism, to mobilize and legitimize the insurgency against the new power brokers of Iraq.

Zarqawi was explicit about the need to attack the Shia to galvanize Sunni support for the insurgency. In early 2004 coalition forces intercepted an internal report sent by Zarqawi to al Qaeda leaders in Afghanistan. (At that time Zarqawi's group was named TWJ.) In the report he outlined his strategy for fighting in Iraq. Some have raised doubts about its authenticity. However, Zarqawi's persistent anti-Shia rhetoric, as well as bombing attacks against Shia before and after he sent the report, lends it credence.[22] This is one of only a few captured strategic documents, so it is important to quote it at length.

Zarqawi based his report on the argument that the ordinary Sunnis in Iraq "have little expertise or experience" in fighting. "For this reason," he wrote, "most of the groups are working in isolation, with no political horizon, farsightedness, or preparation to inherit the land.... With God's praise we are trying to ripen them quickly." Zarqawi was dissatisfied with the insurgency's "safe" tactics.

> Jihad here unfortunately [takes the form of] planting mines, launching rockets, and mortar shelling from afar. The Iraqi

brothers still prefer safety and returning to the arms of their wives, where nothing frightens them. Sometimes the groups have boasted among themselves that not one of them has been killed or captured. We have told them in our many sessions with them that safety and victory are incompatible, the tree of triumph and empowerment cannot grow tall and lofty without blood and defiance of death.... People cannot awaken from their stupor unless talk of martyrdom and martyrs fills their days and nights.

This paragraph reveals an important point. It is the foreign jihadists who are trying to convince their "Iraqi brothers" to adopt tactics of martyrdom. Thus, rather than being an organic development of occupation, suicide attacks have been imported into Iraq by foreign jihadists. Zarqawi himself admitted this in the internal report. "We have been the keys to all of the martyrdom operations that have taken place except those in the north [where AI (and later ASG) operates]. Praise be to God, I have completed 25 [operations] up to now, including among the Shia and their symbolic figures, the Americans and their soldiers, the [Iraqi] police and soldiers, and coalition forces."

Zarqawi went on to reflect on the vulnerabilities of the foreign jihadists: "[The number of immigrant holy warriors] continues to be negligible as compared to the enormity of the expected battle.... There is no doubt that the space in which we can move has begun to shrink and that the grip around the throats of the holy warriors has begun to tighten. With the deployment of [Iraqi] soldiers and police, the future has become frightening."

Key to getting the neutral Sunnis to join the insurgency, embrace martyrdom, and create a base of support for the foreign jihadists is sparking a sectarian war with the Shia.

[The Shia] in our opinion are the key to change. I mean that targeting them and hitting them in [their] religious, political, and military depth will provoke them to show the Sunnis their rabies ... and bare the teeth of the hidden rancor working in their breasts. If we succeed in dragging them into the arena of sectarian war, it will become possible to awaken the inattentive Sunnis as they feel imminent danger and annihilating death at the hands of these Sabeans. Despite their weakness and fragmentation, the Sunnis are the sharpest blades, the most determined, and the most loyal when they meet those [Shia], who are a people of treachery and cowardice.

To strengthen his case for this anti-Shia strategy, Zarqawi reflects on what it would mean to fail: "We pack our bags and search for another land, as is the sad, recurrent story in the arenas of jihad, because our enemy is growing stronger and his intelligence data are increasing day by day." The only chance the jihadists have is to drag the Shia into an overt war with Sunnis.

> If we are able to strike them with one painful blow after another until they enter the battle, we will be able to reshuffle the cards.... This is what we want, and, whether they like it or not, many Sunni areas will stand with the holy warriors. Then the holy warriors will have assured themselves land from which to set forth in striking the Shia in their heartland, along with a clear media orientation and the creation of strategic depth and reach among the brothers outside [Iraq] and the holy warriors within.

Zarqawi's strategy was not too different from what Aymen al-Zawahiri, al Qaeda's second in command after Osama bin Laden, advocated following the 9/11 attacks. In his book *Knights under the Prophet's Banner*, serialized by the London-based *Asharq al-Awsat* newspaper in November and December 2001, Aymen al-Zawahiri wrote: "Victory by the armies cannot be achieved unless the infantry occupies territory. Likewise, victory for the Islamic movements against the world [Zionist-crusader] alliance cannot be attained unless these movements possess an Islamic base in the heart of the Arab region."

He goes on to say that the jihadist movement must seek to "control a piece of land in the heart of the Islamic world on which it could establish and protect the state of Islam and launch its battle to restore the caliphate based on the traditions of the Prophet." He concludes: "If the successful operations against Islam's enemies and the severe damage inflicted on them do not serve the ultimate goal of establishing the Muslim nation in the heart of the Islamic world, they will be nothing more than disturbing acts, regardless of their magnitude, that could be absorbed and endured, even if after some time and with some losses."

It is difficult to say whether Zawahiri inspired Zarqawi's anti-Shia strategy. After all, until 2004 Zarqawi operated separately from the core of al Qaeda's leadership in Afghanistan and held a different strategic vision of jihad. Zarqawi's obsession before the Iraq insurgency was attacking his home government in Jordan and Jewish and Israeli targets wherever he could.[23] This strategy of fighting the "near enemy" represented by apostate regimes and Israel conflicted with bin Laden's and Zawahiri's interest in attacking the "far enemy" represented by the United States.[24] Declaring allegiance to bin Laden and Zawahiri in 2004, therefore, was probably a strategic move to give Zarqawi organizational recognition (only a few of the dedicated jihadists had heard of TWJ, but everyone knew of al Qaeda). Such recognition could bring with it financial support from wealthy sympathizers. He also might have intended to garner support from Saudi and other al Qaeda militants in bordering countries. But the debate about attacking the far or near enemy became moot when the United States occupied Iraq and brought to power a pro-U.S. Shia regime; the far enemy became the near enemy.

In addition, it is not clear whether this strategy stemmed from an inherent anti-Shia stance or if the anti-Shia rhetoric stemmed from Zarqawi's instrumental strategy to spark sectarian civil war in Iraq. There is little evidence that Zarqawi ever planned attacks on Shia before joining the insurgency in Iraq. Bin Laden's al Qaeda has traditionally avoided an anti-Shia discourse despite the popularity of such rhetoric in Saudi Arabia and among jihadi Salafis.

What is clear, however, is that direct attacks on the Shia have indeed precipitated a sectarian civil war in Iraq.[25] Zarqawi's strategy worked according to plan. Containing an emerging civil war has become the number one priority of Iraqis, their government, and the U.S.-led coalition. Ironically, the political marginality of the jihadi Salafis has meant that they are less constrained by the concerns of the broader Iraqi public. Their marginality is at the root of their lethality.

FOCUSED COMPARISON BETWEEN THE IRAQI NATIONALISTS AND JIHADI SALAFIS

It is difficult to draw sharp dividing lines between the insurgent groups, since they all want the United States to leave Iraq and they often deploy similar tactics and use comparable rhetoric. However, a number of factors differentiate Iraqi Islamic nationalists from jihadi Salafis. First of all, Iraqi

Islamic nationalists do not use the language of apostasy in criticizing the current Iraqi regime. They deem the regime illegitimate, but this alleged illegitimacy stems from its cooperation with the occupation forces, not from its failure to apply Islamic law. In contrast, jihadi Salafis always stress that any Muslim government that does not rule in accordance with God's laws is an apostate regime that must be fought.[26]

Second, Islamic nationalists do not emphasize killing Shia for their theological orientation. To the extent they kill Shia, it is because they are part of the security services that engage in counterinsurgency operations or aid the occupiers in stabilizing Iraq. This may appear to be a distinction without a difference, but it does matter that enmity toward the Shia is rooted in nationalist claims about loyalty and collaboration, not religious ones about heresy and apostasy. The former idea suggests that reconciliation with the Shia is possible (at least theoretically) after the occupation ends; the latter that the Sunni–Shia divide never can be bridged peacefully.

On May 28, 2006, the Fatwa Council of Al-Rashidin Army, an Islamic-nationalist group, issued a document entitled "The Religious Ruling on Jihad and its Requirements in Iraq." It makes clear that attacks on Shia civilians are not part of the jihad in Iraq and are a deviation from religion. "According to Islamic law, it is not permissible to kill or fight the Shia or Kurds in general, just because the majority of the militia is either Shia or Kurdish, because the condition for the above ruling was not based on their being Shia or Kurd but on the fact that they fought or practiced aggression. Such description can apply to a Sunni as well as a Shia." It goes on to say, "Concerning others who do not really practice aggression, Islamic law does not permit fighting them just because they are Shia or Kurds."[27]

Third, Islamic nationalists are attuned to ongoing struggles in the Arab world and link some of their operations to the resistance in Palestine and Lebanon to establish their pan-Arab credentials. For example, the IAI, 1920 RB, and CA each issued statements and videos in which they claimed that attacks on U.S. personnel in Iraq were in revenge for Israeli aggression in Gaza and Lebanon.[28] Jihadi Salafis have been conspicuous in their refusal to support Hezbollah in Lebanon.

A televised interview with Dr. Ibrahim al-Shamari, the IAI spokesman, reveals the extent to which Islamic nationalists differ from their counterparts in the jihadi Salafi camp in terms of strategy and ideological emphasis.[29] The IAI is one of the four major groups in the insurgency representing the Islamic-nationalist faction. It is one of the most active in claiming responsibility for attacks, issuing videos of its operations—including the famous "Sniper of Baghdad" montage—and making political statements about events in the country.

During the interview, al-Shamari denies that his group is part of AQI, despite referring to its members as "our brothers," and dispels rumors that the IAI has clashed with Zarqawi. He also denies that his group is linked to Baathists directly or indirectly, "because our orientation and beliefs differ from theirs." He affirms, "We do not have any organizational or institutional ties with the former regime, either as followers or as leaders." However, he does add that the group is open to anyone who accepts its clear Islamic orientation. Whoever wants to join has to be vetted to make sure his intentions and past history are beyond suspicion. The group inquires about the Islamic beliefs of potential cadres during discussions with its Islamic legal committee. If the committee approves the potential member, the military command evaluates him. If the latter accepts him, the new member is assigned to the IAI.

The IAI consists of various departments, such as the general command, which includes the lead commander and his deputies. It has a political bureau that drafts the group's political and strategic positions and a consultative council that formulates the general political orientation of the group. The group also has a military command and various committees on the media, legal issues, security, and intelligence. In this respect, the IAI closely resembles the jihadi Salafis in the AQI and the ASG, both of which are segmented into committees and military brigades. However, the parallel between the IAI and the jihadi Salafis ends there.

Perhaps the biggest division between the IAI and AQI is over the Shia question. AQI, as already indicated, views the Shia as heretics. The IAI limits its criticism to the SCIRI Badr Corps only and has a nuanced view of the Mahdi Army. Regarding the Badr Corps, al-Shamari argues that the Iraqis know who they are and what they did during the war with Iran, especially their torture of Iraqis during interrogations on Iranian territory. The Badr Corps also has aided the occupation forces in taking over the country since 2003. As for the Mahdi Army, some are nationalists and honorable people, but others attack the Sunnis and act on sectarian grounds.

Al-Shamari goes on to say, "This country is for everyone, not just for the Sunnis. All the agencies and militias are controlled by these [Kurdish and Shia] sects and they have used them to harm the people of the Sunna. We recognize that there are sectarian divides and political disagreements, but these should be resolved through *dawa* (preaching) and dialogue and persuasion. We do not use arms against them. It is the other side that has attacked us." He concludes, "If a Shia resistance emerges in Iraq, we will welcome it and be happy for this development." As previously mentioned, the IAI and other Islamic nationalists blame the United States and Iran for fomenting an "unnatural" sectarian conflict in Iraq.

Many other important differences divide the IAI and the jihadi Salafis. Whereas the latter are clear in rejecting elections, the IAI is not. During the August 2005 constitutional referendum, the IAI issued an order to its brigades to avoid targeting electoral sites. According to al-Shamari, the IAI chooses armed resistance to express its opposition to the occupation, but "we wanted people to reject the constitution in their own way. We reject it with force; the people reject it by voting against it."

Moreover, whereas the jihadi Salafis reject the current government in Iraq and all other governments in the region as apostates because they do not rule in accordance with Islamic law, the IAI rejects the government because it is based on sectarianism *(taifiyyah)*, not apostasy. It is interesting to note that Zarqawi's speeches were replete with terms such as *kufr* (impiety) and *riddah* (apostasy), the central concepts of jihadi Salafism. However, in the nearly hour-long interview, al-Shamari did not once mention those terms. Furthermore, al-Shamari refers to the insurgents in Iraq as *muqawama* (resistance), not jihad. This distinction is important because the jihadi Salafis have made it clear that they reject this notion of resistance, which implies a secular nationalist war against the occupation, whereas jihad implies a religious struggle against the occupation and apostate regimes. The only legitimate war in Islam, according to Zarqawi, is jihad.[30]

More blasphemous from a jihadi Salafi perspective is al-Shamari's suggestion that dialogue between the United States and the resistance is possible: "We do not recognize the so called government [in Iraq]. This is nothing more than a body of sectarian gangs that has ill treated the Sunnis. As for dialogue with those who are in control, the U.S., we will not reject negotiations as long as they officially come to us requesting dialogue on the issue of leaving Iraq. The U.S. should come to us directly with an official request for dialogue." He goes on to say that dialogue must be between those who are in control of the situation: the United States and the resistance. For this dialogue to take place the U.S. Congress first must issue an order to leave Iraq at a specified time, and the occupiers must recognize the resistance, not the current government, as the representative of the Iraqi people.[31]

Al-Shamari speaks well of Dr. Muthanna Harith al-Dari, spokesman for the Iraqi Association of Muslim Scholars. He also speaks highly of the association itself, despite denying direct links to it. "We respect it highly; it is a legal Islamic committee and one of the representatives of the Sunni community, but it is not the sole representative [of Sunnis] or the foundation for the holy fighters. They are not the umbrella for the armed resistance." Many in Iraq view the association as a nationalist body interested in equitable inclusion of Sunnis in the emerging political process.[32] The IAI insurgents and others may deny that the Association of the Muslim Scholars speaks for them, but they seem to give it the space it needs to negotiate with coalition forces and the current government in Iraq.[33] This respect for the Association of Muslim Scholars is important because the association has criticized AQI, and Zarqawi in turn criticized the association. It distinguishes between resistance and terrorism, saying the former is the legitimate right of any people under occupation, while the latter is an illegitimate importation by extremists who do not represent the interest of Iraqis. The association condemns attacks on Shia civilians and institutions and downplays the presumed schisms between Sunnis and Shia. It specifically condemned Zarqawi for his official war on Shia communities.[34]

The observable differences between the IAI, the largest and most powerful group within the Islamic nationalist camp, and AQI, the most extreme group in the jihadi Salafi faction, confirm the analysis presented earlier. The Islamic nationalists are seeking system reintegration in the new Iraq, while the jihadi Salafis are seeking a total war that transforms Iraq into a base for extreme Islamists.

CONCLUSION

Jihadi Salafis in Iraq, like their Baathist counterparts, are seeking to collapse the political system through expansive violence and a strategy of sectarian agitation. Their political marginality and extremist worldview guarantee their inability to integrate or compete in any democratic order dominated by Shia and Kurds. Thus they are seeking to spark a civil war through provocative attacks on Shia civilians. Unfortunately, they are succeeding. Iraq is turning into a failed state in which central authority is weak or nonexistent, communities depend on militias for protection and retribution, and violent conflict is depleting the nation of its valuable material and human resources. As I show in the concluding chapter, the failed state in Iraq will be one where the global jihadists associated with AQI have a new safe haven to replace the one al Qaeda lost after the collapse of the Taliban in 2001.

NOTES

1. The following description of jihadi Salafism is based on the words of two of its most respected leaders, Abu Muhammad al-Maqdisi and Abu Basir al-Tartusi. See their documents posted in Arabic on the *Tawhid wal Jihad* Web site (www.tawhed.ws): Abu Basir al-Tartusi, "Principles in Takfir," July 13, 1994; Abu Basir al-Tartusi, "The Conditions of No God but God," October 18, 2000; Abu Basir al-Tartusi, "Islam's Ruling Concerning Democracy and Party Pluralism," 461-page document, no date; Abu Basir al-Tartusi, "This Is Our Creed and This Is What We Call For," March 10, 2002; Abu Muhammad al-Maqdisi, "This is our Creed," October 1997; Abu Muhammad al-Maqdisi, "Democracy Is Religion," 65-page document, no date; Abu Muhammad al-Maqdisi, "Reflections on the Fruits of Jihad: Between the Ignorance of Islamic Law and the Ignorance of Reality," May 2004. This section also refers to the documents produced by AQI and ASG concerning their "creed and methodology." See OSC, "Al-Zarqawi's Legal Committee Publishes Book 'Why Do We Fight, And Whom Do We Fight?'" October 17, 2005; OSC, "Iraq: Ansar al-Sunnah Group Statement on Creed, Objectives," May 8, 2006.

2. International Crisis Group, "Saudi Arabia Backgrounder: Who Are the Islamists," *ICG Middle East Report* 31, September 21, 2004; Quintan Wiktorowicz, "Anatomy of the Salafi Movement," *Studies in Conflict and Terrorism* 29, no. 3 (April–May 2006): 207–39.

3. Khaled Abou El Fadl, *The Great Theft: Wrestling Islam from the Extremists* (San Francisco: Harper, 2005), chapter 3.

4. On the early traditionalists, see Patricia Crone, *God's Rule: Government and Islam, Six Centuries of Medieval Islamic Political Thought* (New York: Columbia University Press, 2004), chapter 11.

5. In classical Islam warfare by Muslims is religiously sanctioned when it has the proper intention of raising the word of God on earth. In practice jihad is the fight to establish Islamic governments in lands not ruled by Islam or to defend Muslim populations, territories, property, and holy sites from non-Muslim aggressors. For a masterly treatment of the subject, see Michael Bonner, *Jihad in*

Islamic History: Doctrines and Practice (Princeton, N.J.: Princeton University Press, 2006).

6. OSC, "Report Explains Presence of Salafis, Ba'thist Arabs in Iraq before Occupation," May 20, 2005; Baram, "Who Are the Insurgents"; Hassan, "Saddam Was the First to Attract Islamic Organizations and Later Regretted It."

7. See Brookings Institution Iraq Index, May 1, 2006, www.brookings.edu/iraqindex.

8. Mashari al-Zaydi, "Jordanian Papers Concerning Fundamentalism and Politics" (Arabic), *Asharq al-Awsat* (London), October 13, 2005, part 4 of 5; Fatih Krekar, "The Zarqawian Vision and its Heavy Load" (Arabic), *Al Jazeera*, June 15, 2006, www.aljazeera.net.

9. Hamd al-Jaser, "Kuwaiti Jihadists in the Sunni Triangle" (Arabic), *Al-Hayat* (London), August 11, 2004; Hazem al-Amin, "Lebanese 'Jihadists' in Iraq: 'Salafis' from Peripheral Regions and Cities" (Arabic), *Al-Hayat* (London), August 11, 2004; Hazem al-Amin, "How Al-Qaeda Searched for a Twin State to the Taliban Emirate" (Arabic), *Al-Hayat* (London), October 10, 2005; Hazem al-Amin, "Strangers Come during 'Al-Qaeda Season' to Recruit Suicide Bombers to Iraq" (Arabic), *Al-Hayat* (London), January 26–27, 2006, parts 1 and 2; Jean Chichizola, "Four Recruiters for Jihad in Iraq Arrested" (French), *Le Figaro* (Paris), January 26, 2005; Muhammad al-Ashhab, "European Networks for Smuggling Jihadists" (Arabic), *Al-Hayat* (London), February 11, 2005; Saud al-Sarhan, "Al-Qaeda in Saudi Arabia" (Arabic), *Asharq al-Awsat* (London), May 20, 2005; Eric Schmitt, "As Africans Join Iraqi Insurgency, U.S. Counters Military Training in their Lands," *New York Times*, June 10, 2005; Peter Beaumont, "Insurgents Trawl Europe for Recruits," *Observer* (London), June 19, 2005; Ahmed al-Arqam, "The Moroccan Judiciary Sentences to Prison Deportees from Syria on their way to Fight in Iraq" (Arabic), *Asharq al-Awsat* (London), July 2, 2005; Ibrahim Hamaydi, "Islamic Trends Advance in Syria and the Authorities Wage 'Preemptive Operations' Against the Takfiris" (Arabic), *Al-Hayat*, January 4, 2006; Nir Rosen, "Iraq's Jordanian Jihadis," *New York Times*, February 19, 2006.

10. Reuven Paz, "Arab Volunteers Killed in Iraq: An Analysis," Global Research in International Affairs Center, *Occasional Papers* 3, no. 1 (March 2005): 2.

11. Nawaf Obaid and Anthony Cordesman, *Saudi Militants in Iraq: Assessment and Kingdom's Response* (Washington, D.C.: Center for Strategic and International Studies, September 19, 2005), 6.

12. This statement was made in a fifty-minute video montage by al Qaeda depicting their operations against U.S. forces and Iraqi security services, www.miraserve.com. Sykes-Picot refers to the secret agreement between France and Britain during World War I to divide the Ottoman Empire into spheres of influence. It was one of the factors that shaped the contemporary Middle Eastern state system.

13. The communiqué was issued September 20, 2003, and signed by Abu Abdullah al-Hassan Ben Mahmoud, the commander of Ansar al-Sunna Army. It appeared in *Ansar al-Sunna*, issue 1 (October 2003): 17–18.

14. OSC, "Al-Zarqawi's Legal Committee Publishes Book." The document was published earlier, perhaps in June 2005. Also see the statement by ASG, which makes many of the same claims made by AQI, in OSC, "Iraq: Ansar al-Sunnah Group Statement on Creed, Objectives," May 8, 2006.

15. The term *al-Rafidah* comes from early Islamic history and refers to the Rafidis, a group opposing the caliph Muawiyyah that emerged in the 680s CE. However, it is not known if the term was coined during this period. The Rafidis claimed that Abu Bakr al-Siddiq and Umar Ibn al-Khattab, the first two caliphs (rulers) following the death of the Prophet Muhammad in 632 CE, conspired to usurp power from Ali Bin Ibi Talib, who should have been the first caliph. According to the Rafidis, the Prophet designated Ali as his successor. However, the traditional Sunni view holds these charges as blasphemy because both Abu Bakr and Umar are highly venerated companions of the Prophet. See Crone, *God's Rule*, 73–75.

16. Sometime in early 2004, a letter by Zarqawi to al Qaeda leaders in Afghanistan was intercepted by the coalition forces. In it he declared the Shia as the real enemy in Iraq, describing them as "an insurmountable obstacle," "spying enemy," and "penetrating venom." He concludes: "Beware of them. Fight them. By God, they lie." His reference was to Shia Islam in general, not specific individuals or parties.

17. OSC, "Al-Zarqawi's Legal Committee Publishes Book 'Why Do We Fight, And Whom Do We Fight?'" October 17, 2005. ASG also rejects democracy as a "religion," not a political system, because it gives rule to the people, not God. See al-Yaman Bin Abdullah al-Sulieman, "Democracy: Religion or Politics?" *Ansar al-Sunna* (sixth issue, Ansar al-Sunna Army in Iraq's monthly journal), (February–March 2004): 15–16.

18. OSC, "Al-Zarqawi's Legal Committee Publishes Book."

19. The document does not have an author or date, but it is dedicated to Yousef al-Ayiri, al Qaeda leader in Saudi Arabia, killed in 2003. It was issued by the Media Commission for the Victory of the Iraqi People (The Mujahidin Services Center) sometime in 2003.

20. ASG's Islamic legal committee affirmed that jihad had become an individual obligation in Iraq in a *fatwa* (religious ruling) entitled "The Ruling Concerning Jihad in Iraq," published in the first issue of its monthly online journal, *Ansar al-Sunna* (September–October 2003), 11–14. Jihad as *fard ayn* (individual obligation) is usually contrasted with jihad as *fard kifaya* (collective obligation).

Islamic scholars construe individual obligation to mean that it is the duty of every Muslim to wage jihad in the path of God in defense of Islam, its lands, religious institutions, people, and property. Individual obligation usually arises when Muslim lands are besieged by powerful foes that cannot be easily repelled with a small force. Under these circumstances, jihad is the religious obligation of every Muslim capable of fighting, just as all Muslims are obligated to pray, fast, and pay alms. In contrast, collective obligation means that the duty of jihad of individual Muslims is fulfilled if a sufficient number of Muslims arise to make additional fighters unnecessary for the task. Collective obligation usually applies in campaigns of conquest *(futuhat)* when Muslims are sufficiently capable of waging war without the need to burden all of society.

21. See Vali Nasr, *The Shia Revival: How Conflicts within Islam Will Shape the Future* (New York: W. W. Norton, 2006).

22. The report was not dated and it is not clear to whom it was sent in al Qaeda. Zarqawi's anti-Shia rhetoric can also be found in his video montages and audio recordings. See, for instance, the transcript of an hour-long recording his supporters entitled "The Descendents of Ibn al-Alqami Are Back" (OSC, "Al-Zarqawi Justifies Killing of Innocent Muslims, Condemns Shi'a 'Betrayal' of Sunnis," May 18, 2005) and the transcript of an audio recording his supporters entitled "Here Is a Message for Mankind, Let Them Take Warning Therefrom" (OSC, "Al-Zarqawi Calls for 'All-Out War' Against Shi'a," September 14, 2005).

23. Peter L. Bergen, *The Osama bin Laden I Know* (New York: Free Press, 2006).

24. Fawaz A. Gerges, *The Far Enemy: Why Jihad Went Global* (New York: Cambridge University Press, 2005).

25. Patrick Cockburn, "On the Frontline: War without End," *Independent* (London), September 18, 2005; Sabrina Tavernise, "As Iraqi Shiites Police Sunnis, Rough Justice Feeds Bitterness," *New York Times*, February 6, 2006; Ellen Knickmeyer, "Shiites Told: Leave Home or Be Killed," *Washington Post*, March 1, 2006; Edward Wong, "Fearful Iraqis Avoid Mosques as Attacks Rise," *New York Times*, August 19, 2006; Edward Wong and Kirk Semple, "Civilians in Iraq Flee Mixed Areas as Killings Rise," *New York Times*, April 2, 2006; Jonathan Finer, "Threat of Shiite Militias Now Seen as Iraq's Most Critical Challenge," *Washington Post*, April 8, 2006.

26. Contrast the following document by IAI concerning the new Iraqi government with the documents of ASG and AQI concerning their creed and method: OSC, "Al-Zarqawi's Group 'Creed and Methodology' Reiterates Mandate of Jihad, Battling 'Infidels, Apostates, Shia,'" March 24, 2005; OSC, "Al-Zarqawi's Legal Committee Publishes Book"; OSC, "Iraq: Ansar al-Sunnah Group Statement on Creed, Objectives," May 8, 2006; and OSC, "Islamic Army in Iraq Issues Statement of Future of Iraqi Coalition Government," June 30, 2006.

27. OSC, "Al-Rashidin Army Explains Religious Ruling on Jihad," May 30, 2006.

28. On July 16, 2006, the 1920 RB issued two videos depicting IED attacks on U.S. military vehicles in western Ramadi. The operations were dedicated to Palestinian and Lebanese fighters (the latter refers to the Shia Hezbollah organization) involved in renewed armed conflict with Israel following the kidnapping of three Israeli soldiers (one by Palestinians and two by Hezbollah). OSC, "Islamic Army in Iraq Claims Attack in 'Revenge' for Gaza Deaths," July 12, 2006; OSC, "Al-Fatihin [Conqueror] Army Claims Attacks 'Avenging Qana [Lebanon] Martyrs' Throughout Iraq," August 1, 2006.

29. Interview conducted by Yasser Abu Hilala, host of the Al Jazeera program *Today's Encounter*, first aired March 24, 2006.

30. Zarqawi was explicit on this point in one of his audiotapes, "Do Ye Know Better than Allah?" See OSC, "Al-Zarqawi Lecture Urges Use of Shari'ah Idioms, Views 'Concept of Jihad,'" October 7, 2005.

31. The 1920 RB issued a similar statement, declaring: "Negotiating with the occupier cannot take place except under certain conditions set by the Movement, such as the official recognition of the resistance as the legitimate representative of the Iraqi people, and the departure of the occupier from our land, and under international assurances. This position of ours is agreed upon by many resistance groups in Iraq." OSC, "1920 Revolution Brigades Reaffirm Position on 'Resistance,' Deny Negotiating with Occupation," March 30, 2006.

32. The 1920 RB also views the Association of Muslim Scholars positively. In a published interview Sayf al-Din al-Baghdadi, spokesman for the movement in Iraq, affirms, "We respect it and we support any party, which rejects occupation and deals with it hostilely. This party has offered martyrs, and many of its cadres have been jailed but it remained patient and firm." See *Al-Sabil* (Amman), "The Road to Jerusalem Begins in Baghdad, and the Land of Iraq Will Not Disappoint the Land of Palestine" (Arabic), January 18, 2005.

33. Borzou Daragahi, "Rebels' Arsenal Includes Politics; Iraqi insurgents seem to time their attacks and informal cease-fires for maximum gain, while distancing themselves from foreign fighters," *Los Angeles Times*, February 19, 2006.

34. Association of Muslim Scholars, communiqué no. 157, "In Regard to the Latest Statements of Abu Musab al-Zarqawi," September 15, 2005.

CHAPTER 3

SUICIDE TERRORISM IN THE IRAQI INSURGENCY

S uicide terrorism in Iraq began with the U.S.-led invasion in March 2003. However, most suicide attacks in Iraq target the new security services and Shia civilians, not coalition forces. From March 22, 2003, to August 18, 2006, 514 suicide attacks took place in Iraq, some separately and some in coordination with other insurgent attacks. Hardly a day passes without news of a suicide attack in Iraq.

Suicide bombings in Iraq differ in three respects from earlier campaigns of suicide terrorism initiated by the other groups such as Hezbollah, LTTE, and Hamas. First, many, if not most, of the suicide bombers in Iraq are not Iraqis. They are Muslim volunteers from Arab and non-Arab countries as near as Saudi Arabia, Kuwait, Jordan, and Syria, and as far away as North Africa and Europe. In previous cases, the suicide bombers tended to come directly from the aggrieved national community (see appendix 2 for a list of some of the known suicide bombers in Iraq). However, some reports suggest that more and more Iraqis are willing to become suicide bombers.[1]

Second, most suicide attacks target Shia civilians in markets, mosques, and religious festivals, as well as Iraqi security services, including newly recruited police officers and personnel from the Iraqi armed forces. Earlier campaigns of suicide terrorism did not exhibit this pattern of targeting compatriots.

Third, the major groups engaging in suicide attacks as the insurgency developed in 2004 and 2005 were not strictly nationalists seeking to liberate Iraq from Western forces. Instead, they tended to represent religious worldviews associated with the global jihad or jihadi Salafism. These groups include Ansar al-Islam (AI); Ansar al-Sunna Group (ASG); and al-Tawhid wal-Jihad (later AQI), which has merged with the MSC, now part of the Islamic State of Iraq (see appendix 4).

It is important to note that both TWJ and ASG were closely associated with AI before it was decimated in 2003, suggesting continuity in tactics despite subsequent organizational differentiation. Their ultimate aim is to oust the newly installed regime and establish an Islamic state capable of representing and defending Muslim interests against the "onslaught" of the "Zionist-crusader" alliance. In practical terms, this means preventing a new regime dominated by the "heretical" Shia and "treasonous" Kurds from maintaining power. It also means depriving the new regime of a monopoly on the use of force and allowing jihadists to establish a base of operations akin to the one al Qaeda had in Afghanistan under the Taliban regime until late 2001. In previous campaigns of suicide attacks by Islamists in Lebanon and the Palestinian territories, suicide bombers pursued narrower agendas related to liberating the land and avoided expanding the number of targets that could potentially entangle these movements in broader conflicts.

The unique features of suicide terrorism in Iraq suggest that analysts may have to refocus to account for its diffusion to previously unaffected arenas. As I argue below, some of the prevailing explanations of suicide attacks do not appear to apply to the Iraqi case.

SUICIDE TERRORISM: ONE TACTIC AMONG MANY

The Iraqi insurgents rely on a diverse tool kit of tactics and deploy them across a range of targets, which makes the tasks of target hardening and counterinsurgency (COIN) much more difficult. It must be made clear at the outset that since January 2005 insurgents in Iraq have carried out an average of 45 to 100 attacks per day, and only a few of these are suicide attacks—usually one or two, but in rare instances as many as eleven. According to data from the Brookings Institution Iraq Index, in 2004 and 2005 alone insurgents deployed a total of 16,560 roadside bombs, 1,293 non-suicide car bombs, and 544 suicide car bombs.[2] These numbers show that suicide terrorism constitutes only a small proportion of insurgent tactics. However, as shown below, the physical and political impacts of suicide attacks are disproportionate to their numbers.

According to a military source, insurgent tactics include intimidation of those who work with coalition forces. This tactic involves direct threats without the use of violence or nonlethal violence against "collaborators,"

SUICIDE TERRORISM IN THE IRAQI INSURGENCY

such as interpreters, heads of tribes or local clerics mediating between foreigners and the local populace, or those who do not adhere to the insurgents' edicts. Insurgents also rely on sabotage of electric stations, oil pipelines and facilities, and coalition reconstruction projects. They use small-arms fire (guns and sniping) against coalition forces and assassinations of public officials and private citizens. Lobbing improvised rockets and mortar shells at fixed coalition positions and firing surface-to-air rockets at airplanes and helicopters are also frequent in the insurgency. Insurgents have deployed ambushes that involve the simultaneous use of mines, small-arms fire, grenades, and rocket-propelled grenades (RPGs). Insurgents also engage in kidnapping local citizens and foreigners to exchange them for ransom or execute them, as well as kidnapping members of the security services and "spies" to interrogate and execute them.

The most lethal weapon in their arsenal, however, is the improvised explosive device (IED). There are several types: roadside bombs detonated with a triggering device, such as a mobile phone, remote-control device for a toy car, or a garage door opener; vehicle-borne IEDs (such as nonsuicide car bombs) and suicide vehicle-borne IEDs (SVBIEDs). Less frequent are suicide attacks using explosive vests.[3]

Insurgents have used these tactics repeatedly against foreigners, Iraqis, and infrastructure targets. Foreign targets include coalition forces, such as personnel on foot or in vehicles, airplanes, or helicopters; military bases; and security checkpoints. They also include foreign contractors, such as personnel employed on reconstruction projects, private security agents, foreign workers offering manual labor, and translators. Other foreign targets include journalists on the road or in hotels, international organizations such as the United Nations, nongovernmental agencies such as the Red Cross, and representatives of foreign governments such as the Jordanian and Turkish embassies and Algerian, Egyptian, and Russian diplomats.

Iraqi targets include the newly formed Iraqi security forces and their bases; police recruitment centers and police stations; Kurdish, Shia, and Sunni political figures participating in the new political process; militia members belonging to the Shia Badr Corps, Mahdi Army, and Kurdish Peshmerga; Shia civilians in markets, mosques, religious ceremonies, and funeral processions; Iraqi interpreters for coalition forces; and journalists and university professors. As for infrastructure targets, they encompass physical infrastructure, such as electric stations and bridges, and economic infrastructure, such as oil pipelines and development projects. The range of Iraqi targets will continue to grow as the country slips further into a civil war and as insurgents adapt to target-hardening measures.

The frequency of insurgent attacks has increased over time. According to data from the Brookings Institution (see chart 2), as of August 2006 the insurgents had sustained high levels of violence throughout the insurgency with no apparent significant drops in attacks from quarter to quarter.[4] Commentators point out that attacks became deadlier as insurgents used armor-piercing IEDs and engaged in major coordinated attacks.[5]

According to data from the Defense Intelligence Agency, as of December 2005 the majority of insurgent attacks targeted coalition forces, with Iraqi security forces next in frequency. However, the majority of the attacks against coalition forces involved conventional IEDs, snipers, and rockets, not suicide bombers.[6] As seen below, attacks by suicide bombers usually target civilians and Iraqi security forces.

A strategic logic governs insurgents' choice of targets. For insurgents seeking system reintegration, such as the IAI, MAI, 1920 RB, and SDAB, attacks on coalition forces, foreign contractors, and the Shia- and Kurd-

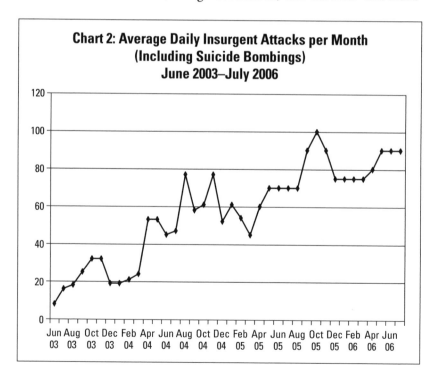

Chart 2: Average Daily Insurgent Attacks per Month (Including Suicide Bombings) June 2003–July 2006

dominated Iraqi security forces are necessary to drive the occupation forces out of Iraq and force the emerging regime to deal with the insurgents on its own. Then these insurgent factions would have tremendous leverage to negotiate new political, security, and economic arrangements in Iraq.

For insurgents seeking system collapse, such as the MSC, ASG, and the ideological Baathists, expansive violence against foreigners, Shia and Kurdish politicians and civilians, Iraqi security forces, international organizations, nongovernmental agencies, journalists, and the physical and economic infrastructure is intended not only to drive the multinational forces out of Iraq but also to create widespread insecurity among the public, engender sectarian polarization, and produce economic collapse. All of these outcomes are intended to delegitimize the new order, allow the insurgents to portray themselves as the sole protectors of Sunnis and thus command their support, and create a failed state in which the central authority does not have a monopoly on the use of coercive force. These conditions would allow jihadists with an agenda beyond Iraq to establish bases of operations, recruitment, and training.

DATA AND ANALYSIS OF SUICIDE TERRORISM IN THE INSURGENCY

Suicide attacks in Iraq began with the invasion, but they substantially increased in late 2004 (see chart 3). These data suggest that the strategy of "martyrdom" was implemented mainly by insurgents, not by the former Iraqi regime when it was still in power or in hiding during 2003. (Saddam Hussein was captured in December 2003 and his two sons, Uday and Qusay, were killed in July 2003.) However, the first two suicide bombers were women dispatched by the Iraqi regime during the invasion phase. The former regime also organized suicide brigades within the Fedayeen Saddam (FS) organization and trained foreign volunteers in suicide attacks before the invasion.[7] Captured documents show the names of individuals who allegedly volunteered for such attacks, as well as foreign volunteers who received official permission from the Baathist state to enter Iraq.[8] Furthermore, Baathists have claimed responsibility for suicide attacks. However, the majority of suicide attacks began taking place more than a year and a half after the fall of the regime, suggesting a lack of eagerness by Iraqis or foreigners to sacrifice for Saddam and his party.

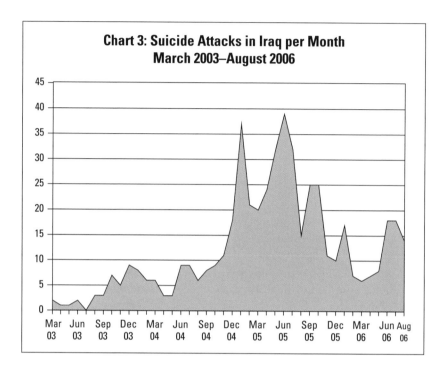

Chart 3: Suicide Attacks in Iraq per Month
March 2003–August 2006

GEOGRAPHY OF INSURGENCY AND LOCATIONS OF SUICIDE ATTACKS

Although the insurgency is associated with rebellious Sunni towns such as Fallujah, Ramadi, and Samarra, it is much more widespread than it appears, ranging as far north as Mosul and Tal Afar and as far south as Najaf.[9] However, it is taking place mainly in the center of the country, around Baghdad and western Al Anbar, Iraq's largest province, which borders on Syria, Jordan, and Saudi Arabia. Al Anbar includes the cities of Ramadi (the provincial capital), Al-Qaim, Haditha, Hit, Fallujah, Abu Ghraib, and several other towns.

According to an August 2006 report by the Department of Defense, four provinces—Al Anbar, Baghdad, Salah al-Din, and Diyala—containing 37 percent of the Iraqi population accounted for 81 percent of the attacks since 2003.[10] The insurgency is weaker in southern Iraq, inhabited mainly by Shia, and northern Iraq, inhabited mainly by Sunni Kurds (except in Mosul). As of January 1, 2006, of the 33,661 Iraqi police and civilian deaths caused by insurgent attacks, 20,125—nearly 60 percent—had occurred in Baghdad.[11] The concentration of casualties in Baghdad results partly from the fact that the police have been operating there longer than anywhere else in the country.

Yet despite the insurgency's concentration in central and western Iraq, the pattern of coalition forces' COIN operations highlights its widespread nature:

- Fallujah, west of Baghdad, April and November 2004;
- Najaf, south of Baghdad in Najaf province, April–May 2004;
- Karbala, southwest of Baghdad in Karbala province, April–May and August 2004;
- Baquba, northeast of Baghdad in Diyala province, June 2004;
- Samarra, north of Baghdad in Salah al-Din province, October 2004 and March 2006;
- Mosul, northern Iraq, November 2004;
- Near Syrian border in Al Anbar province, June 2005;
- Tal Afar, northeastern Iraq, September 2005;
- Baghdad (south and west of the capital), May–June and November 2005, February and June 2006.

The geographic expanse of the insurgency suggests that COIN operations are not likely to result in a decisive defeat of the insurgents without other major political developments. First, the geography of the insurgency suggests that the grievances of the Sunni communities in Iraq are widespread, thus allowing insurgents to gain a broad base of support for their activities.

Second, the fact that attacks are taking place in and around the capital, Baghdad, suggests that the Sunni insurgents are aware of the significance of destabilizing the center of the new Iraqi regime. The insurgents are not interested only in maintaining "no-go zones" in the peripheral regions of Iraq, but are contesting for power, showing their confidence in their cadres and capabilities. They are going after U.S. troops, the core of the coalition forces located predominantly in and around Baghdad. According to one estimate, between March 2003 and April 2006 approximately 25 percent of 2,350 U.S. military deaths occurred in Baghdad. The remaining 75 percent were more evenly distributed across the provinces, and not all of them were due to insurgent attacks.[12] The insurgents recognize that driving U.S. forces out of Iraq will result in a favorable shift in the balance of power between insurgents and Iraqi security forces.

Third, the insurgency's reach suggests that the rebels are mainly Iraqis embedded in their communities, not foreign jihadists. It is difficult for foreigners to establish themselves in various communities without being identified easily by Iraqi security forces and the local population. The Iraqi makeup of the insurgency makes it difficult for the national government to flush out the insurgents without heavy-handed measures, which are likely to intensify the insurgency before quelling it.

Fourth, the availability of multiple battlefields means that the insurgents can retreat from one area to another under the pressure of COIN operations. This explains why a number of major operations to "break the back" of the insurgency have failed to stem the violence.

The majority (52 percent) of suicide attacks in Iraq as of February 20, 2006, had taken place in and around Baghdad, the capital (see chart 4). The remaining 48 percent have been distributed over a wide geographic area in eight other provinces. Between February 20 and August 18, 2006, twenty-seven of seventy-one suicide attacks took place in Baghdad.

TYPES OF SUICIDE ATTACKS

Suicide attackers rely heavily on car bombs or SVBIED, as well as explosive bags and belts (see chart 5). Insurgents have used cars made by Opel, such as the Cadet or Omega, because they are inexpensive and many Iraqis drive them, thus making them hard to distinguish.[13] Insurgents have also used ambulances because they can hold much more explosive material than a sedan could and can speed up or maneuver between cars without raising suspicions. As many as 500 ambulances have been stolen since the fall of Baghdad, and insurgents can purchase these vehicles at a significantly reduced price.[14] Suicide attackers have also used pickup trucks, cement-mixing trucks, and sport utility vehicles stolen from fleeing NGOs.

The car bombs are usually prepared in residential "factories." First the cars are gutted to make room for large numbers of projectiles, usually mortar rounds taken from unguarded ammunition supply points, packed tightly with TNT, PE4 (plastic) or C4 explosives, and other "sympathetic" explosives (which detonate as other explosions occur). Some vehicles are rigged to explode on impact by means of a plunging device in front of the

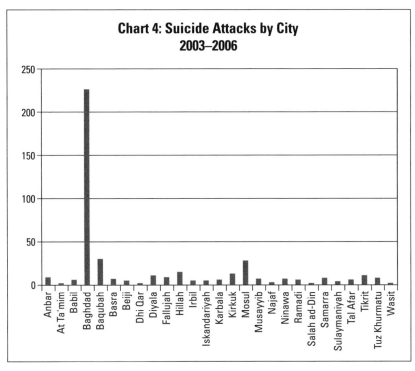

Chart 4: Suicide Attacks by City
2003–2006

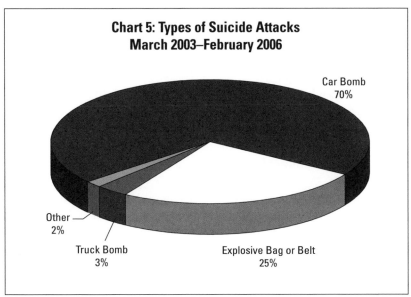

Chart 5: Types of Suicide Attacks
March 2003–February 2006

Car Bomb
70%

Other
2%

Truck Bomb
3%

Explosive Bag or Belt
25%

car. Others have a button or switch controlled directly by the suicide bomber driving the vehicle. There have been reports of remote detonators controlled by another person from a distance in case the suicide bomber had second thoughts about proceeding with the mission.[15]

According to one source, insurgents in charge of car bombs sometimes operate in cells to avoid major security failures that could result in their capture. For instance, COIN operations revealed that car bombs are prepared in one place and taken to another "factory" or farm on the periphery of Baghdad, where they are loaded with explosives before being sent to another location where the suicide bombers are briefed on their missions.[16]

The biographies of the "martyrs" and some videos of operations reveal that surveillance squads prepare elaborate briefings for bombers before the operation. They use videos and hand-drawn diagrams to illustrate vulnerabilities in the targets, and they even do practice runs to make sure the operation will be successful.[17] Moreover, some of the videos of suicide attacks reveal that the bombers often go in groups of two or three, followed by the surveillance team.[18] In at least one instance, the recruiter drove behind the bomber until he was close to the target and witnessed the detonation.[19]

Why do many operations involve several suicide bombers at a time? First, sending more than one suicide bomber is the hallmark of al Qaeda's mass-casualty, mass-destruction attacks. This tactic of simultaneous detonations developed during the 1990s with the Kenya and Tanzania U.S. embassy bombings and continued with the 9/11 attacks and the London bombings of July 7, 2005.

Second, sending more than one suicide bomber is likely to generate a more powerful attack that will kill scores of people and capture headlines nationally and internationally. If the strategy is to create chaos and insecurity to shake people's faith in the new regime, demoralize the occupiers, and deter other countries from joining the fray, then simultaneous attacks make sense.

Third, sending more than one suicide bomber offers a tactical advantage by breaching fortifications and creating a gap for the other bombers to attack the main target. Many of the biographies of the suicide bombers and some of the videos of their operations reveal how one bomber is to destroy a guard post or a fence while the others penetrate the breach to attack the main target.

Fourth, sending bombers together lessens the chance of a bomber retreating during an attack. A lone bomber is more likely to respond to the instinct of self-preservation than a group, for whom failure to carry out the attack might jeopardize the team. Group reinforcement is heightened by the fact that a camera crew often follows the attacker to film the operation for propaganda and training purposes. Failure to act under these circumstances is likely to make one feel cowardly, shameful, and dishonorable.

TIMING OF SUICIDE ATTACKS

Suicide attacks in Iraq tend to spike in response to two developments, one on the battlefield and the other in the political arena (see chart 6). On the battlefield, COIN operations are usually followed by a wave of suicide attacks. Of ten major COIN operations ending in June 2006, seven were followed by a rise in suicide attacks from the previous level. Insurgents are keen to show their enemies and supporting public that they will not be deterred or give up the struggle in the face of repression. Suicide attacks are the most dramatic way to illustrate the failure of the COIN campaign. Immediate mass-casualty attacks deliver the message that insurgents are defiant and able to strike back with a vengeance. They also capture media attention and send the message that insurgents are determined to die for their cause. The disproportionate attention given to suicide attacks shifts the focus away from successes in COIN to the failure of the coalition forces to protect ordinary people.

Furthermore, since COIN operations invariably involve "excesses" and collateral damage that capture headlines in the Iraqi and worldwide media, insurgents can capitalize on this emotional reaction to build local support, enabling them to strike back with little concern for the consequences of their deadly bombings. The best example of this dynamic occurred in September 2005. While coalition forces were waging a major COIN operation in Tal Afar, in two days AQI unleashed ten suicide bombings, eight of which took place in Baghdad and six of which happened on the same day, September 14, 2005. As these bombings were occurring, Zarqawi issued the famous declaration of an "all-out war" against the Shia in Iraq. He added, "Since yesterday, the battles for revenge started all over the land of the two rivers. The raid for avenging the Sunni people in Tal Afar has started."[20]

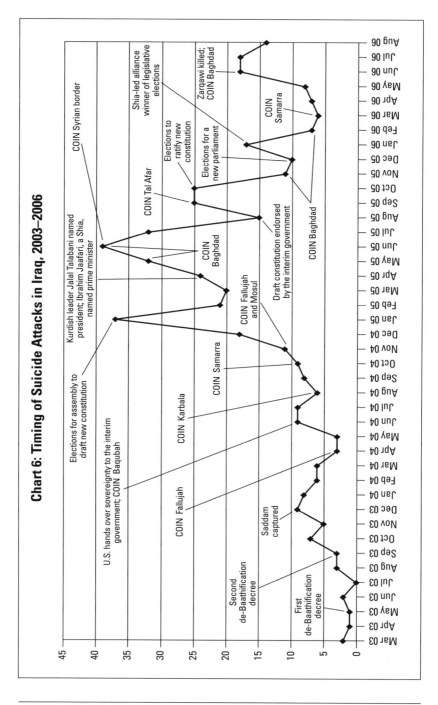

Chart 6: Timing of Suicide Attacks in Iraq, 2003–2006

On the political front, suicide attacks tend to spike when major institutional developments give the impression that Iraq has reached a "turning point" and stability is "around the corner." Suicide attacks rose rapidly during or immediately after the January 2005 election of an assembly to draft a new Iraqi constitution; endorsement of the draft constitution in August 2005; and the election of the new Iraqi parliament in December 2005. After the Iraqi parliament approved the first elected government since the fall of the regime, on April 28, 2005, the following day insurgents exploded at least seventeen car bombs, killing at least fifty people and injuring more than a hundred.[21]

The primary reason suicide attacks rise during or in response to these political developments is that insurgents want to show the Iraqi people and the world in general that these "political games" will not change the reality on the ground. Creating chaos through suicide attacks shows all concerned that the insurgents, not the political establishment, control the tempo of the struggle. These attacks are powerful reminders that ultimately the new power brokers in Iraq will not manage to consolidate their authority through "imposed" political arrangements.

On June 8, 2006, U.S. forces killed Abu Musab al-Zarqawi, the head of AQI, in a targeted air strike. That same day Iraqi lawmakers approved three key security positions in Prime Minister Nuri al-Maliki's cabinet, ending an extended controversy over who would lead the interior, defense, and national security ministries. A week later al-Maliki and coalition forces unveiled a new security plan for Iraq, including amnesty for insurgent groups willing to end the violence and engage in talks with the government and beefed-up security for Baghdad. All these security and political developments gave rise to optimism that Iraq might be turning a corner.

Unfortunately, the month of July saw an unprecedented surge of violence, featuring at least eighteen suicide attacks and daylight massacres of Sunnis by Shia militias. According to Iraq's health ministry and the Baghdad morgue, an average of 110 Iraqis were killed per day during that month, a 9 percent increase over the preceding month (the morgue's tally put the increase at 18 percent). Much of this violence was associated with Shia militias and death squads, but insurgents also stepped up their attacks, sparking Shia retaliation and avenging Shia massacres.[22]

According to a Pentagon report issued in August 2006, from May 20 to August 11, 2006, when the new Iraqi government was forming and Zarqawi was killed, Iraq witnessed a substantial rise in the average number of weekly attacks, from nearly 650 (from February 11 to May 19) to about 800. In the same period, Iraqi civilian and security casualties increased 51 percent over the previous period, reaching nearly 120 a day.[23]

These events and death toll confirm the hypothesis that insurgents escalate their violence in response to counterinsurgent operations on one hand and political progress on the other. This finding is daunting and does not bode well for an expeditious resolution of the crisis in Iraq.

LETHALITY OF SUICIDE ATTACKS

The lethality of suicide attacks also increased as the insurgency developed from 2003 to 2006 (see chart 7). According to the Brookings Institution, as of August 27, 2006, suicide attacks had accounted for 335 (or 37 percent) of 900 multiple-fatality bombings in Iraq (bombings causing more than one fatality at a time).[24] This finding confirms earlier studies that showed suicide attacks to be more lethal than any single conventional tactic.

TARGETS OF SUICIDE ATTACKS

Suicide bombers in Iraq strike at different types of targets (see chart 8). Moreover, these targets changed as the insurgency developed (see chart 9). Initially a high proportion, including some spectacular attacks on U.S., Italian, and Romanian forces in 2003, targeted coalition forces. Next insurgents began to attack targets such as the United Nations, Red Cross, and Jordanian and Turkish embassies, which could have given the occupation stability and legitimacy.

Attacking these targets is particularly important for insurgents pursuing a system-collapse strategy. First, attacking support organizations makes it difficult to reestablish order in society, thus preventing them from making the lives of Iraqis more palatable under the occupation. Second, these attacks heighten the sense of chaos and insecurity, making people dread the transformational changes taking place in society and yearn for someone to provide stability. Finally, attacking such targets sends a powerful message to neutral countries and organizations contemplating aiding the occupation that no one is safe in Iraq.

It did not take long for insurgents to expand the circle of violence to Iraqi police and security forces that were responsible for reestablishing public order and offering protection to the Iraqi Shia and Kurdish politi-

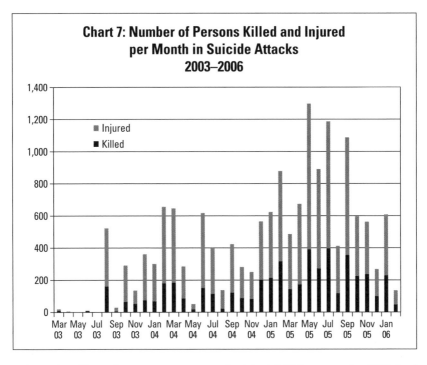

Chart 7: Number of Persons Killed and Injured per Month in Suicide Attacks 2003–2006

cal parties. These forces were not attacked in 2003 because the CPA had not yet recruited and deployed them. As Iraq's new security forces began deploying and it became more difficult for suicide bombers to attack coalition forces, the proportion of such attacks against Iraqi forces and civilians increased substantially. From June 2003 to April 30, 2006, approximately 4,550 Iraqi military and police personnel were killed. The average number of monthly deaths in 2004 was about 160; in 2005 it was nearly 212.[25] According to one source, attacks on police stations are not random.[26] Rather, insurgents target police stations that act effectively against the insurgents and cooperate directly with security forces.

These developments suggest two conclusions. First, as suicide attacks on coalition forces became much more difficult and much less effective, insurgents shifted to softer targets. To be sure, nonsuicide attacks on coalition forces remained constant and even increased as the insurgency developed, but insurgents relied on "safer" weapons such as mortars and rockets, snipers, and IEDs. As of August 27, 2006, of the 2,629 U.S. troops killed in Iraq, 896 (34.1 percent) died in IED attacks. Another 819 (31.2 percent) died in hostile fire that might have included suicide vests, but not car

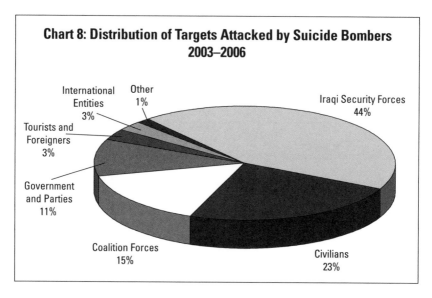

Chart 8: Distribution of Targets Attacked by Suicide Bombers 2003–2006

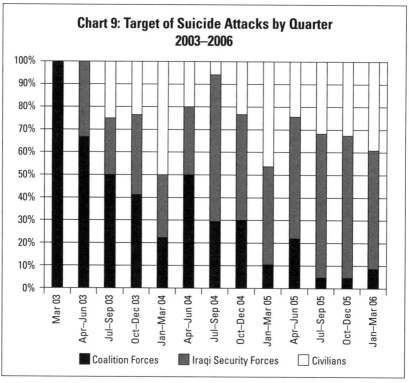

Chart 9: Target of Suicide Attacks by Quarter 2003–2006

bombs. The latter killed 126 U.S. personnel (4.8 percent).[27] Given that the overwhelming majority of the suicide attacks (70 percent of 440 attacks as of February 2006) used car bombs, it is safe to conclude that most suicide attacks in Iraq do not target U.S. forces.

According to my interviews with two U.S. servicemen who served in Iraq, suicide attacks on U.S. forces have become largely ineffective. U.S. forces acquired better armor following the initial wave of attacks. This armor made suicide attacks against U.S. forces less lethal. Also, fixed U.S. positions and checkpoints have been fortified with concrete barriers, cement blocks, and "dragon's teeth" (steel-reinforced concrete) defenses to prevent the penetration of vehicle-borne suicide bombers. Other measures include building dual (exterior and interior) gates and entry-control points with guard shacks.

Moreover, starting in mid-2004, as the insurgency escalated, U.S. commanders sent fewer troops on patrol in hot zones, to avoid creating targets of opportunity for insurgents. Patrols have been limited largely to protecting supply convoys. Thus U.S. forces became harder to attack. In addition, U.S. forces have become better able to detect potential suicide bombers. They are suspicious of cars with single drivers; they monitor vehicles that seem to be weaving erratically between cars or speeding up toward U.S. vehicles or positions; they look for cars that seem weighed down by heavy objects that may include explosives; and they attempt to read the faces of drivers, looking for signs of nervousness or anxiety, as they approach checkpoints or U.S. vehicles.[28]

Finally, U.S. forces warn drivers to keep a safe distance between their vehicles and U.S. vehicles, and they do not hesitate to fire warning shots at vehicles that get too close or are speeding toward their convoys. Most Iraqis now know the perils of getting too close to U.S. vehicles; tragically, many innocent Iraqis have been killed by coalition forces who mistook them for insurgents and suicide bombers.[29]

The second conclusion is that the insurgents recognize the importance of the Iraqi security forces in creating stability for the new regime. While the U.S.-led coalition forces have made it clear that their exit strategy depends on the formation of a capable Iraqi security force that can secure the nation's borders and provide internal security and order, insurgents believe that the Iraqi security forces are actually intended to serve as a cover for the occupation, encouraging Iraqis to take the frontlines in the war against the insurgency while the United States and its local allies in the Shia and Kurdish parties shape the new order to benefit their narrow sectarian interests.

Zarqawi said in one of his video messages, "The failure of the U.S. [forces] to keep order led them to a new chapter. With the help of the traitorous leaders, they began to set up a new government and forces to do their dirty work. The cowardly Americans now stay back in their bases like masters, hiding away from the fighting. They have recruited thousands of Iraqis to fight the Muslims and trample all over their nation."[30]

PERPETRATORS OF SUICIDE ATTACKS

It is not clear who is carrying out most of the suicide attacks in Iraq (see chart 10). However, a large percentage of attacks have been claimed by AQI (including attacks attributed to TWJ), ASG, AI (which is no longer active), and Baathist groups that initially fell under the rubric of Saddam loyalists (including al-Faruq Brigades, FS, Leaders of the Iraqi Resistance and Liberation, and Muhammad's Army). All of these groups are pursuing a system-collapse strategy because they do not see themselves playing an influential role in the new Iraqi political order dominated by Shia and Kurds. Concealing the identity of individuals and groups responsible for suicide attacks, particularly those that kill scores of civilians, makes sense to insurgents for several reasons. First, many attacks on civilians are unpopular among ordinary Iraqis, even Sunnis with grievances against the new regime. Thus, although some groups want to spark a sectarian war, they do not necessarily want to take credit for it.

Second, in light of suspicions that many of the suicide bombers in Iraq are not Iraqis, insurgents may wish to conceal this fact if it is indeed the case. Many Iraqis are adamant that suicide bombings are not part of "Iraqi culture" and insist that outsiders have brought in this phenomenon for their own purposes. Some accuse AQI, but many more accuse the Israeli Mossad, the Central Intelligence Agency, and Iran of plotting to divide Iraq to create new spheres of influence. Moreover, since the United States initially argued that the insurgency was led by unpopular Baathists and foreigners affiliated with AQI, implying that it was not a legitimate liberation movement, it makes sense for insurgents to conceal the identity of the bombers if they are indeed foreigners and Baathists.

Third, it makes sense to conceal the identity of bombers for security reasons. If the bombers come from inside Iraq, insurgents are well advised

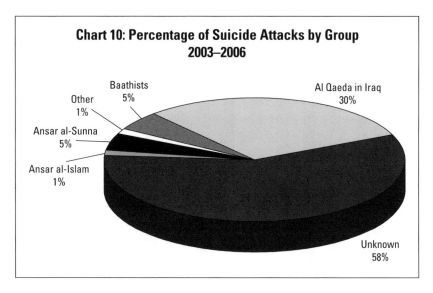

Chart 10: Percentage of Suicide Attacks by Group 2003–2006

to hide their identity to avoid retribution against their families; if they are coming from outside, it is equally wise to hide their identity to avoid tipping off security services in foreign countries about radical networks sending terrorists to Iraq.

Finally, because of the manifest acceptability of conspiracy theories in Iraq and many parts of the Muslim world, concealing the identity of suicide bombers gives groups such as AQI and others plausible deniability when the outcomes of those attacks do not fit well with their political calculations. They can always blame (and indeed have blamed) the CIA, Iran, or the Mossad for sparking sectarian strife and shedding the blood of the Iraqi people to divide the country and keep it weak.

As the insurgency developed, claims of responsibility for suicide attacks began to manifest a pattern (see chart 11). After September 2004 claims of responsibility by groups loyal to the Baathist regime disappeared completely, and claims by AQI dropped significantly. There are several explanations for this development. First, it could be an error in attribution, whereby coalition forces and reporters assumed that Baathists and Saddam loyalists had perpetrated initial suicide attacks, when in fact unknown others had carried them out. As it became clear that the insurgency had the widespread support of large segments of the Sunni population, people paid more attention to who was actually claiming responsibility for suicide attacks.

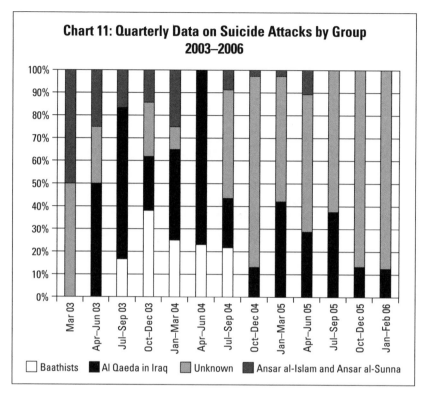

Chart 11: Quarterly Data on Suicide Attacks by Group 2003–2006

Second, it could be that Saddam loyalists willing to engage in suicide attacks melted into other groups, given the improbability of a return to the old Baathist regime. Earlier COIN efforts focused on capturing former Baathist elements that could be financing or leading the insurgency. By mid-2004 many of the wanted Baathists had been captured or killed, fled into secret exile, or turned themselves in. As this was happening, new groups were emerging with Islamic and nationalist names. Also, some, such as Zarqawi's TWJ, were capturing major headlines with their spectacular suicide attacks and beheadings. It is possible that the cadres of the Baathist party joined these new formations for leadership and ideological cover.

Third, since suicide attacks against coalition forces decreased after September 2004 and attacks on Iraqi security forces and Shia civilians increased, Baathists and AQI might have ceased to claim responsibility for suicide attacks for fear of being blamed for massacring their own people and Muslims in general. It is interesting to note that the proportion of unclaimed suicide attacks after September 2004 increased significantly, while claims by Baathists and AQI diminished significantly. The International Crisis Group pointed out that many insurgents ceased claiming responsibility for controversial attacks on civilians.[31]

WHY JIHADI SALAFIS ARE THE MAIN SUICIDE BOMBERS IN IRAQ

Why do the jihadi Salafis and, to a lesser extent, Baathists rely on suicide terrorism while the other factions do not? First and foremost, the strategy of the Islamic nationalist faction does not involve sparking a civil war. Mass-casualty attacks against the Shia only heighten the threat facing Sunnis in Iraq and reduce their chances of reintegration into the political system. A civil war with the Shia majority means the Sunnis will bear the brunt of the casualties. In contrast, AQI is interested in sparking a civil war because only then can it collapse the system, operate as the protector of the Sunnis, and create a new base for regional and global jihad in a failed Iraqi state.

Second, the jihadi Salafis and ideological Baathists are politically weak in Iraq (as they are everywhere else in the Muslim world). ASG emerged out of a split with AI, a marginal group in Kurdistan that formed in December 2001. AQI formed, at least initially, from predominantly foreign jihadists led by Zarqawi, a Jordanian national. The Baathists have brought Iraq misery, poverty, and isolation through their wars. Sparking sectarian strife through suicide attacks on Shia communities allows them to position themselves as the main representatives of Sunni grievances in Iraq. As AQI became more "Iraqi" in terms of its leadership, it began to distance itself from major attacks on Shia civilians.

In contrast to the jihadi Salafis and the Baathists, the Islamic nationalist faction is based on solid political foundations in the Sunni community. It receives the tacit support of the Association of Muslim Scholars, and its cadres come from the disbanded armed forces and the Sunni tribes. Sunni Iraqis are interested in ending the occupation, protecting themselves against Shia reprisals, and having bargaining power in the face of Shia and Kurdish dominance of the new political process. They are not interested in fighting a global jihad or installing a Taliban-like regime.

Third, jihadi Salafi ideology, which has been developing at least since the end of the Soviet occupation of Afghanistan, emphasizes martyrdom.

The focus on martyrdom, combined with virulent anti-Shia discourse, makes it easier for its cadres to dehumanize their targets and justify killing them in suicide operations. Only recently has the discourse of the Islamic nationalist faction in Iraq emphasized martyrdom in the path of God, and it does not focus on the Shia–Sunna split as an inherent division in Iraq. Therefore, it is not easy to dehumanize Shia civilians. This attitude is likely to change as Iraq continues to slide into a civil war.

CONCLUSION

Insurgency and suicide terrorism in Iraq are difficult to defeat in the short term because insurgents rely on multiple tactics against a wide range of targets in numerous areas covering a vast geographic space. Insurgents are not restrained in their choice of targets. They attack coalition forces, foreign contractors, Iraqi security forces, physical and economic infrastructure, Shia and Kurdish civilians, militias, political parties, and Sunnis who "collaborate" with the coalition and the new Iraqi regime. It is difficult to harden all these targets. Suicide attacks in Iraq became more frequent as the insurgency developed and especially after the removal of major figures associated with the old regime. This pattern suggests that non-Baathists are probably behind most suicide attacks in the Iraqi insurgency. Although most of the bombers are still unknown, the jihadi Salafis in AQI, ASG, and the now-defunct AI have claimed a large percentage of suicide attacks.

Suicide attackers initially targeted coalition forces, but they quickly shifted to softer targets such as Iraqi security forces and Shia civilians. Suicide bombings are heavily concentrated in and around Baghdad, which shows that the insurgents are taking the fight to the new regime's center of gravity. Chaos and insecurity in the capital capture national, regional, and international headlines, put pressure on coalition forces to leave Iraq, and deter other countries from joining the coalition. These conditions make the new regime appear impotent in the face of the insurgency. Suicide attackers rely heavily on vehicle-borne bombers and are eager to attack following COIN operations or during major political developments in the country to show they are not defeated and political "theatrics" will not end the insurgency. Therefore, political solutions and institutional restructuring are not likely to end the violence in the immediate future because the jihadi Salafis are not interested in an integrative political process; they aim to collapse the emerging political order.

NOTES

1. Patrick J. McDonnell and Sebastian Rotella, "Making Bombers in Iraq," *Los Angeles Times*, February 29, 2004; Peter Beaumont, "Turmoil in Iraq: Al-Qaeda's Slaughter Has One Aim: Civil War," *Guardian* (London), September 18, 2005; Carol J. Williams, "Suicide Attacks Rising Rapidly: Increasingly, the Bombers are Iraqis instead of Foreign Infiltrators," *Los Angeles Times*, June 2, 2005; Jamal Halaby, "Iraqi Woman on Trial in Jordan for Bombing," *Associated Press*, April 24, 2006.

2. www.brookings.edu/iraqindex, August 28, 2006. It is not clear how the Brookings Institution derived a total of 544 suicide attacks in 2004–05. This number seems inflated, and unfortunately Brookings does not provide a list of suicide attacks to make it possible to evaluate the reliability of the data.

3. January 5, 2006, interview in Fort Leavenworth, Kans., with a company commander in the First Cavalry Division who served in Baghdad and North Babel between February 2004 and March 2005. The major requested anonymity.

4. www.brookings.edu/iraqindex, August 28, 2006.

5. Bryan Bender, "U.S. Military Worried over Change in Iraq Attacks," *Boston Globe*, April 24, 2005; John Barry, Michael Hastings, and Evan Thomas, "Iraq's Real WMD," *Newsweek*, March 27, 2006.

6. See the United States Government Accountability Office report, *Rebuilding Iraq: Stabilization, Reconstruction, and Financing Challenges*, GAO-06-428T, February 8, 2006, 6, www.gao.gov/new.items/d06428t.pdf. An August 2006 report by the Pentagon confirms, "Coalition forces continued to attract the majority (63 percent) of attacks." See Department of Defense report to Congress, "Measuring Security and Stability in Iraq," August 29, 2006, 31, http://hosted.ap.org/specials/interactives/wdc/documents/Iraq/Security-Stability-ReportAug29r1.pdf.

7. A captured top-secret Iraqi government document reveals that Baathist officials gave instructions to subordinates on how to train Arab volunteers for suicide attacks and whom to assign to the task. The document, ISGP-2003-00028868 (in Arabic), is posted on the Pentagon/FSMO Web site (http://fmso.leavenworth.army.mil/documents-docex/Iraq/Released-20060317/ISGP-2003-00028868.pdf); see 20–22.

8. The documents were made public by coalition forces in 2006 and are stored at Fort Leavenworth, Kans. They are also available in the OSC database. See, for example, the six-page document, ISGQ-2003-00002783, "Correspondence regarding Fedayeen Saddam suicide missions team," n.d., no author. (http://fmso.leavenworth.army.mil/documents-docex/Iraq/).

9. James Glanz and Thom Shanker, "Iraq Study Sees Rebels' Attacks as Widespread," *New York Times*, September 29, 2004; Thomas E. Ricks, "In the

Battle for Baghdad, U.S. Turns War on Insurgents," *Washington Post*, February 26, 2006.

10. See Department of Defense report, "Measuring Security and Stability in Iraq," 32.

11. www.brookings.edu/iraqindex, May 1, 2006.

12. John Ward Anderson and Jonathan Finer, "The Battle for Baghdad's Future: Three Years after Its Fall," *Washington Post*, April 9, 2006; "Capital Is Pivotal to U.S. Success in Iraq, Officers Say," *Washington Post*, April 9, 2006.

13. *Asharq al-Awsat* (London), February 5, 2004.

14. *Azzaman* (London), March 24, 2005.

15. January 5, 2006, interview in Fort Leavenworth, Kans., with company commander in First Cavalry Division. See note 3.

16. Ibid.

17. AQI issued a video of the October 24, 2005, suicide attack on the Palestine Hotel, where many foreign reporters were staying. The video contains extensive footage of pre-attack plan briefings, which included actual video of the target before it was attacked, as well as a practice run on the target.

18. AQI issued a video of the November 18, 2005, suicide attack on the al-Hamra Hotel by three suicide bombers: Abu Ayoub al-Iraqi (Iraqi), Abu Abdel al-Malik al-Najdi (Saudi), and Abu Samir al-Tunisi (Tunisian). The hotel was said to be a "base for foreign intelligence" and the Badr Corps. It is not clear if this was the case, but the hotel did house foreign reporters.

19. See first issue of *Biographies of Eminent Martyrs*, an online magazine issued by AQI and distributed through jihadi Web forums. His handler narrates the story of the suicide bomber Abu Osama al-Maghribi (Moroccan).

20. OSC, "Al-Zarqawi Calls for 'All-Out-War' Against Shia," September 14, 2005.

21. Rory Carroll, "17 Bombs Greet New Iraqi Cabinet," *Guardian* (London), April 30, 2005.

22. Edward Wong and Damien Cave, "Number of Civilian Deaths Highest in July, Iraqis Say," *New York Times*, August 16, 2006.

23. Department of Defense report, "Measuring Stability and Security in Iraq."

24. www.brookings.edu/iraqindex, August 28, 2006.

25. Ibid.

26. January 5, 2006, interview in Fort Leavenworth, Kans. See note 3.

27. www.brookings.edu/iraqindex, August 28, 2006.

28. January 5, 2006, interview in Fort Leavenworth, Kans. See note 3.

29. According to a major in the 130th Engineer Brigade serving in Victory Base (Baghdad) and LSA Anaconda (Balad) since October 25, 2005, "Suicide attacks are not effective against U.S. forces.... We do not allow civilian vehicles to get close to our convoys, we are very disciplined about wearing individual protective gear, we have armored vehicles that can protect occupants from most blasts, and we don't allow civilians to intermingle with troop formations. Unfortunately, this has distanced us from the population. It's an unfortunate tradeoff." E-mail correspondence, February 28, 2006. The major requested anonymity.

30. The forty-five-minute montage was issued around June 29, 2005. It is in five parts, and Zarqawi's statement appears in part 2.

31. International Crisis Group, "In Their Own Words: Reading the Iraqi Insurgency."

PART II

THE ALCHEMY OF MARTYRDOM: IDEOLOGY, THEOLOGY, AND MYTHOLOGY OF SUICIDE TERRORISM

CHAPTER 4

THE IDEOLOGY AND THEOLOGY OF MARTYRDOM

Jihadi Salafis strategically use utilitarian arguments, ideology, emotion, and theology to appeal to potential recruits inside and outside Iraq, justify the killing of civilians and fellow Muslims in insurgent attacks, deactivate self-inhibiting norms against killing oneself and others in suicide attacks, legitimize the organizations that engage in violence, and counter the claims of authorities in Iraq and around the Muslim world.

Justifications for suicide attacks in Iraq against coalition forces closely parallel justifications by Hamas in the Palestinian territories and Hezbollah in Lebanon. Insurgent groups argue that this is a defensive war against a powerful and arrogant aggressor. Given the disparity in capabilities between coalition forces and the insurgents, the latter have to strike with the best weapons available to them. Human bombs are powerful weapons that kill scores of enemy soldiers in a single strike; they also demoralize the enemy and exhibit the resolve of the insurgents.

However, because suicide bombers in Iraq have been striking mainly at Iraqi security forces and Shia civilians, jihadi Salafis in Iraq, especially al Qaeda in Iraq (AQI), have adopted a number of ancillary arguments to justify attacks on fellow Iraqis and Muslims. These arguments may be divided into three categories: ideological, theological, and emotional.

Ideological justifications emphasize a conspiratorial worldview featuring a "crusader-Zionist" alliance against Islam and Muslims helped by "local collaborators" who do the "dirty work" of the invaders. Theological justifications revolve around Islamic traditions that appear to legitimize suicide, killing civilians, and Muslims killing Muslims. They cite three traditions in particular to justify suicide attacks in Iraq: the wars against apostates in the formative period of Islam *(hurub al-Riddah),* the ruling concerning killing Muslim human shields *(qatl al-turse),* and the rule concerning plunging into the ranks of enemies in battle *(al-inghimas fi al-saf).*

Emotional appeals focus the attention of Muslims on the enduring humiliation and oppression suffered at the hands of foreigners and their "lackeys" in the Muslim world. Personal sacrifice is framed as the only means to erase this shame and redeem the nation.

Despite the elaborate ideological and theological arguments jihadi Salafis make to justify their violence, it is the more emotive element of their discourse—highlighting Muslim humiliation and suffering in video clips and audio recordings—that galvanizes support for their cause. The more complex theological arguments are intended for a smaller circle of jihadi Salafis who may question the legitimacy of suicide attacks in general and suicide bombings against Muslims in particular. Therefore, it is important to pay careful attention to the emotional appeals of jihadists in Iraq.

IDEOLOGY, THEOLOGY, AND MYTHOLOGY IN THE SERVICE OF DEATH

How do the ideological, religious, and emotional appeals of jihadi Salafis in Iraq translate into violence on the ground? Insurgents deploy ideology, religion, and cultural identities in three ways. First, religion and cultural identities serve as tool kits from which organizers of collective action strategically select texts, narratives, traditions, symbols, myths, and rituals to imbue risky activism and extreme violence with morality. Research on insurgency and social movement activism suggests that political actors must align their rhetoric and ideological appeals with cultural norms and expectations, lest these appeals fail to resonate with their target recruits.[1]

Cultural or religious framing is always strategic and ideological, in the sense that political actors selectively use traditions or symbols that can motivate mobilization in line with political objectives. Moreover, religious and cultural framing invariably involves a degree of innovation, whereby old ideas are presented in new ways that appear authentic and relevant for contemporary times. As Sidney Tarrow eloquently put it, "Symbols of revolt are not drawn like musty costumes from a cultural closet and arrayed before the public. Nor are new meanings unrolled out of whole cloth. The costumes of revolt are woven from a blend of inherited and invented fibers into collective action frames in confrontation with opponents and elites."[2]

Ideology, religion, and emotion also can serve to deactivate self-inhibiting norms against murder and mayhem. These discursive ploys allow jihadists to appear as moral agents even when they are acting in immoral ways. Engaging in conduct that violates accepted moral standards and contravenes years of socialization can generate self-devaluation associated with guilt feelings. However, as social psychologist Albert Bandura explained, many psychological maneuvers can selectively disengage moral self-reactions from unethical conduct. He began with a premise widely accepted by experts on political violence: Terrorists are not abnormal individuals or psychopaths who lack morality and are bent on bloodletting. Rather, they are normal, ordinary people who are capable of selectively disengaging their moral codes in the service of inhumane conduct under certain circumstances or inducements.[3]

Just as soldiers can go to battle to fight and kill for their country, terrorists can engage in violence to promote a cause. To be sure, soldiers must be trained to overcome their inhibitions to kill others, but most societies do not see this behavior modification as immoral; indeed, it is rewarded with medals, venerated in public ceremonies, and idealized as heroic sacrifice when soldiers are killed in action. Similarly, terrorists can frame their violent deeds as moral acts in the service of their people, country, or God. Selective moral disengagement is not equivalent to setting aside one's values as if they are personal baggage that can be stowed away to free one's hands temporarily. Rather, it involves the cognitive reconstruction of unethical conduct as socially or morally acceptable.

Those who perform cruel acts can justify them through several mechanisms of moral disengagement. The most common is the ethical justification of violence through resolution of moral dilemmas. Terrorists frame their conduct as a necessary evil to end social injustices such as economic exploitation, foreign domination, or exposure of one's religious community to deleterious influences. This form of moral disengagement does not deny that cruel violence is an undesirable aberration, but it frames it as a necessity to overcome a greater evil. Jihadi Salafis in Iraq use this mechanism of moral disengagement by emphasizing the threats facing the Sunnis in Iraq and the Muslim world in general: Given the magnitude of the crisis, extraordinary means to repel the greatest evil facing Muslims are both permissible and necessary.

Another mechanism of moral disengagement involves exonerating comparisons. The purveyors of violence rationalize their actions by framing their violent conduct as a minor transgression compared with the cruelties the enemy inflicts on them. As Bandura explained, "Self-deplored acts can be made to appear righteous by contrasting them with flagrant inhumanities. The more outrageous the comparison practices, the more likely it is that one's own destructive conduct will appear trifling or even benevolent."[4] Jihadi Salafis in Iraq frame their actions as a response to the great cruelty and humiliation imposed on the Sunnis by the invaders and their Shia collaborators. The emphasis on women being mistreated, men tortured, mosques destroyed, and the Quran defiled is intended to reassure jihadists that their violence pales in comparison to the transgressions of their enemies.

Perhaps the most powerful mechanism of moral disengagement is the dehumanization of one's target. Recognizing the humanity of others, including enemies, can obstruct the perpetration of cruelties against them. Attributing subhuman qualities to others is one way to dehumanize them. Thus they fall outside the "universe of moral obligation and, therefore, are not deserving of compassionate treatment."[5]

Dehumanization not only entails rendering others subhuman or making them symbols of iniquity and malevolence; it also erases differences inside the enemy camp and attributes an unchanging essence to an entire category of people. Others become part of a monolithic bloc that possesses unredeemable characteristics, values, or habits. The other is a category— "class enemies" and "reactionaries," "apostates" and "infidels," "crusaders" and "Zionists." Essentializing the enemy involves combining immutability with heredity.[6] The enemy is incapable of change and bequeaths its vile characteristics to its offspring. This mental construction of the enemy allows militants to attribute collective guilt to the enemy. It removes one's capacity for empathy with the other by creating an emotional distance. The sharp dividing lines between "us" and "them" exaggerate the inability of conflicting parties to reconcile differences. This process is invariably accompanied by a devaluation of the other; we are separate, but we are not equal. "We" are morally superior even if temporarily weak; "they" are morally corrupt even if they possess all the power and wealth in the world.

AQI and other insurgent groups in Iraq portray the Shia as irredeemable people who are inherently antagonistic to Sunnis and have been a threat to Islam since time immemorial. They draw parallels between the alleged betrayal of Ibn al-Alqami, the Shia minister during Hulagu's attack on Baghdad in 1258, with current Shia leaders aiding the coalition forces in the occupation of Iraq. Ibn al-Alqami was accused of betraying the Abbasid caliph and helping the Tartar invaders sack the heart of the Muslim empire. Going further back, AQI repeatedly raises the claim that the Shia insult the honor of the Prophet's family by accusing the Prophet's favorite wife Aisha of adultery. This "original sin" of the Shia is sufficient to condemn them today. Their enemies point to alleged links between Iran and Shia parties and organizations during the Iraq-Iran war of the 1980s to show that the Shia are forever treasonous and treacherous.

INSTRUMENTAL AND IDEOLOGICAL JUSTIFICATIONS FOR SUICIDE TERRORISM IN IRAQ

As of February 2006, AQI had claimed responsibility for 30 percent of the suicide attacks in Iraq for which claims of responsibility were made. Abu Musab al-Zarqawi offered an instrumental justification for these attacks in one of his audio recordings.

> [The holy warriors] faced the strongest and most advanced army in modern times. They faced its arrogance, tyranny and all its big numbers and advanced weapons.... When the holy warriors noticed this huge disparity in numbers and armaments between them and the enemy, they looked for alternatives to amend this deficiency and fill this gap so that the light and the fire of jihad would not be extinguished. Brigades of martyrs, whose sole goals are to please God and rush to the heavens, have set out and attacked the sanctuaries of infidelity and broken its armies. They inflicted severe punishment and injuries on the enemy and hurt its reputation. They mobilized the sons of this nation against this enemy and revived hope in the souls once again, praises and gratitude be to God.[7]

Abu Dujana al-Ansari, the head of AQI's al-Bara Bin Malik Brigade (suicide bombing squad), similarly justifies suicide attacks in a montage dedicated to Zarqawi. Al-Ansari says that the suicide brigade was created following the earlier advice of Sheikh Osama bin Laden to terrorize the enemy, penetrate its defenses, and demoralize its soldiers.[8] Al-Ansari declares that such attacks instill fear in enemies' hearts and make them cower in the face of the Muslim fighters.

But how do they justify attacking Iraqi security forces? Insurgents in Iraq, not just those associated with AQI and ASG, argue that the Iraqi security forces are a mere extension, an appendage, of the coalition forces in Iraq. Just as the United States recruited the Northern Alliance fighters in Afghanistan against the Taliban regime, it is relying in Iraq on the Shia militias of the Badr Corps (which they derisively call the "Ghader"—betrayal—Corps) and the Kurdish Peshmergas. The same goes for the newly formed Iraqi security services (which they derisively call *al-haras al-wathani*—the idol-worshipping guard, as opposed to *al-haras al-watani*, the National Guard).[9] Striking at these "collaborators" is nothing less than striking at the U.S.-led forces.

In a forty-six-minute video montage dedicated to the theme of fighting the Iraqi police and security forces, Zarqawi rhetorically asks, "Why is it permissible to strike the enemy when he has blonde hair and blue eyes, but it is not permissible to strike him when he has dark hair and black eyes?" He concludes, "An American Muslim is our beloved brother, and an Arab infidel is our depraved enemy, even if we share with him the same spot of land."[10]

In justifying attacks against Shia militias, AQI and other insurgent groups argue that these militias attack and kill Sunnis, torture them, abuse and humiliate them at checkpoints, and serve as spies for the occupation forces. Many video clips issued by ASG and AQI are dedicated to this theme. Therefore, the operations against the Shia are in self-defense to protect the Sunni communities as well as take revenge on those who would harm Sunnis and turn them over to the coalition forces. AQI formed the Umar Brigade specifically to attack members of the Shia Badr Corps.[11]

In justifying attacks against the ruling government, the nationalists and jihadi Salafi insurgents argue that it is an illegitimate government—indeed a puppet regime—that came to power under unacceptable circumstances with the help of aggressive enemies of the Iraqi people. It rules only because the coalition forces allow it to, not because it is a genuine Islamic representative of the people of Iraq. The Iraqi government gives cover and legitimacy to the occupation when it should be fighting it and demanding the withdrawal of foreign forces from Iraqi land. Without the charade of parliamentary politics and constitutional conventions, the occupation would be exposed for what it is to the Iraqi people and the world.

Moreover, this government is part of a global conspiracy against Islam led by "crusaders" and "Zionists." These forces fear the truth of Islam and the unification of Muslim lands under a single leader, or *khalifa* (caliph), and consequently conspire to distort Islam and weaken the faith of Muslims. If Muslims were united in one entity they could counter the hegemony of the West and revive the glories of the golden age. Secularism, nationalism, and Shia sectarianism are instruments of this nefarious plot to divide and conquer Muslims.

Secularism divides the world into religious and nonreligious spheres antithetical to Islam, which is a comprehensive religion that regulates both matters of faith *(ibadat)* and social relations *(muamalat)*. Furthermore, secularism violates God's sovereignty *(hakimiyyat allah)* by allowing someone other than God to legislate right and wrong, permissible and forbidden. Nationalism, in turn, fosters narrow identifications with language, land, and borders, not a broader unity among the community of the faithful and brotherhood of Muslims. As for Shia sectarians, they give ascendancy to a heretical creed, not Islamic law based on the proper *manhaj* (method or orientation). The Shia are the most dangerous tool against the true believers because they appear Islamic, authentic, and of the people. In reality, they loathe the people of the Sunna and wait for the opportunity to betray them.[12]

RELIGIOUS JUSTIFICATIONS OF SUICIDE ATTACKS

It is supremely ironic that jihadi Salafis embrace "martyrdom operations" and deploy this tactic against the Shia in Iraq. Martyrdom is a central feature of Shia ethos, theology, and commemorative rituals; it is less prominent in Sunni orthodoxy and the classical jihad discourse of Sunni scholars and caliphs. Every year the Shia publicly mourn the martyrdom of Imam Hussein in the ceremonies of *ashura* (tenth day of Muharram in the Islamic calendar).

The son of the fourth caliph, Ali, and Fatima, the Prophet's daughter, Hussein was thus the grandson of the Prophet. This pedigree gives him special status among the Shia. However, it is not his lineage that is commemorated every year, but the events that led to his martyrdom and the symbolism therein. According to the tradition, Hussein challenged the powerful army of the Umayyad caliph Yazid in the battle of Karbala (now in Iraq) in 680 CE. Hussein was responding to the urgings of the people of Kufa to reclaim leadership from the Umayyad "usurpers."[13] On the tenth day of battle, he was slain and his head was severed and presented as a gift to the ruling caliph. The symbolism of Hussein's martyrdom contains elements of both pessimism and optimism about social activism and rebellion that can be exploited to promote either quietism or revolt in Shia Islam.

On the optimistic side, these events speak of the courage and heroism of a righteous leader who challenged powerful forces, regardless of the consequences. Hussein is venerated because he did not cower in the face of inequity and did not allow the asymmetry of power between his forces and those of Yazid to deter him from seeking to redress injustice. On the pessimistic side, these events exemplify the limits of courage and heroism in reversing the unfairness of the powerful. They are an allegory for the tragic reality of historical experience in which the virtuous are doomed to endure suffering at the hands of the immoral.

The Shia mourn the martyrdom of Imam Hussein by dressing in black and participating in mass processions. Men and women beat their chests (matam) to symbolize their grief. Self-flagellation with chains, whips, and swords is a common aspect of the commemoration. Mourners engage in the ritual of tatbir, whereby they nick their upper forehead with a razor to induce bleeding that symbolizes Hussein's suffering and martyrdom. Actors perform public plays in complete historical attire to represent the events of the first ten days of Muharram, while preachers lecture on the meaning of Hussein's sacrifice in the battle of Karbala. In these mourning ceremonies, women and men often break down in tears.[14]

None of these rituals is found in Sunni Islam, nor do Sunni scholars commemorate the martyrs during the time of the Prophet Muhammad. The recent veneration of martyrdom by Sunnis in Palestine and jihadi Salafis in Iraq is an innovation in Sunni orthopraxy. To be sure, as shown below, the Quran and the traditions of the Prophet contain many positive references to jihad and martyrdom in the path of God. Muslims in the formative phases of Islam relied on these verses and traditions to inspire offensive jihads (futuhat) and defensive ones.

In premodern times, Sunni communities in southwestern India, Aceh in present-day Indonesia, and Mindanao in the southern Philippines engaged in suicide attacks to resist Western colonial rule.[15] Yet, despite ubiquitous references to martyrdom in Islamic texts, martyr rituals, symbols, and ceremonies never achieved the prominent status in Sunni Islam that they have in the Shia tradition. It took mass martyrdom by Iranian (Shia) youth in the bassidj organization during the Iran-Iraq war of 1980–1988 and successful suicide missions by the Shia Hezbollah in Lebanon during the 1980s and 1990s against U.S., French, and Israeli forces to revitalize the spirit of martyrdom among Sunni groups, principally the Palestinian Islamic Jihad and Hamas. Thus, paradoxically, jihadi Salafis are mimicking Shia martyrdom to attack their most reviled enemy: the Shia.

Jihadi Salafis have to contend with more than a paradox in Iraq. Suicide terrorism poses a serious theological challenge. Salafis tend to be strict constructionists when it comes to interpreting Islamic texts and traditions. In Islam there are clear and widely accepted prohibitions against Muslims killing themselves, civilians or noncombatants, or other Muslims.[16] Yet jihadi Salafis have engaged in attacks intentionally involving self-immolation and have killed civilians and Muslims. How do they square their tactics with their strict constructionist jurisprudence? How do they justify contravening three clearly established Islamic prohibitions commanded by God and the Prophet Muhammad?

AQI relies on a number of religious arguments that allow it, at least in theory, to circumvent the aforementioned prohibitions while continuing to claim Islamic legitimacy. These arguments revolve around who is a Muslim and who is an apostate in Islam, the role of human intentionality in action, and analogous reasoning based on historic Islamic traditions and rulings concerning killing civilians in battle and killing Muslim human shields.

THE MEANING OF PIETY AND APOSTASY IN ISLAM

AQI and ASG make it clear that not everyone who calls himself a Muslim can be considered a Muslim. Islam is not a mere utterance with the tongue (*iqrar);* it is also sincere belief in the heart *(niyah)* and manifest deeds *(a`amal al-jawarih).* The three must be present for a person truly to be a Muslim. AQI and ASG cite the example of Abu Bakr, the first caliph in Islam, who fought wars with tribes that claimed to be Muslim but refused to pay the alms tax *(zakat).* Abu Bakr judged them on their deeds, not their words. Given this precedent from the pious ancestors *(al-Salaf al-Salih),* it is permissible to judge the "so-called Muslims" of Iraq on the basis of their deeds, not their words alone.[17]

When jihadi Salafis insist that they constitute the saved denomination *(al-firqa al-najiyyah)* or the victorious sect *(al-taifa al-mansura),* they refer to two Prophetic traditions. In one the Prophet Muhammad tells his followers that the Muslim nation will be divided into seventy-three sects;

all of them will end up in the fire of hell except the one that follows the Prophet and his companions. In the other the Prophet speaks of a group of people from the Islamic nation who would continue to fight in defense of the truth and be triumphant until Judgment Day.

In a document entitled "The Markers of the Victorious Sect in the Land of the Two Rivers [Iraq]," Abi al-Fadhl al-Iraqi and Abu Islam al-Ansari distinguish between "true" Muslims and all the other doomed sects.[18] The victorious sect believes that

- Legislation belongs to God alone. Anyone who rules or legislates on the basis of something other than what God has revealed in his book and the traditions of his Prophet Muhammad is a usurper of God's dominion and an infidel outside the creed. He must be fought, and fighting him is an individual obligation *(fard ayn)* of every Muslim.
- Engaging in *takfir* (declaring Muslims to be in violation of the creed and outside the community of the faithful) is a religious imperative that must be exercised to protect religion and its adherents from error.
- Individuals are considered infidels if they express or engage in major impiety *(kufr kabir),* even if they do not intend to be infidels.
- Genuine Muslims do not support non-Muslims over Muslims because such action is a great impiety.
- The Shia sect is apostate and an evil on earth.
- Muslim lands that are ruled by un-Islamic laws are considered an amalgam of Islam and infidelity *(diyar murakabah).* In these lands, Muslims should be treated as Muslims and infidels as infidels. In other words, this land is not considered a house of war, in which everyone is considered outside the community of the faithful and, therefore, can be fought. Nor is it a house of Islam, in which fighting is not permissible and where non-Muslims are protected subjects.
- Muslims do not participate in elections and do not enter parliaments.
- Jihad is continuous until Judgment Day, either with or without a Muslim leader. Jihad is not merely a defensive struggle against invaders, but an aggressive striving to reestablish the Islamic caliphate and spread Islam to all of humanity.

These elements are used in different ways to justify expansive violence in Iraq. In the case of the Iraqi security services, Zarqawi and others argued that in verse 5:51 the Quran states, "O you who believe! Do not take the Jews and the Christians for friends; they are friends of each other; and whoever amongst you takes them for a friend, then surely he is one of them; surely Allah does not guide the unjust people." Taking the Americans and British as protectors—indeed as "masters"—violates this verse. According to AQI, one of the violations that put Muslims outside the creed is giving support to unbelievers over believers. By siding with the non-Muslims against the Muslim insurgents, the Iraqi forces have forfeited their claim to being Muslims and have become apostates. In Islam, it is permissible for Muslims to kill apostates for abandoning the faith unless they repent.

However, according to AQI and ASG, even the opportunity for repentance—giving people a chance to abandon what they are doing in support of the occupation before killing them—is not applicable in Iraq. An opportunity for repentance, AQI argues on the authority of the Hanbali scholar Ibn Taymiyyah (1263–1328), is possible when Muslims are in a position of power and control. Otherwise, apostates may be killed without being given a chance to repent.

ASG similarly refers to the authority of the venerated classical scholar Ibn al-Qayyim al-Jawziyya (1292–1350): "According to the jurists, an apostate, who has committed aggravated apostasy, may be killed without being given the chance to repent."[19] Moreover, according to AQI, fighting against the apostates "takes precedence over fighting against the original infidels. Apostasy is a greater transgression than original unbelief, and the apostate is a greater enemy."[20]

As for others outside the security services and the government, they are safe as long as they refrain from aiding the regime and the occupation forces in any way. However, AQI defines support for the occupation and the existing regime in very broad terms that put nearly every Iraqi who is not an insurgent in the circle of enemies:

- Those who give aid by "word of mouth," such as the "evil Islamic scholars," chief among them the Shia cleric "al-Sistani, his followers, his troops, and his sympathizers. All of these persons are like a sword hanging over our heads."
- Those who give aid by their actions, not just soldiers and police forces, but also those who "maintain public order in the state,"

those who "defend constitutional legitimacy," and those who uphold the law by "carrying out the verdicts passed by the tyrannical, manmade courts."

- Anyone who assists the enemy in any way, even if "he might be a Muslim in his heart, might have no thoughts in his mind against Islam, and there might be no suspicions surrounding him."[21]

ASG also has a broad list of "collaborators" who may be killed for working with the occupation forces. It includes anyone who

- Works for the police and security services. It is not permissible to work for the army and police of the "unbelievers," because it provides them with stability, peace, and security. It is not permissible to take the occupation forces as guardians or superiors. Offenders are considered unbelievers and apostates punishable in accordance with Islamic law (by death). Even those who participate out of need for money, position, or any other reason are considered apostates, even if in their hearts they do not wish to support the invaders.
- Spies for the enemy. They are considered apostates and will be killed.[22]
- Sells the occupation forces food, water, clothes, arms, or any form of sustenance, either directly or indirectly.
- Translates for the occupation forces or gives them assistance that could make them comfortable, safe, or in good spirits.
- Provides them with security or constructs anything that will give them safety, even if it is a small part of a project.[23]

As for the Shia, Zarqawi argued that they are heretics outside the creed because they reject the first two caliphs of Islam—Abu Bakr al-Siddiq and Umar Ibn al-Khattab—the core of the pious ancestors for Sunni Muslims. The Shia question the honor and chastity of Aisha, the Prophet Muhammad's favorite wife, despite the fact that the Quran insists on her pure character. The Shia also hurl invectives at Abu Hurayrah, one of the most prolific transmitters of Prophetic traditions in Sunni Islam. Since they are heretics, which is worse than being original infidels, Shia blood is not sacrosanct and may be shed for the interest of the broader Islamic community.

The ruling government is composed of apostates who must be fought. Not only has it taken the "crusaders" as protectors in violation of aforementioned Quranic verses, it does not rule in accordance with Islamic law *(sharia)*, despite the fact that the dominant parties in government have an Islamic orientation. These two major transgressions against the faith *(kufr kabir)* make the existing ruling regime a *taghout* (which has the dual meaning of being a tyrant and an idol worshipper). Fighting the government is just as important as fighting the invaders, because it appears Islamic when in reality it is creating dissension *(fitna)* among Muslims and diverting believers from the proper path.

HUMAN INTENTIONALITY AND THE ISLAMIC PROHIBITION AGAINST SUICIDE

Suicide is strictly prohibited in Islam, as it is in other Abrahamic traditions. The jihadi Salafis reject the use of the term "suicide operations" *(amaliyyat intihariyya)* and insist on the euphemistic label "martyrdom operations" *(amaliyyat istishhadiyya)*, "sacrifice operations" *(amaliyyat fidaiyya)*, or "jihadi operations" *(amaliyyat jihadiyya)*. Such labeling, however, has not been sufficient to circumvent the prohibition against self-immolation. A stronger argument was necessary to parry the criticisms of the traditional Salafi scholars, such as Sheikh Naser al-Din al-Albani, Sheikh Ibn Uthaimin, Sheikh Abdel Aziz bin Baz, and Sheikh Abd al-Aziz al-Shaykh.[24]

Jihadi Salafis begin by pointing out that the Quran recognizes and venerates the martyr. They cite the following Quranic verses:[25]

> 9:111 – Allah hath purchased of the believers their persons and their goods; for theirs (in return) is the garden (of Paradise): they fight in His cause, and slay and are slain: a promise binding on Him in truth, through the Law, the Gospel, and the Quran: and who is more faithful to his covenant than Allah? Then rejoice in the bargain which ye have concluded: that is the achievement supreme.

> 2:154 – And call not those who are slain in the way of Allah 'dead.' Nay, they are living, only ye perceive not."[26]

Moreover, God commanded the Muslims to fight the unbelievers with whatever capabilities they could muster, including their lives:

> 8:60 – Against them make ready your strength to the utmost of your power, including steeds of war, to strike terror into (the hearts of) the enemies, of Allah and your enemies, and others besides, whom ye may not know, but whom Allah doth know. Whatever ye shall spend in the cause of Allah, shall be repaid unto you, and ye shall not be treated unjustly.[27]

Since God commands fighting and recognizes and elevates the status of martyrs, how does one evaluate the permissibility of suicide operations? The major innovation of the jihadi Salafis was the notion of human intentionality. As they put it, there is a fundamental qualitative difference between the intention of a person committing suicide to kill him- or herself and one committing suicide to kill "enemies of Islam and Muslims." The former is a depressed person who has given up on life and cannot bear its hopelessness. That person's suicide is about escapism, the deviation of a weak mind. Martyrs, on the other hand, are strong-willed individuals who sacrifice themselves. Whereas suicide is the pathetic end to depression and despair, martyrdom is a new beginning of hope and deliverance. Suicide is shameful and something to be discouraged; martyrdom is honorable and worth emulating.

The argument is best exemplified by Abu Qatada al-Falistini.[28] He argues that during the time of the Prophet Muhammad, two paradigms presented themselves. The first involved a Muslim killing himself by leaning on his sword after suffering an unbearable wound in battle. Rather than endure the pain, he intentionally killed himself to bring relief only to himself. When the Prophet Muhammad was asked about him, the Prophet declared that he was forever in hellfire, the judgment on any person who commits suicide.

The second paradigm involved what is termed "plunging into the ranks" *(al-inghimas fi al-saf)*.[29] After hearing the Prophet Muhammad cite the rewards of martyrdom, Muslims intentionally took extraordinary risks in battle against unbelievers; single fighters rushed headlong into a group of combatants to achieve martyrdom.[30] In this paradigm, these people were considered devout Muslims who would be rewarded abundantly in paradise.

According to Abu Qatada, what distinguishes the first paradigm from the second is the intention of the acting agent. In the first paradigm, the person's intention was to escape the pain of this world, whereas in the second paradigm the intention was to fulfill God's command to fight in his path even if it entailed one's death. In both paradigms the end result is the same, the death of the Muslim fighter, but their intentions differ significantly. The wounded fighter violated God's command for his own benefit. The fighter "plunging into the ranks" of the infidels believed in the words of God and his Prophet; otherwise why would he take such an action to benefit other Muslims?

Abu Qatada's intentionality claim is anchored in the notion of Muslim interests. Plunging into enemy ranks cannot be done for its own sake. It must contain a benefit for Islam and Muslims. In other words, martyrdom is never simply for its own sake; its goal must be to raise God's word on earth and advance the cause of Muslims. Abu Qatada defines Muslim interests broadly. For instance, it is permissible for a person to take extraordinary risks by plunging into enemy ranks if only to show the enemies of Islam that Muslims are courageous and do not fear death. This action benefits the Muslims because the enemy might be deterred from attacking or might even surrender after perceiving the determination of Muslims. Plunging into the ranks might also encourage other Muslim fighters to become equally courageous and follow in the footsteps of the "martyr." Under such a broad conception of Muslim interests, it is easy to see how virtually any suicide attack today could be considered beneficial to Islam and Muslims.

THE "PERMISSIBILITY" OF KILLING CIVILIANS IN ISLAM

Jihadi Salafis point to Prophetic traditions and Hanbali rulings that they say permit the killing of civilians in warfare.[31] These traditions refer to firing catapults (manjaniq) at enemy positions where civilians are present and "the night raid" (qatl al-bayat) found in Sahih Muslim, Book 019, Number 4321: "It is reported on the authority of Sa'b b. Jaththama that the Prophet of Allah (may peace be upon him), when asked about the women and children of the polytheists being killed during the night raid, said: They are from them."

To the jihadi Salafis, this passage proves that the Prophet recognized the need for civilian collateral damage in war. They supplement their argument by citing Quranic verse 16:126, "And if you take your turn, then punish with the like of that with which you were afflicted." Since Shia militias are killing Sunnis in Iraq, they argue, it is permissible for the Sunni insurgents to kill Shia civilians in revenge.[32]

However, it is important to note that other jihadi Salafis, especially Abu Basir al-Tartusi and Abu Muhammad al-Maqdisi, question the appropriateness of applying this tradition in Iraq and elsewhere. Abu Basir, for instance, argues that unequivocal *(muhkamat)* verses and traditions are absolute *(qatiyyah)* in their command not to kill civilians intentionally. Therefore, one should not use verses subject to multiple interpretations *(mutashabihat)* or rulings by scholars to override the clear and absolute Quranic and Prophetic commands.[33]

Similarly, al-Maqdisi, Zarqawi's mentor in Jordan, raises objections about the use of the "night raid" tradition to justify killing civilians. He argues that the night raid covers an exception to the general rule of avoiding harm to noncombatants. Yet the jihadists in Iraq have applied this tradition as if it were the rule, not the exception. More important, the tradition concerning the night raid suggests that the Muslim fighters cannot distinguish between enemies and their civilians because the raid is carried out at night. Therefore, the tradition affirms the need to avoid harming civilians to the extent that one can distinguish between combatants and civilians. It is not a blanket statement to support killing civilians during war. Al-Maqdisi concludes that if all this caution is given to avoid harming the civilians of the unbelievers, imagine how much more caution fighters must exercise when it comes to the possibility of killing Muslim civilians.[34]

THE "PERMISSIBILITY" OF KILLING MUSLIM HUMAN SHIELDS

The most complex argument for the permissibility of Muslims killing other Muslims is based on a historic ruling of Islamic scholars concerning killing human shields *(qatl al-turse)*. According to this tradition, the scholars ruled that it is permissible for Muslims to kill Muslims serving willingly or unwillingly as human shields to benefit the broader struggle against the unbelievers.

AQI has used this ruling to justify Muslims killing other Muslims in public spaces. It argues that the occupation forces are hiding behind ordinary Muslims in markets and other public places so that it is nearly impossible for the jihadists to fight the enemy without inflicting unintentional harm on other Muslims. If the attacks, especially suicide bombings, were to stop in Iraq to save the lives of these innocent Muslims, the struggle would come to an end and the unbelievers would triumph. This outcome harms the "collective" interests of Muslims by allowing unbelievers to control Muslim lands and wealth and inflict humiliation and suffering on the entirety of the Muslim community. On the other hand, operations that kill ordinary Muslims result in "private" harm of individuals while they bring "collective" benefits to the entire Muslim community in Iraq—indeed, to Muslims around the world.[35] This logic, according to AQI, is the essence behind the ruling of the pious ancestors concerning killing human shields.

Jihadi Salafis extend this argument to justify self-sacrifice, which some Salafis equate with suicide. According to one jihadi Salafi scholar, in accordance with the "human shields" ruling, if it is permissible for Muslims in certain circumstances to inflict harm on other Muslims to benefit the entire Muslim community, then certainly it is permissible for Muslims in certain circumstances to inflict harm on themselves to benefit the entire Muslim nation.

Muslims killing other Muslims is a greater sin in the eye of God than Muslims killing themselves. Although both are grave sins that warrant eternal damnation in the eyes of God, Muslims who kill other Muslims cause two types of harm. The first is to the injured Muslim who did not wish to be killed, and the second is to the murdering Muslim who violated God's command. The act of suicide, on the other hand, involves a singular harm to the perpetrator of the act. The suicidal individual harms him- or herself and no one else. Given this hierarchy of sins, if the ruling permitting the killing of Muslim human shields is applicable, then certainly the ruling concerning the lesser sin of committing suicide is valid if done to benefit Muslims in the path of God.[36]

Other radical Salafis, however, have taken issue with the applicability of the ruling concerning human shields in Iraq. They argue that this rule comes with stringent conditions that must be met before Muslims are allowed to kill fellow Muslims. Abu Basir al-Tartusi lists four such conditions. First, it must be impossible to fight the aggressor except through harming the human shields. If there are other ways to repel the invaders, then it is not permissible to harm the human shields or to seek to fight them directly. Second, it must be clear that avoiding harm to the human shields results in a bigger harm to Muslim lands and Muslims. Islamic principles command that the believer repel the greater harm with the lesser harm if one or the other is unavoidable. Third, the benefit stemming from killing human shields must be absolutely clear and undisputable, not a mere possibility or a probable outcome. Finally, if the three conditions are met, it is permissible to attack the enemy being shielded by Muslims, but the intent must be to kill the enemy, not the Muslims.[37]

CONCLUSION

Jihadi Salafis use a variety of instrumental, ideological, and theological arguments to justify suicide attacks against Muslims and non-Muslims in Iraq. Instrumentally, they insist this is the best tactic to instill fear in the hearts of the invaders and demoralize their ranks. Also it deters others from cooperating with the occupiers. Ideologically, they insist that there is a conspiracy against Islam and Muslims led by "crusaders and Zionists" and aided by local collaborators who do their dirty work. Therefore, extraordinary measures—including killing nominal Muslims—are necessary to foil this conspiracy.

Jihadi Salafis frame ambiguous Quranic verses, Prophetic traditions, and historic Islamic rulings to justify suicide, killing civilians, and killing fellow Muslims. These arguments involve complex historical traditions that are open to multiple interpretations, yet jihadists have retrieved and presented them as unproblematic justifications for suicide terrorism in Iraq.

NOTES

1. Richard L. Wood, "Religious Culture and Political Action." *Sociological Theory* 17, no. 3 (1999): 307–32; Rhys H. Williams and Timothy J. Kubal, "Movement Frames and the Cultural Environment: Resonance, Failure, and the Boundaries of the Legitimate," *Research in Social Movements, Conflicts and Change* 21 (1999): 225–48; Rhys H. Williams, "From the 'Beloved Community' to 'Family Values': Religious Language, Symbolic Repertoires, and Democratic Culture," in *Social Movements: Identity, Culture, and the State,* David S. Meyer,

Nancy Whittier, and Belinda Robnett, eds. (New York: Oxford University Press, 2002).

2. Tarrow, *Power in Movement*, 118.

3. Albert Bandura, "Mechanisms of Moral Disengagement," in *Origins of Terrorism: Psychologies, Ideologies, Theologies, States of Mind*, Walter Reich, ed. (Washington, D.C.: Woodrow Wilson Center Press, 1990), 161–91; Albert Bandura, "Moral Disengagement in the Perpetration of Inhumanities," *Personality and Social Psychology Review* 3, no. 3 (1999): 193–209; Albert Bandura, Claudio Barbaranelli, Gian Vittorio Caprara, and Concetta Pastorelli, "Mechanisms of Moral Disengagement in the Exercise of Moral Agency," *Journal of Personality and Social Psychology* 71, no. 2 (1996): 364–74.

4. Bandura et al., "Mechanisms of Moral Disengagement," 171.

5. James Waller, *Becoming Evil: How Ordinary People Commit Genocide and Mass Killing* (New York: Oxford University Press, 2005), 245.

6. Clark McCauley, "The Psychology of Group Identification and the Power of Ethnic Nationalism," in *Ethnopolitical Warfare: Causes, Consequences, and Possible Solutions*, Daniel Chirot and Martin E. P. Seligman, eds. (Washington, D.C.: American Psychological Association, 2001), 343–62.

7. Audio entitled "The Descendents of Ibn al-Alqami Are Back," issued by the Ana Muslim Forum (www.muslm.net), in May 2005 (translated from Arabic by the author; accessed July 15, 2005).

8. The montage is about seventy-eight minutes long, entitled "Commander of the Slaughterers," issued by the Global Islamic Media Front in November 2005, and available at the OSC, "GIMF Issues 'Amir of the Slaughterers' Video," December 14, 2005.

9. This analysis is in the document "Jihad in Iraq: Hopes and Dangers." It does not have an author or date but was dedicated to Yousef al-Ayiri, al Qaeda leader in Saudi Arabia, killed in 2003, and issued by the Media Commission for the Victory of the Iraqi People (The Mujahidin Services Center) sometime in 2003. Also, see article by Salah al-Muatasim, "The Truth about the Americans and the Collaborating Regime" (Arabic), *Ansar al-Sunna* (online magazine), issue 11, June 2004, 8–10.

10. Montage entitled "And Worship Shall Be Only for Allah," issued by the Media Division of al Qaeda in Iraq, June 2005. This argument was repeated in the aforementioned "Commander of the Slaughterers" video, in which Zarqawi says, "After the Americans suffered major losses, they began to create the local police and security services to do their work. They have become infidels and apostates for serving the Americans.... Those that say you can kill those with blue eyes, but not those with black eyes love nationalism, not monotheism; they want this world, not the next. The Iraqi Army is the army of apostasy."

11. Zarqawi announced the formation of the Umar Brigades in an audiotape released July 5, 2005. OSC, "New Al-Zarqawi Message," July 11, 2005.

12. See Abi Aisha al-Hashimi, "Bush ... The Angelical Crusader" (Arabic), *Zarwat al-Sinam* (al Qaeda in Iraq's online magazine), issue 3, n.d., 18–22; OSC, "Al-Zarqawi Justifies Killing of Innocent Muslims, Condemns Shia 'Betrayal' of Sunnis," May 18, 2005; OSC, "Text of Al-Zarqawi's Statement of Operations Against Iraqi Forces, President Bush's 'Holy War,'" July 6, 2005; OSC, "Al-Zarqawi Calls for 'All-Out-War' Against Shia," September 14, 2005.

13. Ali established his caliphate in Kufa from 656 to 661 CE and fought against the founder of the Umayyad dynasty, Mu'awiyyah bin Abi Sufyan, in what came to be known as the first civil war in Islam. In 661 Ali was assassinated by the extremist *Khawariji* sect, which opposed Ali's acceptance of arbitration with Mu'awiyyah's forces. According to the Shia position, Imam Hassan, Ali's son, should have been selected as caliph. However, he relinquished the position and allowed Mu'awiyyah to claim the title.

14. For a vivid depiction of Shia rituals of *ashura*, see Augustus Richard Norton, "Ritual, Blood, and Shii Identity: Ashura in Nabatiyya, Lebanon," *The Drama Review* 49, no. 4 (Winter 2005): 140–55. On the meaning of martyrdom in Karbala, see the documentary *The Living Martyr: Inside the Hezbollah* (Films for the Humanities and Social Sciences, 2000).

15. Stephen Frederic Dale, "Religious Suicide in Islamic Asia: Anticolonial Terrorism in India, Indonesia, and the Philippines," *Journal of Conflict Resolution* 3 (March 1988): 38–59.

16. Quranic verse from Surat al-Nisa' (4:29–30): "Nor kill (or destroy) yourselves: for verily Allah hath been to you Most Merciful! If any do that in rancor and injustice, soon shall We cast them into the Fire: And easy it is for Allah." Prophetic tradition cited in Sahih Muslim and Sahih Bukhari: "And whoever commits suicide with a piece of iron will be punished with the same piece of iron in the Hell Fire." Quranic verse 2:190: "Fight in the path of God those who fight you, but do not transgress limits, for God does not love transgressors." Prophetic tradition quoted in Sahih Muslim (Book 019, Number 4319): "It is narrated on the authority of 'Abdullah that a woman was found killed in one of the battles fought by the Messenger of Allah (may peace be upon him). He disapproved of the killing of women and children." Ibn Taymiyya, the Hanbali scholar, wrote, "As for those who cannot offer resistance or cannot fight, such as women, children, monks, old people, the blind, handicapped and their likes, they shall not be killed, unless they actually fight with words and acts." He cited a report about the Prophet: "That he once passed by a woman who had been slain. The Messenger of God halted and said: 'She was not one who would have fought.' Then he said to one of [his companions]: 'Catch up with [the commander] Khalid ibn al-Walid and tell him not to kill women, children, and serfs.'" Quranic verse from

Surat al-Nisa' (4:93): "If a man kills a believer intentionally, his recompense is Hell, to abide therein (For ever): And the wrath and the curse of Allah are upon him, and a dreadful penalty is prepared for him."

17. OSC, "Al-Zarqawi's Group 'Creed and Methodology' Reiterates Mandate of Jihad, Battling 'Infidels, Apostates, Shia,'" March 24, 2005; OSC, "Al-Zarqawi's Legal Committee Publishes Book 'Why Do We Fight, And Whom Do We Fight?'" October 17, 2005.

18. The document is dated 25 Shawal 1425 (Islamic calendar, 2004) and is posted on the *Tawhid wal Jihad* Web site (www.tawhed.ws). See also on the same Web site, Abdel Munim Mustapha Halima (Abu Basir al-Tartusi), "Features of the Victorious Sect" (Arabic), February 6, 2002.

19. OSC, "Iraq: Ansar al-Sunnah Group Statement on Creed, Objectives," May 8, 2006.

20. OSC, "Al-Zarqawi's Legal Committee."

21. Ibid. This form of expansive *takfir* (declaring other Muslims as apostates) is not new; it appeared in Algeria and Egypt during the 1990s. Jihadi Salafis in those countries used the same arguments to justify killing Muslim government officials, policemen, state workers, intellectuals, tourists, and ordinary civilians. See Mohammed M. Hafez, *Why Muslims Rebel: Repression and Resistance in the Islamic World* (Boulder, Colo.: Lynne Rienner, 2003).

22. ASG issued several video clips of "confessions" of spies—usually Shia in the Badr Corps—before they were executed.

23. See the *fatwa* by the Islamic legal committee of the ASG, "The ruling concerning Jihad in Iraq," published in the first issue of its monthly online journal, *Ansar al-Sunna* (September–October 2003), 14–18.

24. Al-Albani ruled that this tactic could be ordered only by an agreed-upon Islamic commander under an Islamic state. Organizations and individuals cannot call for suicide attacks on their own. The others simply ruled it a form of suicide prohibited by Islam.

25. See Yahya Hashim Hasan Farghal, "Uncovering the Intentions behind Martyrdom Operations" (Arabic), on the *Tawhid wal Jihad* Web site (www.tawhed.ws), n.d.; and Abu Saad al-Amili, "Martyrdom Operations: The Highest Form of Martyrdom" (Arabic), www.tawhed.ws, n.d.

26. See also verses 9:20-22: "Those who believe, and suffer exile and strive with might and main, in Allah's cause, with their goods and their persons, have the highest rank in the sight of Allah: they are the people who will achieve (salvation)"; 2:207: "And there is the type of man who gives his life to earn the pleasure of Allah: And Allah is full of kindness to (his) devotees"; 4:74: "Let those fight in the path of God who sell the life of this world for the other. Whoever fights in the path of God, whether he be slain or victorious, on him We shall bestow a vast reward"; 3:169: "Think not of those, who are slain in the way of Allah, as dead.

Nay, they are living. With their Lord they have provision"; and 4:95–96: "Not equal are those believers who sit (at home) and receive no hurt, and those who strive and fight in the cause of Allah with their goods and their persons."

27. See also verse 2:216: "Fighting is commanded upon you even though it is disagreeable to you. But it is possible that you dislike something which is good for you and that you love something which is bad for you. God knows, but you know not"; and 4:75: "What is wrong with you that you do not fight in the path of God when weak men, women and children are crying: 'Our Lord! Bring us out of this town of evil people and give us from Your presence a protector! Oh, give us a defender!'"

28. Abu Qatada al-Falistini, "The Permissibility of Martyrdom Operations: They Are Not Suicide" (Arabic), www.tawhed.ws, November 6, 1995.

29. Jihadi Salafis rely on a ruling issued 25 Muhram 1319 (Islamic calendar) by Ibn Taymiyyah (1263–1328), a medieval Hanbali scholar, "The Basis for Plunging into the [Ranks of the] Enemy: Is it Permissible?" This ruling was posted on www.tawhed.ws, n.d.

30. For copious citations of prophetic traditions and stories from the Prophet's companions regarding plunging into the ranks of the enemies, see the tract by Yousuf al-Ayiri, "Did Eve Commit Suicide or Martyrdom" (Arabic), www.tawhed.ws, n.d.

31. Nawaf Hayel al-Takrouri, *Martyrdom Operations in Islamic Jurisprudence* (Arabic) (Damascus: Dar al-Fikr, 2003): 238–244; Sulieman Bin Nasr al-Alwan, "The Ruling to Kill Women and Children in Martyrdom Operations" (Arabic), www.tawhed.ws, February 24, 1422 (Islamic calendar); Hamid al-Ali, "The Ruling Concerning Killing Jewish Women and Children in Palestine" (Arabic), www.tawhed.ws, n.d.

32. The Global Islamic Media Front, affiliated with AQI, begins a short video, *They Kill Our Women and Children, So We Will Kill Their Women and Children*, with this Quranic verse.

33. Abu Basir al-Tartusi, "Warnings Concerning Martyrdom or Suicide Operations" (Arabic), www.tawhed.ws, August 24, 2005.

34. Abu Muhammad al-Maqdisi, "Reflections on the Fruits of Jihad: Between the Ignorance of Islamic Law and the Ignorance of Reality" (Arabic), www.tawhed.ws, April 2004.

35. Zarqawi made this claim explicit in his audio recording, "The Descendents of Ibn al-Alqami Are Back." However, the claim is largely derived from jihadi Salafi scholars who made the argument long before he did. See, for example, Hamoud Bin Aqla al-Shuaybi, "Ruling Concerning Martyrdom Operations" (Arabic), www.tawhed.ws, February 2, 2001; and Abu Jandal al-Azdi, "Passages of Jurists about the Rules Concerning Raiding and Human Shields (Bombings and Ambushes)" (Arabic), www.tawhed.ws, May 20, 2003.

36. Al-Shuaybi, "Ruling Concerning Martyrdom Operations."

37. Abu Basir al-Tartusi, "Warnings Concerning Martyrdom or Suicide Operations."

CHAPTER 5

MARTYRDOM MYTHOLOGY IN IRAQ

I nsurgents in Iraq do not depend solely on the force of instrumental arguments, ideology, or theology to mobilize support for martyrdom. They also seek to mythologize martyrdom through the image of heroic martyrs who erase the shame of defeat and redeem the honor of the Muslim nation. Mythologizing martyrdom is not about fabricating facts, but rather entails the invention of tradition by selectively highlighting some aspects of religion, culture, and history to frame contemporary self-sacrifice as part of the venerated jihad and martyrdom of the pious ancestors of Islam. It also entails framing martyrdom as the heroic response to nonreligious transgressions such as female dishonor, treasonous collusion, or collective humiliation. Martyrdom mythology also involves attributing to the "martyrs" superhuman characteristics, including extraordinary devotion to God and religion, unselfish willingness to abandon material fortune and loved ones, ability to foretell martyrdom in dream visions, and astonishing success in killing the "enemies" of Islam.

Insurgents seek to bridge ideological and political divides by appealing to emotional and personal themes embedded in the culture and ethos of Arabs and Muslims in Iraq and around the world. The dominant narratives in insurgent videos, audio recordings, and online magazines revolve around three themes, which they often present in sequence, like a play in three acts. Act 1 depicts the unmerciful humiliation and suffering inflicted on Muslims in Iraq and throughout the world, suggesting a conspiracy by the Western "crusaders" to target Muslims and single them out for punishment. The second act shows the impotence of existing Muslim regimes and their collusion with the West, suggesting they are not the true leaders of the Muslim world, but "servants of their Western masters." The final act insists on the inevitability of Muslim victory because pious and heroic cadres have stepped forward to redeem the suffering and humiliation of their fellow Muslims through faith in God, sacrifice on the battlefield, and righteousness in their cause. The three acts convey a crisis, a causal explanation of the crisis, and the solution to alleviate the suffering of Muslims.

How and why do insurgents engage in this type of emotional discourse? Chapter 4 introduced the communicative challenges of insurgents: to appeal to potential recruits, justify violence, deactivate self-inhibiting norms against killing civilians and fellow Muslims, legitimize insurgent groups, and counter the claims of opposing religious and secular authorities. Insurgents use ideology and theology to achieve those communicative tasks, but they risk overwhelming their audiences with information and complex arguments. Moreover, ideological and theological arguments depend on some knowledge of Islamic jurisprudence *(fiqh)* not always available to the wider Muslim public.

Consequently insurgents supplement their messages with culturally resonant themes as well as emotional imagery to reach out to those less committed to the cause and to demonize their opponents. Their framing of the conflict suggests that insurgents, including jihadi Salafis, are astute cultural actors who know how to segment their messages and tailor them for different audiences.

HUMILIATION

At the heart of insurgents' mobilizing narratives is the theme of humiliation at the hands of callous and arrogant powers. Act 1 begins with video footage from the "shock and awe" phase of the invasion of Iraq in 2003. It depicts the imperial arrogance of the invaders and reflects the asymmetry in power between the aggressors and their victims. It also shows photos of Iraqi women and children killed or wounded by the bombardment, usually accompanied by chilling melancholic chants embedded in the clip; mosques and minarets purposely destroyed by shelling while they are issuing the calls to prayer *(adhan),* suggesting a war on Islam, not just a war on Iraq; coalition forces storming into homes while women and children are crying out in terror, beseeching the foreigners to let their fathers and brothers go free; a U.S. soldier shooting a wounded insurgent inside a mosque or coalition forces stepping with their boots on the backs of men bound and forced to the ground with black sacks covering their faces; and, above all, men and women enduring humiliating torture in Abu Ghraib prison. All these images personalize the suffering and heighten the sense of powerlessness and indignation that many Muslims feel.

The Mujahidin Army in Iraq issued an hour-long video entitled *Courageous Men or Lions (Usud al-Shara)*.[1] It contains footage of destruction inside a mosque, a torn Quran, and another Quran with the Christian cross spray-painted on its cover. As these images appear, a child's voice is heard reciting poetry.

Where are our mosques?
Where are our schools?
Why do I see them in ruins after they were beacons?
Where are my countrymen?
Why are they not moving to free our captive brothers? Defend the honor of our sisters?
Is this not in our religion?

These images from Iraq are usually combined with stock images from other conflicts in Muslim countries, especially Palestine. We see the killing of the little boy Muhammad al-Durah in the arms of his father during the opening days of the Aqsa uprising in 2000. These images galvanized the world's attention and epitomized the suffering of the Palestinian people. Along with others it is intended to deliver two messages. First, the suffering and humiliation of Muslims around the world are not unconnected, but part of a series of transgressions by the "crusader-Zionist" alliance against Islam and Muslims. The images portray the war in Iraq as one of many wars on Islam. Thus the insurgents are heightening the sense of threat facing the Muslim world to justify extraordinary measures to resist the manifest conspiracy against Islam.

As Zarqawi declared in one of his video montages:

Our Jihad in Iraq is the same as in Afghanistan, Kashmir, Chechnya, and Bosnia, an honorable jihad.... We shed the dust of divisive nationalism and hopeless patriotism that tears asunder the ranks of Muslims and turns them into tasty bites for the infidels.[2]

In one of the biographies of "martyrs," the Kuwaiti suicide bomber Abdel Rahman Bin Shuja al-Utaybi (Abu Awf) is said to have been moved by suffering in Palestine: "One day we were watching a videotape of young stone throwers in Palestine and the tragedy there. There were heartbreaking scenes and one of the brothers shed so many tears. He was Abdel Rahman (Abu Awf), who could not stand the tragedies of Muslims."[3]

In his last will and testament, the Saudi suicide bomber Abu Ans al-Tahami al-Qahtani wrote:

> Whoever looks at the condition of the Islamic nation will find it is torn asunder and its cuts bleeding in every place. There is the wound of Palestine for nearly 50 years; and there are the wounds of Chechnya, Afghanistan, Kashmir, Indonesia, Philippines, and Iraq. We are immersed in our wants and desires while the sanctuaries are violated, the mosques demolished, and the holy books insulted. I do not know how we are living inside ourselves; do these wounds pain us or do we not care?[4]

The second message delivered by linking suffering in Iraq to other Muslim conflicts is that the struggle in Iraq is the central battlefield on which to fight the war against the enemies of Islam. Fighting in Iraq, in effect, is the same as fighting in Palestine, Chechnya, Kashmir, Saudi Arabia, and elsewhere in the Muslim world. These are all one struggle, not many separate wars. In framing the conflict in this light, insurgents can call on jihadists to come and fight in Iraq without feeling guilty that they have abandoned their struggle at home. Victory in Iraq is victory in every Muslim land. A hymn chanted over and over in one of the insurgent videos reflects this presumed unity in the struggles of Muslims:

> *With the Sharp Weapon of Truth*
> *We will liberate the lands of the free*
> *And bring back purity to the land of Jerusalem*
> *After the humiliation and shame.*[5]

Linking the war in Iraq to the liberation of Jerusalem "after the humiliation and shame" appeals to the emotional need for unity and solidarity among Muslims; it reaches out to an identity rooted in shared suffering and collective yearning for a victory following decades of failure and defeat.

Jihadists in Iraq also rely on the theme of female dishonor and suffering at the hands of foreigners and Iraqi security forces to justify violence and mobilize people. Images of women terrified in their homes as soldiers storm in to search for insurgents; videos of women being frisked by foreign men; rumors of women abducted or taken into custody where they are humiliated or even raped; and stories of women being handed over by

Iraqi forces as hostages to be exchanged for wanted insurgents are plentiful in jihadists' video clips and montages, audio recordings, and online magazines.

Insurgents undoubtedly are appealing to notions of masculinity that pervade tribal culture, in which *sharaf* (nobleness), `ird (honor), and *muruah* (chivalry or manliness) are of vital importance. These notions of masculinity are often defined by one's zealous protection of and control over women so they do not risk straying in their relations with men and thereby bring shame to the entire family or tribe. Shame brought about by violations of honor and norms of decency associated with the separation of the sexes can impel the traditionally minded to engage in violence to redeem the honor of the violated female, including killing the "offending" woman. Failure to take vengeance raises questions about one's nobility and sense of manhood. As shown below, jihadists exploit this aspect of Arab culture to the hilt.

IMPOTENCE AND COLLUSION

Part of the mobilizing narrative in Iraq is the depiction of the "arrogance" of the invading forces and the collusion of "so-called" Muslim governments. Insurgent videos often show the clip of the gloating President George W. Bush on board a U.S. battleship, declaring victory in Iraq. This image is often followed by images of U.S. troops marching in the streets of Iraq or walking through Saddam Hussein's palaces, smiling, confident in their triumph. Occasionally one sees the famous image of a U.S. soldier placing the American flag atop the head of Saddam's statue in the center of Baghdad on the day the city fell. All these images are intended to portray the United States as an arrogant power proud of its unjustified aggression against a Muslim nation.

These images are closely followed by others showing Arab leaders— King Abdullah of Saudi Arabia, King Abdullah II of Jordan, Hussni Mubarak in Egypt, and the post-Saddam leadership of Iraq (Iyad Alawi, Ibrahim al-Jaafari, Jalal Talabani, and Abdel Aziz al-Hakim, among others)—in the company of coalition officials, President Bush, and British Prime Minister Tony Blair. These leaders are laughing and sometimes embracing their Western "masters." The most commonly used image is that of King Abdullah of Saudi Arabia clasping hands with President Bush, suggesting a tight bond among the closest of friends. Another image shows the late King Fahd of Saudi Arabia giving former U.S. President Bill Clinton a medallion. Other images include Arab or Western leaders in the company of Israeli leaders. A common image is that of President Bush shaking hands with former Israeli Prime Minister Ariel Sharon in the White House during the Aqsa uprising, suggesting approval of Israel's "iron fist" policies against the Palestinians.

In one of the videos of the Ahl al-Sunnah wal-Jamaah Army, images of Muslim leaders in the company of Western dignitaries are contrasted in alternating frames with images of Iraqi fighters. Muslim leaders and their guests are enjoying themselves in lavish palaces and comfortable settings. The holy fighters are donning modest clothes and fighting in desolate towns and villages. While the official leaders are laughing and smiling with their Western "masters," the fighters are offering supplications to God, praying in the battlefield next to their weapons. Western leaders are shown with a Star of David on their foreheads, suggesting they are agents of Israel, while the fighters are chanting, "God is great, glory to Islam." [6]

The overall message of these images is that the Arab and Muslim worlds are led by "puppets" that cannot be relied on to liberate Iraq and end the suffering of the Muslim people. The puppets are illegitimate governments that sold out to the arrogant occupiers who are conspiring against the Muslim world. This imagery is important for five reasons. First, it portrays anyone working for the official leaders and government in Iraq as part of the collusion with the Western aggressors. Since these leaders are illegitimate sellouts, it is not acceptable to work for them under the pretext of working for a Muslim or Iraqi government, not the occupation. Those who persist in working for the official Iraqi government are fair game and may be killed without compunction.

Second, since these leaders are collaborators working for foreign powers, their moral criticism of the jihadists and their tactics is without effect; who are they to challenge the legitimacy of the insurgents? Third, since these governments are impotent in the face of the suffering of Muslims, it is necessary for other Muslims to step forward to fight in their stead. Jihad is an individual obligation *(fard ayn)* because the existing governments have abdicated their duty to protect Muslim lands and liberate them from unbelievers. Fourth, since jihadists do not have the support or resources of official governments, they have to rely solely on their faith and limited capabilities to repel the arrogant aggressors, justifying their demands for extraordinary measures and calls for martyrdom. Finally, these images frame the struggle more broadly than simply liberating Iraq from a foreign occupation. Instead, they portray the struggle as replacing the entire corrupt and "mercenary" regimes that currently rule in the Muslim world with ones that are truly Islamic and protect Muslim interests, not those of their Western "masters."

INEVITABLE VICTORY THROUGH FAITH AND SACRIFICE

The first two themes (or acts) can be disempowering if not followed by the third theme of redemption and victory through martyrdom. Act 1 shows unbearable suffering and humiliation that has afflicted the Muslim world, and the second act portrays existing rulers in the Muslim world as impotent individuals who cannot reverse the suffering of Muslims in Iraq. Act 3 presents the necessary solution for the salvation of Muslims around the globe. Victory and redemption come through faith in God and a desire to sacrifice in his path.

An important part of the third theme is the mythology surrounding martyrdom and martyrs. AQI promotes the image of a heroic Muslim willing to make the ultimate sacrifice to redeem his nation and avenge the personal suffering inflicted on helpless Muslims, especially women. The propaganda surrounding the "martyrs" is disseminated on Web postings, in videos of operations, and in AQI's online journal, *Biographies of Eminent Martyrs*. These productions reveal five themes that make up the mythology of martyrdom:

- Sincere devotion to religion;
- Willingness to sacrifice one's wealth and personal ties for God;
- Eagerness to carry out a "martyrdom operation";
- Success in sacrifice operations;
- Confirmation of martyrdom through dream visions.

These biographies are often short, inconsistent in the information they present, and highly propagandistic. The point of the following analysis is to show how groups seek to promote the myth of heroic martyrdom through such stories, not to suggest that the biographies reflect the true motivations of the suicide bombers.

SINCERE DEVOTION TO ISLAM

Insurgent videos are replete with images of pious Muslims praying, chanting "God is great" *(allahu akbar)*, even as they are in the midst of an operation or planting IEDs. These "true" Muslims are intent on reversing the humiliation of their Muslim brethren around the world. One of the melodic hymns repeated over and over in several insurgent videos declares:

> *We shall not accept humiliation,*
> *We shall not accept humiliation,*
> *We shall not accept humiliation or subjugation;*
> *We will not bow our heads,*
> *We will not bow our heads,*
> *We will not bow our heads to the depraved.[7]*

Suicide bombers are portrayed almost invariably as genuinely religious people who love jihad more than they love life and fear God more than they fear death. The biographies often detail at length how the "martyr" used to pray incessantly and spent his time reading the Quran. The bombers are said to have prayed in the mosque, the best option in the eyes of God, as opposed to praying at home. They often pray more than the average Muslim, certainly more than God expects them to. They wake up to make their predawn prayers *(qiyam)*—not a religious obligation but a voluntary expression of devotion. Some are said to have memorized the Quran at a very young age; others fast every Monday and Thursday although they are not required to do so by religion (although it is part of the Sunna).

The Kuwaiti bomber Abu Awf al-Kuwaiti (Abdel Rahman Bin Shuja al-Utaybi) is said to have cried as he was entreating God to grant the holy warriors victory everywhere.[8] The same is said of the Saudi suicide bomber Muhammad Bin Rahayman al-Tawmi al-Shamari (Abu Salih).[9] In the biography of Abu Umayr al-Suri (Syrian), the narrator mentions in passing that one of the martyrs did not want to stay in the same house as Abu Umayr because "he felt shame [out of guilt]; every time he woke up he would find Abu Umayr up already in the middle of his prayers."[10]

The emphasis on sincerity in devotion is important for AQI and jihadi Salafis in general. Suicide bombings can be considered martyrdom in Islam only if the individual bomber is a devout Muslim fighting out of faith in God and dying for his sake. One cannot expect to receive the rewards of martyrdom if he or she is motivated by something other than love of God and striving in his path. Perhaps more important, jihadi Salafis are aware that Muslim governments attempt to portray jihadists as "deviants" and misguided individuals who know little about Islam and have been brainwashed into carrying out suicide attacks. Stressing the religiosity of the bombers, therefore, is AQI's attempt to counter the claims of existing governments and assure their supporting public that they are genuine Muslims doing their share to save the nation.

A video recording by Ansar al-Sunna Group shows an unidentified suicide bomber declaring in his last will and testament:

> This is our religion and this is our path, to it we call, and for it we die, with God's blessings in order to meet him.... What kind of a world is this where a nation's sanctity and honor are violated, its wealth robbed, and its scholars, pardon me, I mean the scholars of the sultans, discourage the youth from joining the jihad and raise doubts in their minds about jihad. Go forward my brothers and pay no heed. The land of jihad is calling you. How nice it will be if you answered the call. Oh God, accept me as a martyr....[11]

The suicide bomber is shown smiling as he waves good-bye to his brothers-in-arms.

The final will and testament sent by the Saudi suicide bomber Abu Hareth Abdul Rahman al-Dousry to his family reads: "To my mother, father, wife and brothers.... I did not leave you to punish you, but instead to heed God's call to jihad. How can I live happily knowing that this country is being violated, usurped and raped, and that the infidels are storming our homes and sanctuaries and violating our religion? If we do not meet again on this earth, we shall meet in heaven."[12]

These and other insurgent productions affirm that the bombers were genuinely concerned Muslims who put their trust in God and sacrificed to redeem the suffering of their people.

WILLINGNESS TO SACRIFICE PERSONAL WEALTH AND FAMILY TIES

AQI propaganda portrays the "martyrs" as people who have given up all things dear to fulfill a higher, more noble obligation: jihad and martyrdom in the path of God. Many of the bombers are said to be wealthy or from wealthy families (such as the previously mentioned Abu Umayr al-Suri, an electrical engineer). Even those who are not wealthy made personal sacrifices, such as selling their cars or spending their meager savings, or relied on donations to make the trip to Iraq. Perhaps the most powerful image is that of a father leaving his newborn child or a husband leaving his bride to fight and die in the path of God.

The biography of Abu Osama al-Maghribi, a Moroccan from the city of Tanja, is instructive. Abu Osama, the reader is told, was twenty-six when he carried out an operation. He worked with his father in a "fancy" restaurant that brought in about three thousand dollars a month. At the age of twenty he bought a piece of land and married. However, for six years he was unable to father a child. When the war broke out in Iraq, he decided to join the jihad. Abu Osama sold the piece of land and bought a ticket to "an Arab" country. As he was about to depart for Iraq, he found out his wife was pregnant. He was overwhelmed with joy. However, this news did not stop him from leaving for jihad.

After arriving in the Arab country, Abu Osama moved from mosque to mosque seeking someone to take him to Iraq. He ran into a group of Moroccans led by Abu Khbab al-Falastini. They took him to Iraq to Abu Ismail al-Muhajir, who became Abu Osama's handler. Abu Osama made a vow with others to die in the path of God and eventually was the bomber in the operation against the UN headquarters in Baghdad.

Like many of the other bombers, he was eager to do the operation. On the day he found out he was chosen for a suicide mission, he also received news that his wife had borne a son. She named him Osama after bin Laden. This news did not deter him from going ahead with his operation. On the contrary, he was happy for "two good pieces of news in the same day." On the day before the operation, he was left alone with his handler to reflect, pray, and cry. When the day came, he and his handler went to survey the target one more time. Abu Osama took hold of his new "wife," the explosive-laden vehicle, and drove toward his target.[13]

This theme of leaving behind one's family is repeated over and over. The biography of Abu Wadha al-Kuwaiti (Mansur al-Hajari) notes that he was married but did not father any children for four years. Then he had a little girl he named Wadha. A week later he went to Iraq and eventually died in a suicide operation. The biographer draws the following lesson from the story of Abu Wadha: "The man was married and he did not have any children for four years. However, one week after he had a child he went to jihad. It is devotion and the love of faith."

A similar narrative describes Abu Ahmed al-Kuwaiti (Abdel Aziz al-Shamari): "The hero got married to a relative, but when he heard the call of God and saw the door of paradise open wide he could not sit around while his brothers were racing to reserve places in the highest paradise. The price of these places is sincere blood, truthful prayer, and tireless effort." Abu Hamza al-Kuwaiti (Said al-Hajari) also gave up the good life for jihad: "His wedding was supposed to take place within a few months but he opted to marry the virgins of paradise."[14] The same is said of the Saudi suicide bomber Abu Ans al-Tahami al-Qahtani.[15]

These narratives are intended to set a new standard for heroism and devotion to the faith. It is not enough to be a good Muslim, pray regularly, and carry out one's ritual obligations. Even mere desire to join the jihad is not enough. One should exert as much effort as necessary to reach the land of jihad. These themes undoubtedly are intended to inspire others, particularly people in the Persian Gulf who are relatively well off, to abandon material wealth and join a more rewarding path in life.

EAGERNESS TO CONDUCT A "MARTYRDOM OPERATION"

Over and over the biographies of the "martyrs" declare that they are eager to die in the path of God and are frustrated when they are denied or delayed. Almost every clip of the suicide bombers in Iraq shows the bombers as happy, eager to do the will of God. They usually wave good-bye with smiles on their faces, running toward their explosive-laden vehicles, reflecting the theme of joy in sacrifice in the path of God and assured of the rewards they will earn in paradise.

The Kuwaiti volunteer Abu Bara (Faysal Zayd al-Mutiri) is said to have declared to a friend, "My brother, I cannot wait to meet God Almighty, can you?" When he died, "Abu Bara had an extraordinary smile on his bright face." Another Kuwaiti, Abu Muad (Abdel Aziz Abdel Hadi Dayhani), is said to have told his friends: "I do not care if I get killed. I will not sit motionless while my brothers are under attack every day.... We should starve when the nation starves. We should share its joys and sorrows and we should die with it and for it.... God willing, we will meet in paradise if we do not meet in the land of dignity."[16] An Iraqi named Abu

Faris al-Anbari is said to have been eager to go on a suicide mission and pestered Zarqawi to send him. He even cried profusely when he was wounded in a conventional operation. He cried out not in pain but because God did not bless him with martyrdom. Eventually he was killed by American forces on the way to a hospital after suffering a wound in an aerial bombardment.[17]

This theme of eagerness to carry out a suicide operation and joy expressed on the day of the operation is intended to counter the claims of authorities that the bombers are coerced or brainwashed into carrying out suicide attacks. Iraqi satellite channels often air "confessions" of foiled bombers who claim they did not know they were about to engage in a suicide operation because someone else was in control of the detonator, while they were merely delivering the truck to the target. Some are said to have had their hands handcuffed to the steering wheel or to have been given drugs before their operations and shown pornographic materials to excite them about meeting heavenly maidens.

The theme of eagerness to die is intended to dispel these allegations and elevate the status of the suicide bombers to that of faithful and heroic martyrs fully in control of their choices and destinies. Many of these volunteers are said to have tried to go to Chechnya or Afghanistan following the 9/11 attacks, but they were prevented for one reason or another, suggesting a deep-rooted desire to engage in a jihad even before they went to Iraq.

The biography of Azzad Akanji (Abu Abdullah al-Turki) is illustrative. A Turk, he went to Pakistan for two years and then to Afghanistan for combat training before joining the jihad in Iraq. Following a stint in jihadi training camps, he returned to Turkey to make his way to Georgia. His ultimate goal was to join the jihad in Chechnya. However, he was unable to enter Chechnya and returned to Turkey.

While in Turkey Abu Abdullah wanted to carry out a suicide operation against Jewish tourists. When this operation did not materialize, he wanted to participate in other suicide missions. However, he was not chosen for the operation against British and Jewish targets. Subsequently he was wanted by the authorities in connection with the suicide bombings in Turkey. Undeterred, he made his way to Iraq and carried out an operation with two other bombers against the Khan Bin Saad police station in Diyali.[18]

The theme of eagerness to die is also intended to reinforce the idea that the bombers in Iraq are faithful Muslims who do not fear death because they know what awaits them in the afterlife. Like Hamas and Hezbollah members, jihadi Salafis in Iraq promote the idea that martyrdom is a gateway to another life, not an end to life. Dying in the path of God will gain the martyrs all the rewards of martyrdom, including the following:

- Remission of one's sins at the moment the martyr's blood is shed;
- Immediate admission into heaven, so martyrs do not suffer the punishment of the tomb;
- The privilege of accompanying prophets, saints, and righteous believers;
- Marriage to heavenly maidens *(houri al-ayn)*;
- The right to intercede with God on behalf of seventy relatives;
- Protection against the pain of death;
- Entry into the highest gardens of heaven *(jannat al-firdaous)*.

The bombers are happy because they are abandoning this world of disgrace and shame for one where they are venerated along with the honorable and righteous believers, enjoying for eternity all the fruits of their sacrifice. As proof of such happiness, jihadists often post on the Web photos of dead jihadists who appear to be smiling or peacefully asleep. One caption points out that the martyr "is happy in the company of the heavenly maidens."

SUCCESS IN MARTYRDOM OPERATIONS

AQI repeatedly conjures up the symbolism of the battle of Badr, the first major military confrontation between the Muslims of Medina and the unbelievers of Mecca, in 624 CE. During the first twelve years of his mission, beginning in 610, the Prophet Muhammad preached monotheism to the polytheists of Mecca. He endured ridicule and persecution without calling for a violent jihad against his oppressors. When the danger to the embryonic Islamic community of Mecca grew to an unbearable level, the Prophet Muhammad and his followers left for the town of Yathrib (or al-Medina al-Munawara, Medina for short). In the ten years before the death of the Prophet in 632, God gave the Muslims permission to fight back against the onslaught of Meccan invasions.[19] Despite being initially outnumbered, the Muslim community in Medina was able to stave off the superior Meccan forces and ultimately triumph over them and conquer Mecca.

The first of these battles was Badr. This battle exemplifies how a few believing individuals can face powerful enemies and prevail over them because of their faith in God and desire for martyrdom. Muslims could muster only 314 fighters for the battle of Badr; they faced an invading Meccan army of about 1,000 men. Before the battle, the Muslims of Medina faced tremendous uncertainty as to their personal fate and the destiny of their new community. After the battle, they were assured that God was on their side and they should never question his commitment to them as long as they remained faithful.

One of the most cited Quranic passages in jihadist literature is verse 8:17: "So you slew them not but Allah slew them, and thou smotest not when thou didst smite (the enemy), but Allah smote (him), and that He might confer upon the believers a benefit from Himself. Surely Allah is Hearing, Knowing." The verse speaks of direct divine intervention as angels were sent from heaven to fight alongside the Muslims. This was God's way of showing his blessings to the faithful.

Militants frame their contemporary struggle against powerful enemies as part of the Islamic tradition of jihad and martyrdom by the weak against the strong, the righteous over the unjust. Had the first Islamic community succumbed to persecution, Islam as a world civilization would have died in its infancy. The dominant symbolism of this narrative is the defeat of unjust authority by dispossessed, righteous victims who did not recoil at the prospect of martyrdom and relied on their faith to help them triumph over a superior enemy.

The first issue of AQI's publication *Zarwat al-Sinam* (The Pinnacle) features a letter by Osama bin Laden to the holy warriors of Iraq. Bin Laden writes: "In a Prophetic tradition, the Angel Gabriel asks our Prophet, peace and blessings upon him, 'Who among the companions participated in the battle of Badr?' The Prophet answered: 'Our Best.' The Angel Gabriel replied: 'And that is who participated from among the angels.'" He goes on to declare, "Know that this is a great war similar to the immense Badr conquest in its wonderful results and enduring influence.... Today I consider the holy warriors who resist America's fighter planes and tanks, and who strike with missiles in Palestine and Iraq, to be the best of this Islamic nation. Success comes from God the almighty who granted success in the Badr of Palestine, Badr of Iraq, Badr of Afghanistan, Badr of Chechnya, and all other fields of jihad."[20]

The biographies of the martyrs invariably emphasize, or often exaggerate, the success of the suicide mission as if to assure potential recruits that their worldly sacrifices will not be in vain. The numbers of "apostates," "crusaders," and "CIA agents" reported killed in these operations are often in the hundreds. One finds repeatedly in the biographies of the bombers that they killed more people than are mentioned in news reports, which "rely on American numbers." One often hears that the Americans dump their dead in rivers or in hastily prepared graves to cover up their real losses. Because of this "success," the biographers term each operation a "conquest" (*ghazwah*), such as *ghazwahit al-Nasiriyah* (the attack on Italian forces in Nasiriyah, which killed thirty-one people). The term *ghazwah* is an intentional allusion to battles in early Islamic history when the Prophet Muhammad triumphed over his enemies in Mecca and later, when Muslim armies at the height of their strength invaded and conquered other lands.

Success, however, is not always only in numbers. The idea of vengeance against those who would violate the honor of Muslim women is important, playing on masculine expectations in the highly patriarchic Arab world. Insurgent groups often portray their attacks as revenge for personal violations of honor. In a communiqué declaring responsibility for an attack on a security building in Tikrit in April 2005, AQI congratulates one of its "lions" in the Martyrs Brigades for demolishing the site where "our women were imprisoned, and our elderly were humiliated, severely beaten, and tortured."[21] In another AQI video of a suicide attack on the Palestine Hotel in Baghdad, the suicide bomber is shown declaring before his operation that he will "regain the life of honor once more" and "we shall redraw for Islam a map, its borders are honor, might, and triumph."[22] The message delivered in this clip is that sacrifice is not merely for Iraq, but for the entire Muslim world. Martyrdom in Iraq is the key to redeeming the Muslim nation the world over.

A clip by the Mujahidin Shura Council in Iraq, entitled "Fatimah's Fiancé," is illustrative. It shows Abu Muawiyah al-Shamali, a Saudi suicide bomber in his twenties. His operation was a direct response to a letter allegedly sent by a female detainee named Fatimah at Abu Ghraib prison. In December 2004 Fatimah called on the holy warriors to come to rescue all the female prisoners who were subjected to daily rape, torture, and humiliation at the hands of the "sons of the pigs and the monkeys" [Jews and Christians].

After describing torture and humiliation, she asks the insurgents to save the prisoners. "Brothers," Fatimah wrote, "I tell you again, fear God! Kill us with them so that we might be at peace. Help! Help! Help!" Abu Muawiyah al-Shamali then appeared with a big smile on his face and read a poem, with a gun and the Quran nearby. After reciting the poem, he entreated God to grant him Fatimah's hand in marriage in paradise: "Oh, Lord, marry me to Fatimah who was martyred after they had violated her honor." The suicide bomber was smiling broadly throughout the taping of his farewell message. As he sat in the booby-trapped car, he smiled and patted the explosives that were going to end his life: "This is Fatimah's dowry." Waving to his friends who were taping the operation, Abu Muawiyah drove his car toward an unidentified target.[23]

After portraying the jihadists as pious, self-sacrificing individuals eager to carry out the responsibilities abdicated by their nominal Muslim leaders, the filmmakers show the results of their sacrifice. Image after image shows humiliation in reverse. Now it is the American soldiers who are bloodied, crying out in fear, embracing their fallen buddies. We see rows of coffins draped in American flags and families crying back in the United States. The "arrogant" have been humbled. One of the Islamic Army in Iraq videos begins with images of blown-up Humvees followed by images of President Bush, Secretary of Defense Donald Rumsfeld, Secretary of State Condoleezza Rice, and former Secretary of State Colin Powell appearing anxious and disturbed, suggesting that jihadi operations have shaken them and removed their exultant confidence.

In another insurgent video that was number two in a montage of "top ten" attacks by the Islamic Army in Iraq, seven American soldiers are shown casually talking and walking as they converge on an object in the middle of a barren field with palm trees in the background. Suddenly, an IED explodes. All the soldiers fall. The person taping the operation is overwhelmed with joy as he is heard sobbing uncontrollably, repeating over and over, "God is great, God is great, God is great." Finally he regains his composure and calmly says, *"Al-hamdu lil-lah"* (praise be to God). This clip ranked number two undoubtedly because of its powerful message: God will reward the believers by punishing the unjust.[24]

CONFIRMATION OF MARTYRDOM IN DREAM VISIONS

One of the surreal aspects of the martyrs' biographies is the narration of dream visions. Two types of dreams appear in these biographies. The first involves suicide bombers dreaming about their operations or previous suicide bombers, usually their friends, appearing in front of them. They sometimes hold conversations with the phantoms. The second type of dream involves the senders of the bombers confirming that they dreamt of a fallen martyr. The biographies of three Kuwaiti volunteers in Iraq are instructive.

Abu Bakr al-Kuwaiti (Faysal Ali Musa al-Rashidi) "saw a dream that he was in a waiting room in a hospital where a sign read: 'Martyr Faysal Ali Musa al-Rashidi.'" Abu Hamza al-Kuwaiti (Said al-Hajari) also had a dream: "I saw myself swimming in a river with other people. The river led to a cave or a tunnel on which it was written: 'To the Highest Paradise.' The closer I came to the tunnel the fewer the swimmers. When I approached, something was dragging me to the bottom of the river. It was a beautiful young maiden of paradise. We hugged each other underwater."

Abdel Rahman (Abu Awf), we are told, had a dream of his friend Mansoor al-Hajari, who had died in an earlier operation. Al-Hajari was sitting next to him. He asked, "How are you, Mansoor?" His friend replied, "Good, praise be to God." Abu Awf said, "I would like to ask you what you witnessed immediately after you pressed the button that set off the explosion." His dead friend smiled and said, "Come here, come here. God is generous. God is generous."

A friend of Abu Awf begged him to pay him a visit in his dreams after Abu Awf completed his mission. After the operation, in which "more than sixty apostates" were killed, Abu Awf fulfilled his friend's wish and came to visit him in his dream. The friend asked, "Where are you, Abdel Rahman? Are you alive?" Abu Awf replied, "I am alive. I am alive."[25]

The notion of visions *(ru'yah)* in dreams has symbolic weight in the Muslim tradition, especially when the recipients of these visions are devout Muslims. Visions in dreams imply that God is communicating directly with his faithful. In the Quran, God communicated with the Prophets Abraham and Muhammad through dreams.[26] Dreams in Islam offer the faithful divine guidance, warn them of impending danger, and can fore-tell specific events. When facing tough decisions many Muslims today rely on a Prophetic tradition that urges them to say a prayer for guidance *(istikhara)* in hopes that God will reveal the correct choice in a dream.[27]

The emphasis on bombers appearing in dreams is intended to assure future recruits that those who went before them were genuine and righteous Muslims who are still alive, in paradise, near God, who is "gen-erous." These visions appear to confirm the Quranic verses: "Whoever fights in the path of God, whether he be slain or victorious, on him We shall bestow a vast reward" (4:74) and "Think not of those, who are slain in the way of Allah, as dead. Nay, they are living. With their Lord they have provision" (3:169). Dream visions allow jihadists to circumvent the fact that the living cannot inquire of the dead what life is like after they have died. Not only is communication with the dead possible through dreams, it is also comforting because the dead appear happy, calling on others to "come here." Moreover, the mythology surrounding dreams is intended to counter the claims of authorities that the suicide bombers are misguided fanatics who unjustly kill themselves and other Muslims. If these claims were true, how could these "martyrs" appear in dreams over and over?

WEAVING A GRAND NARRATIVE OF MARTYRDOM AND MAYHEM

The jihadists in Iraq weave together the three narratives of humiliation, collusion, and redemption to present a diagnosis of existing conditions in Iraq, suggesting a deleterious situation that requires immediate action; a prognosis that spells out how these conditions will persist and become worse if nothing is done to correct them; and a motivation or incentive to act and sacrifice to overcome the collective problem.[28] The emotive ele-ments of their discourse are intended to galvanize support for their cause, not just by a small circle of activists, but also by the broader Muslim pub-lic. Emotional appeals reach out to the wider Muslim world. The themes of humiliation, collusion, and redemption are intended precisely to demon-ize enemies, exhort jihadists to self-sacrifice, and reduce psychological inhibitions against killing fellow Muslims.

One of the most powerful series of clips that capture the three narra-tives of humiliation, collusion, and redemption through sacrifice can be found in a montage issued by AQI, which contains approximately forty-six minutes of footage about fighting the Iraqi security forces.[29] The clips begin with an Iraqi woman donning the *hijab* (implying she is a pious "sister") and obscured by a black shadow to hide her identity (implying she is not safe and needs continuous protection). In a tearful voice, she describes suffering at the hands of an Iraqi policeman intent on turning her over to foreign forces as a hostage to be exchanged for her wanted husband. According to her story, she begged her compatriot: "I'm an Iraqi and you're an Iraqi; why are you doing this to me? Why?" She breaks down, sobbing uncontrollably, and cannot continue telling her story.

As her voice fades, a melancholic hymn accompanies images of Iraqi policemen smiling, singing, and dancing with American forces, apparently during a training session. The scene is juxtaposed with the clip of the Iraqi woman as she continues telling how she was bound and handed over to the Americans. In a tearful but powerful voice, full of faith in God, she declares: *"Hasbiyah allah wa niama al-wakil"* (Allah is sufficient for me, and he is an excellent guardian). Yet, despite her faith in God, she is not strong enough to endure this suffering: "I would rather have died than suffer the humiliation and degradation that I saw." A few seconds of silence follow, giving viewers time to reflect on the woman in tears, letting her story sink in and her image reach out to their conscience. As her image slowly fades, she is heard from once more: *"Hasbiyah allah wa niama al-wakil, hasbiyah allah wa niama al-wakil."*

The tenor of the video clip changes; now it takes an upbeat tone with more intensity, suggesting a turning point in the narrative. A new set of images shows the jihadists marching in line, as if they came purposely to save none other than the suffering sister; these images give the impression that they are heroic and determined. The images are accompanied by sounds of marching feet, and underneath a voice repeats: "They are coming, they are coming." Next come clips of suicide operations and jihadi attacks along with images of destroyed military vehicles belonging to the occupation forces and dead Iraqi security forces. These images are accompanied by a hymn that honors fighting in the path of God and venerates the sacrifice of one's blood for religion. Humiliation has turned into victory, powerless suffering into willing sacrifice, and shame into honor.

A poem recited by Zarqawi in one of his audio recordings also evokes the themes of humiliation, impotence, and redemption through faith and martyrdom:

Baghdad, we are shedding tears of sorrow and grief for you
A Muslim town struck with humiliation at the hands of the worst of
mankind, the crusaders.
I grieve for a girl as pure as snow, who is crying,
Her chastity was violated by a dog and a pack of wolves.
We go where thunder strikes but no Harun [al-Rashid] to stop them,
And the heart is full of grief
We go where thunder strikes while the [rest of the] Arabs bend their
heads to them,
But how can mice ever rise up.
Woe unto my people, for they have strayed from the [right] path,
By falsehoods and idols.
Alas, there is no peace to unite us toward the great One,
Nor do we have leaders among the people.
Baghdad, do not be astonished, for the Arabs have no shame any longer;
They live in sin and when the war heats up they abandon the battle.
Dry your tears, for the people have strayed;
The ammunition of war is faith before the sword.
Where are the voices of the evil clerics whose rubbish we hear only when
they are speaking against the holy warriors? Where are they? Why are
they not defending the honor of Muslim women?
I wish they at least fight out of pride for the honor of [Muslim] women,
Since they do not fight for religion.
And [I wish] they at least join the battlefield even for material gains,
Since they do not care to gain God's blessings.
Here I am, oh mother,
Here I am, oh sister,
Here I am, oh honorable and pure one,
By God, we shall not rest, nor sleep, nor put our swords back in their
sheaths, until we avenge your honor and dignity.[30]

CONCLUSION

Justifications for killing fellow Muslims in Iraq are anchored in poignant narratives that link the suffering and humiliation of Muslims to the collusion of nominal Muslim leaders and their agents with Western oppressors seeking to destroy Islam and subjugate Muslim lands. By framing the struggle in those terms, the jihadists make the point that it is logical to strike at those who make Iraq safe for the invaders. The Iraqi security services and the

Shia and Kurdish political parties—and even Sunnis willing to participate in the "farcical" democracy—are the other side of the crusader-Zionist coin. Given the nature of the threat facing Muslims and the impotence and collusion of governments, it becomes necessary for a heroic cadre to step forward and redeem the honor of the nation and erase the shame of humiliation. These themes of humiliation, collusion, and redemption are woven together to pose a problem, suggest a solution, and present a motivation to fight.

NOTES

1. Issued in January 2006 at www.jaishalmugahideen.net.

2. Montage entitled "And Worship Shall Be Only for Allah," issued by the Media Division of AQI in June 2005, www.alaflam.ws/wdkl/index.htm, accessed July 15, 2005.

3. Abu-Maryam al-Kuwayti, "A Cry in the Face of Deception," n.d. This 68-page pamphlet contains the biographies of ten Kuwaitis killed in Iraq. It was posted on al-Sham Islamic Forum (www.islam-syria.com/vb) in February 2006.

4. From a 157-page document, *Martyrs in Iraq*, posted on Majdah Forum (www.majdah.com/vb) with information about 394 volunteers, mostly Arabs, who perished in Iraq. Abu Ans al-Tahami al-Qahtani is 150th on the list.

5. This fifty-five-minute video, entitled *Persist* or *Continue*, was issued by the Islamic Army in Iraq and distributed through al-Meer Forum (www.almeer. net/vb) in January 2006.

6. This thirty-eight-minute video, entitled *Takbir al-Id*, was issued by the media division of Ahl al-Sunna wal-Jamaah, and distributed through al-Meer Forum (www.almeer.net/vb) in January 2006.

7. See, for example, the two-minute video by AQI, *Hy al-Adl Martyrdom Operation*, distributed by Al-Saqifa Forum in February 2005.

8. Al-Kuwayti, "A Cry in the Face of Deception."

9. From Majdah Forum, *Martyrs in Iraq*. Muhammad al-Shamari is 256th on the list.

10. See issue 3 of AQI's *Biographies of Eminent Martyrs*, distributed by al-Meer Forum (www.almeer.net/vb), November 2005.

11. OSC, "Ansar al-Sunnah Posts Video of 'Martyr's' Will Before Attack in Balad," January 13, 2005.

12. Hala Jaber, "Suicide Bombers Stream into Iraq," *Sunday Times* (London), May 8, 2005.

13. See issue 1 of AQI's *Biographies of Eminent Martyrs*, distributed by Global News Network Forum (www.w-n-n.net/), October 2005.

14. Al-Kuwayti, "A Cry in the Face of Deception."

15. From *Martyrs in Iraq*.

16. Al-Kuwayti, "A Cry in the Face of Deception."

17. Information from *Martyrs in Iraq*. Abu Faris al-Anbari is 160th on the list.

18. See issue 10 of AQI's *Biographies of Eminent Martyrs*, distributed by Hanein Net Forum (www.hanein.net), January 2006.

19. See Reuven Firestone, *Jihad: The Origin of Holy War in Islam* (New York: Oxford University Press, 1999), for an excellent description of the history of persecution, jihad, and martyrdom in the first Islamic community.

20. "The Sheikh Osama bin Laden's Welcome to the Holy Warriors in Iraq," *Zarwat al-Sinam*, Issue 1, Muharam 1426 (Islamic calendar), 4.

21. OSC, "Al-Zarqawi's Group Details Suicide Attack on 'US Intelligence Building' in Tikrit, Posts Video," April 25, 2005. See also OSC, "Mujahidin Shura Council Claims 'Revenge for You, Sister' Attacks in Al-Ramadi," August 5, 2006.

22. A fourteen-minute video, *Baghdad Badr Raid*, issued by AQI and distributed by Ana al-Muslim Forum (www.muslm.net/vb), November 2005.

23. Nine-minute video distributed by al-Meer Forum (www.almeer.net/vb), February 2006.

24. The sixteen-minute video was issued by the Global Islamic Media Front and distributed by the al-Muntada Forum in August 2005.

25. Al-Kuwayti, "A Cry in the Face of Deception."

26. Abraham was commanded to sacrifice his son Ishmael in a dream vision. God rewarded his willingness (and his son's) to fulfill the divine command, which was a mere test of faith, by stopping Abraham's hand as he was about to carry out the deed: "We called unto him: O Abraham! Thou hast already fulfilled the vision. Lo! thus do We reward the good" (Quran 37:102–105). God also communicated to the Prophet Muhammad in dreams to strengthen his resolve before the battle of Badr, in which the Muslim forces were outnumbered 3 to 1 by the unbelievers: "Remember in thy dream Allah showed them to thee as few: if He had shown them to thee as many, ye would surely have been discouraged, and ye would surely have disputed in [your] decision; but Allah saved [you]: for He knoweth well the [secrets] of [all] hearts" (Quran 8:43).

27. The tradition is narrated by Jabir bin Abdullah in *Sahih Bukhari*, Vol. 2, Book 21, No. 263, in USC-MSA Compendium of Muslim Texts (www.usc.edu/dept/MSA/).

28. Snow and Benford, "Ideology, Frame Resonance, and Participant Mobilization."

29. Montage, *And Worship Shall Be Only for Allah*, issued by the media division of AQI, June 2005.

30. OSC, "Al-Zarqawi Uses Western Press, Poetry to Criticize US, Encourage 'Mujahidin,'" May 11, 2005.

PART III

MARTYRS WITHOUT BORDERS: TRANSNATIONAL NETWORKS AND VOLUNTEERISM IN IRAQ

CHAPTER 6

ARAB FIGHTERS IN IRAQ

Recruiting suicide bombers from outside Iraq requires preexisting social and organizational ties. The new security environment produced by the war on terrorism after late 2001 meant that global jihadists had to be extra-cautious in their recruitment efforts. They could not openly recruit people for jihad in Iraq; they had to draw on their earlier affiliations to recruit trustworthy militants.

Networks of radical Salafis served as the conveyor belts for moving militants into Iraq. Many of these networks had their origins in Afghanistan following the 1979 Soviet invasion. Arabs and Muslims from around the world volunteered to help their besieged Muslim brothers in Afghanistan. Ties developed during that period led to the rise of the first generation of global jihadists associated with the venerated leader Sheikh Abdullah Azzam. When the Soviet occupation of Afghanistan ended in 1989, many of the volunteers returned to their home countries. Some played an active role in the Islamic movements of their countries, while others attempted to foment rebellion and terrorism. Consequently many were rounded up by vigilant security services that imprisoned, exiled, or executed them.

Feeling unsafe and hunted at home, many of these "Arab Afghans" returned to Afghanistan and Pakistan in the early and mid-1990s. The armed lawlessness of Afghanistan presented them with an opportunity to set up a safe haven and acquire valuable combat skills. Their goal was to create cadres of well-trained and experienced jihadists who could take the fight to their home countries and the Western allies that backed their governments. These militants trained the second generation of global jihadists, some of whom went on to join insurgencies in Chechnya, Tajikistan, or Bosnia. Others formed cells in Europe to plan or support insurgencies in their home countries.

Networks developed during this period revolved around Osama bin Laden and other, less-known leaders. These second-generation jihadists constitute the nodes of the transnational Salafi networks that play a vital role in mobilizing volunteers for operations in Iraq; suicide terrorism is only one tactic in their repertoire of violence.

These networks enabled the relational diffusion of movement ideology, strategy, and tactics. Four preexisting jihadi Salafi networks were vital for the growth of volunteerism and suicide terrorism in Iraq: the Jordanian network associated with the Salafi movement in the towns of al-Zarqa and Salt; Saudi and Kuwaiti networks associated with al Qaeda in the Arabian Peninsula; Syrian and Lebanese networks associated with Salafis in Hums, Dayr al-Zayr, and al-Ladhikiyah (Syria); the Ayn al-Hilwa refugee camp and Majdal Anjar (Lebanon); and European networks led by North African dissidents from Morocco and Algeria. All four networks have direct links to the second generation of jihadists trained in Afghanistan and Pakistan in the 1990s.

FACTORS FACILITATING VOLUNTEERISM IN IRAQ

A number of developments set the stage for the recruitment of jihadi Salafi militants and ordinary Muslims to carry out operations, including suicide missions, in Iraq. First, the war in Afghanistan following the 9/11 attacks forced many jihadi Salafi militants to seek a new haven like the one they had under the Taliban regime. In 2002 many of them scattered in Iran and along the Pakistan–Afghanistan border. Many knew that returning to their home countries was not an option because they were hunted (they had gone to Afghanistan in the 1990s precisely for this reason). This is the quintessential story of Abu Musab al-Zarqawi and his Jordanian cohort. Iraq became an ideal place to gather immediately before and after the invasion. Mullah Krekar (Najmuddin Faraj Ahmad), the former leader of AI in Iraq, confirms that his organization absorbed jihadists coming out of Afghanistan via Iran.[1]

Second, the war on terrorism, with its emphasis on combating Islamic extremism, enraged many Muslims who felt targeted because of their religion. During travels in Jordan and the West Bank in 2003 and 2005, I often heard ordinary Muslims describe the war on terrorism as a war on Islam. Part of this feeling stemmed from pervasive reliance on conspiracy theories to explain world politics and deny Muslim responsibility for events like 9/11; but it also reflected genuine feelings of anger at having Islam linked to terrorism and suspicion cast on Muslims.

Perhaps more important, Muslims around the world perceived the conflict in Iraq, which the United States presented as part of the war on terrorism, as an unjust war that could only be explained as an attack on Islam by a hegemonic bully. They juxtaposed Western rhetoric of liberating Iraq from tyranny and removing weapons of mass destruction against Western acquiescence at the ongoing oppression of the Palestinians in the Aqsa uprising raging in the Occupied Territories, which amounted to the subjugation of Muslims by a non-Muslim country (Israel) known to have WMDs. Perhaps this, more than anything else, drove thousands of ordinary Muslims to volunteer to fight in Iraq in the weeks leading up to the war.[2]

Survey data gathered by the Pew Research Center in 2003 and 2004 reveal the extent of the gap in perceptions between the United States and large segments of the Muslim world. In June 2003 Pew surveyed eight Muslim countries as part of a twenty-country study. An additional 16,000 respondents were interviewed in a postinvasion survey. The results reveal that large majorities responded negatively to the Iraq invasion. In Jordan, Zarqawi's homeland, 97 percent said Islam was under threat; 80 percent said Iraq was worse off than before the invasion; 91 percent were disappointed by the lack of resistance in Iraq; and 78 percent felt greater solidarity with the Muslim people. Unfortunately the Pew survey data did not include Saudi Arabia.[3]

The March 2004 study surveyed four Muslim populations (Pakistan, Turkey, Morocco, and Jordan). The overwhelming majority expressed distrust of U.S. intentions in Iraq and felt the purposes of war in Iraq were largely to control oil reserves in the Middle East and protect Israel. Substantial majorities were less confident about U.S. intentions to promote democracy in the Middle East. With the exception of Turkey, substantial numbers viewed suicide attacks on American and Western forces in Iraq as justified. Even in Turkey a significant minority (31 percent) felt such attacks were justified.[4] One cannot link these numbers directly to volunteerism in Iraq, but the broader political environment must have contributed to inspiring those who volunteered to fight and die in Iraq.

The third development that contributed to volunteerism in Iraq was related to the legitimacy crisis of many Muslim regimes, which appeared impotent in the face of the United States' resolve to attack Iraq. Arab governments had virtually no say in the United Nations or other public arenas. The Arab League summit before the invasion of Iraq was the scene of major disputes between member states. Proceedings dramatically broke down as country representatives shouted at each other and could barely agree on a simple statement of condemnation of the impending war.[5] Countries such as Qatar, Bahrain, and Kuwait appeared to be colluding with the United States by providing its forces with access to their territory. When the war began, Arab states stood helplessly on the sidelines. As shown in chapter 5, this legitimacy crisis allowed jihadists to present volunteerism as a solution to the impotence and collusion of their governments.

Volunteering to fight in Iraq, however, is not the same as becoming a suicide bomber. The fourth development that contributed to suicide attacks in Iraq was the Palestinian–Israeli struggle. The Aqsa uprising spawned hundreds, if not thousands, of volunteers for "martyrdom operations" against Israel. Thus volunteering became the ultimate expression of faith and heroism in the eyes of the Muslim world. Religious scholars from various traditions and political orientations hailed the suicide bombers in the Palestinian territories as martyrs destined for paradise and eternal salvation in the company of prophets, saints, and adored martyrs.[6]

Support for martyrdom came not only from radical bastions of Islamism such as Iran or Hezbollah in southern Lebanon, but also from traditionally conservative institutions such as Egypt's al-Azhar. Notable religious figures such as Sheikh Ahmed al-Tayyeb, mufti of Egypt, and Sheikh Muhammed Tantawi, imam of al-Azhar, affirmed the right of Palestinians to carry out "martyrdom operations" against Israelis. Yusuf al-Qaradawi, a widely respected Muslim leader who has a weekly program, *al-Sharia wal-Hayat* (Islamic Law and Life), on Al Jazeera satellite television, repeatedly issued religious rulings upholding the legitimacy of "martyrdom operations."[7]

Although al-Qaradawi and other religious authorities did not endorse suicide attacks in Iraq, their support for these attacks in the Palestinian–Israeli context was sufficient to lead jihadists in Iraq to ask, "What is different about occupation in Palestine and occupation in Iraq?" The culture of martyrdom spawned by earlier waves of suicide attacks had created the template necessary for justifying suicide terrorism in Iraq.

Fifth, the rapid collapse of Iraq's internal security apparatus, the insufficient size of coalition forces in Iraq, and the dismissal of former

Iraqi soldiers created, on the one hand, porous borders through which volunteers could easily move into Iraq and, on the other hand, widespread grievances that facilitated cooperation between Sunni nationalists and foreign insurgents. As the new political alignment shifted in favor of the Shia and Kurds, the Arab Sunnis felt justified in supporting—or at least not objecting to—insurgents willing to strike at the new power brokers of Iraq.

Sixth, one cannot underestimate the role of satellite television and the Internet in appealing to Muslims—both experienced jihadists and fresh recruits—to join the fray in Iraq. The spread of satellite television, which delivered images of Muslim suffering to the living rooms of their coreligionists almost daily, fostered an "imagined community" across borders. Anyone who regularly travels in the Middle East observes the proliferation of satellite television even among the poorest sectors of society. It is not uncommon to see a dilapidated house with one or two satellite dishes on its roof. Satellite television channels such as Al Jazeera, Al Arabia, and Al Manar (produced by Hezbollah in Lebanon) not only transmit uncensored images of Muslim suffering in Iraq, they also present editorials that reflect the sympathies of Muslim reporters for their besieged coreligionists. Just as important, satellite television regularly transmits videos of insurgent attacks, as well as video and audio statements by al Qaeda leaders in Afghanistan and insurgents in Iraq.

As governments in the Muslim world and Europe looked askance on promoters of jihad in Iraq and took steps to limit their freedom of maneuver in mosques and other recruitment sites, jihadists turned to the Internet, online forums, and chat rooms to circumvent the physical and legal limits on reaching new recruits. The Internet became the source of nonrelational diffusion of movement ideology, strategy, and tactics. In Iraq the Internet provides basic information on the insurgent groups (what they stand for and what they hope to achieve). Groups also use the Web to engage in debates over strategies and tactics, denounce the "scholars of the sultan" and other groups for not supporting jihad in Iraq, and transmit religious rulings (*fatwas*) and statements about their theological stance on controversial issues.

The groups distribute video clips, montages, and even video games to publicize their deeds and promote the image of heroic martyrdom. They also elaborate their theological and ideological positions in online magazines. More ominously, perhaps, jihadists present training videos and manuals on how to manufacture IEDs, including anti-armor IEDs, and equip them with various types of detonators; prepare different types of explosives; conceal IEDs under everyday objects (such as piles of trash, rocks, or animal carcasses) that do not raise suspicions; position car bombs for maximum effect; make suicide vests and stand so as to achieve the maximum kill rate; and kidnap and assassinate people.[8]

To be sure, the Internet is not likely to be *sufficient* to recruit people to go to Iraq. After all, the country is a highly risky war zone where only the foolish would venture without taking precautions against traps set by vigilant security services. Rather, the Internet serves a number of core purposes in the recruitment process. First and foremost, it provides propaganda necessary to persuade potential recruits to consider the legitimacy and necessity of fighting in Iraq. In this respect, the Internet serves the same function as the pamphlet served for Russian revolutionaries in the first two decades of the twentieth century and the audiocassette served for Iranian revolutionaries during the 1970s. The interactive nature of Web forums and chat rooms, as opposed to asynchronous online content, creates a sense of belonging to a community that is likely to appeal to some alienated individuals. Furthermore, the Internet presents vivid imagery of Muslim suffering in Iraq, fostering righteous indignation among potential recruits and shaming them into avenging their coreligionists.

In addition, images of jihadi operations serve to show potential recruits that people are acting and that success is possible. This is especially important in light of the failure of Muslim governments to halt the invasion of Iraq and stand up to the United States. Moreover, the Internet transmits practical advice to those who want to join the fight in Iraq. Insurgents at one point advertised how to move people to Iraq through an online publication by "the Islamic Doctor" entitled "This Is the Way to Iraq: To whoever wants to reach the jihadists in the Land of the Two Rivers." Islamist Web sites give volunteers valuable tips on how to make their way to Iraq without attracting the attention of security services. The Web sites instruct volunteers to look like secular Western tourists by wearing jeans, being clean-shaven, and carrying a Walkman. The Islamic Doctor points out that the Syrian authorities focus only on the main roads to Iraq and border cities and ignore the less obvious routes. Another important piece of advice is to have all the necessary legal documents and carry a Turkish visa in one's passport, "so you can pretend that you're in transit to Turkey."[9]

The preceding analysis suggests that volunteerism in Iraq is a complex phenomenon. Just as militant organizations might employ suicide attacks for a variety of reasons, individuals might have various motivations for accepting the role of martyr. Although the aforementioned factors are necessary to explain transnational volunteerism in Iraq, they are not sufficient. Such conditions affected millions of Muslims, but only a few hundred or thousand made it to Iraq. A seventh factor is necessary for volunteerism: network ties.

THE JORDANIAN NETWORK

The long border between Jordan and Iraq facilitates the movement of volunteers. In 2004 approximately 450 Jordanians were missing in Iraq. Many came from the Zarqa and Salt regions of Jordan, fewer from Maan and Irbid. These volunteers are indigenous Jordanians, many from the Bani Hassan tribe from which Zarqawi originated, as well as Jordanians of Palestinian refugee origins. The stories of most of those individuals are not yet known, and it is not clear if many or even some became suicide bombers. Of the 102 known suicide bombers in Iraq, only three came from Jordan. In April 2006 the Mujahidin Shura Council issued the biographies of six Jordanian "martyrs" in Iraq—Abu-Hammam al-Urduni, Abu al-Bara al-Urduni (Ans Jamal al-Ashqari), Abu Radwan al-Urduni (Raed Mansoor al-Banna), Abu al-Abbas al-Urduni (Safwan al-Ibadi), Abu al-Walid al-Urduni, and Abu al-Yahya al-Urduni—but only two (al-Ashqari and al-Banna) were suicide bombers. There is little doubt that the movement of Jordanian volunteers to Iraq was facilitated by the jihadi Salafi network that developed in Jordan during the 1990s.[10]

Jihadi Salafism made its way to Jordan, particularly Zarqa, as a result of two developments. First, the end of the Soviet occupation of Afghanistan in 1988 encouraged some Jordanians to go to Afghanistan to participate in the postoccupation factional struggles. Some were lost individuals seeking a path in life; others trying to escape from the security services sought a safe haven in Pakistan and Afghanistan. Still others were true believers who wanted to acquire skills in jihad to fight their own governments. Some of the key individuals who went to Afghanistan between 1989 and 1993 were Abu Musab al-Zarqawi, Khaled Mustafa al-Aruri, Mohammed Wasfi Omar Abu Khalil, Suleiman Taleb Damra, Mohammed Rawashdeh, Naser Fayez and his brother Nafez, and Nasri

Izzedin Tahayinah. They returned to Jordan and later formed a small group known as *Bay'at al-Imam* (literally, declaring allegiance to the prayer leader). They were arrested and sent to prison. Some of these names appear again in connection with Zarqawi's training camp in Herat, Afghanistan, between 1999 and 2001, and again in Iraq following the fall of the Saddam regime.

The second development was the Gulf War of 1990–1991. Following the liberation of Kuwait from Iraqi occupation, many Palestinians were forced to leave Kuwait because of their actual or alleged sympathies for Saddam Hussein. Many returned to Jordan and settled in the Zarqa region. Among them were Salafi scholars trained by the Islamic Heritage Association, a center of Salafi thought in Kuwait. They included Abu Muhammad al-Maqdisi (Issam Muhammad Tahir al-Barqawi), of Palestinian origin and one of the most influential jihadi Salafi scholars. He was Zarqawi's personal mentor in prison. Another important figure who came out of Kuwait is Abu Qatadah (Omar Mahmoud Abu Omar), of Palestinian origin. He spent time in Afghanistan before eventually settling in London, where he became the principal ideologue for the Algerian Armed Islamic Group. As of this writing he is imprisoned in Britain.

Two less-known individuals who came out of Kuwait were Abu Ans al-Shami and Abu Qutaybah (Talib al-Dulaymi). Abu Ans al-Shami was a disciple of al-Maqdisi. He fought in Bosnia before returning to Jordan and eventually became one of Zarqawi's religious advisers in Iraq. Al-Shami was one of the lead advocates of the anti-Shia strategy in the insurgency. He died in September 2004 in a coordinated attack to "liberate" Abu Ghraib prison. Abu Qutaybah was one of Zarqawi's military commanders and was killed in Iraq.

The returnees from Afghanistan in the early 1990s became the foot soldiers of Jordan's militant Islam, and the returnees from Kuwait were the ideologues who gave them a utopian vision to pursue. In 1999 the Jordanian government released many of the radical Islamists from prison under a general amnesty by King Abdullah II, who succeeded his father, the late King Hussein. Their release was in accordance with a custom showing the new monarch's magnanimity.

Zarqawi and some of his associates set up the training camp in Herat, Afghanistan, for militants from the Fertile Crescent *(bilad al-sham),* including Palestine, Jordan, Lebanon, and Syria. They called their camp al-Tawhid wal-Jihad (Monotheism and Jihad). This name reflects the affinity between Zarqawi and al-Maqdisi. The latter has a popular Web site called al-Tawhid wal-Jihad, a portal for some of the most important documents of jihadi Salafi thought. Moreover, al-Tawhid wal-Jihad (TWJ) was the name of Zarqawi's first group in Iraq, which claimed responsibility for many suicide attacks.

Some of the key individuals in the Herat training camp reflect the continuity in jihadist activism from Afghanistan in 1989 to Iraq in 2003. (See appendix 3 for a list of Zarqawi's associates in the Herat training camp and Iraq.) When the Taliban regime fell in Afghanistan, many jihadists were looking for a new haven. For wanted terrorists such as Zarqawi and his associates, returning to their country of origin was not an option because they would have been arrested. In late 2001 Zarqawi made plans to move his cadres to northern Iraq under the protection of Mullah Krekar, the head of the Kurdish Islamist faction AI.[11] The latter was initially formed by the merger of two factions of radical Islamists in Kurdistan, one of which was the Islamic Movement of Kurdistan. Mullah Krekar headed this group, which competed with other Kurdish groups in northern Iraq, including the Democratic Party of Kurdistan under Massoud Barzani and the Patriotic Union of Kurdistan led by Jalal Talabani. The second faction was Jund al-Islam (The Soldiers of Islam), founded in September 2001 and formed by Afghan War veterans headed by Abu Abdullah al-Shafii (Wayra Salih Abdullah), an Iraqi and a veteran of both Afghanistan and Chechnya. In December 2001 the two groups merged under the name AI and Mullah Krekar became its leader. After Krekar was deposed, al-Shafii took over the leadership of the now-defunct group.

AI took in escapees from Afghanistan via Iran. Initially Zarqawi and his Jordanian associates were planning to launch attacks against Jordan, but the war in Iraq created a more attractive target. Air attacks on AI positions in the beginning of the U.S.-led invasion of Iraq, combined with ground attacks by Kurdish militias, nearly eliminated AI. Within a few months, remaining AI cadres joined one of three groups: AI, which hardly exists today; Ansar al-Sunna Army (later ASG), one of the most active jihadi Salafi groups in Iraq; and TWJ, led by Zarqawi (it later changed its name to al Qaeda in Iraq) and one of the most active jihadi Salafi groups in Iraq. All three groups have deployed suicide bombers and were collectively responsible for 36 percent of the claimed suicide attacks in Iraq as of February 2006.

THE SAUDI AND KUWAITI NETWORKS

Many of the suicide bombers in Iraq come from Saudi Arabia and some from Kuwait. Most go to Iraq through Syria and join AQI. Those who go through the northwestern borders between Iran and Iraq join ASG. According to one report, of 1,200 detainees in Syria, 85 percent are Saudi nationals.[12] On the list of 102 known suicide bombers in Iraq, forty-four come from Saudi Arabia and seven from Kuwait (see appendix 2). Moreover, many of the bombers come from well-known families and tribes found in both countries, as well as other Gulf countries: al-Mutayri (three bombers), al-Utaybi (four bombers), al-Dousari (two brothers who became bombers), and al-Shamari or al-Shmari (eleven bombers). To be sure, these are large families with thousands of members in several countries; bombers with these names are not necessarily brothers or cousins.

The presence of Saudi and Kuwaiti militants in Iraq is not unprecedented. Saudis and Kuwaitis volunteered to fight in other conflicts, especially Afghanistan and, to a lesser extent, Chechnya. On the list of 413 known foreigners captured in Afghanistan following the collapse of the Taliban regime in late 2001, 132 (32 percent) were from Saudi Arabia and twelve (3 percent) from Kuwait.[13] Of course, fifteen of the nineteen suicide hijackers on 9/11 were from Saudi Arabia.

Several factors may explain the large presence of Saudi and, to a lesser extent, Kuwaiti bombers in Iraq. First, Wahhabism in Saudi Arabia is a form of Salafism with strong anti-Shia sentiment. The founder of Wahhabism in the eighteenth century, Muhammad Ibn Abdul Wahhab, was a strong critic of Shia theology and practices, equating them with innovations *(bida)* and heresy.[14] So for insurgents seeking to foment sectarian strife in Iraq, Saudi militants are ideal candidates to carry out suicide missions against Shia targets.

Second, the 9/11 attacks on the United States were awe-inspiring for many young Saudis, who could not help admiring the courage and audacity of their countryman Osama bin Laden. This "courageous" attack, combined with anger toward the United States for its support of Israel and invasions of Afghanistan and Iraq, undoubtedly helped inspire some Saudis to action.

Third, Saudis and Kuwaitis tend to be richer on average than Jordanians and Syrians. Consequently, recruiters prefer to take Saudis and Kuwaitis because they bring with them their own resources and perhaps cash for the other insurgents. According to a Syrian handler of volunteers, "Our brothers in Iraq are asking for Saudis [because they] go with enough money to support themselves and their Iraqi brothers. A week ago we sent a Saudi to the jihad. He went with 100,000 Saudi riyals [approximately US$27,000]. There was celebration amongst his brothers there."[15]

Fourth, because conscription into the armed forces does not exist in Saudi Arabia and Kuwait, volunteers from these two countries tend to lack military skills. Thus they are better suited for suicide operations, where they can do the most damage with the least amount of training.

One other major reason helps explain the high proportion of bombers coming from Saudi Arabia. Al Qaeda's struggle in Saudi Arabia apparently reached a dead end by 2004. Having experienced terrorist attacks in the 1990s, the Saudi security services have become efficient in tracking militants inside the kingdom. As a result, the authorities reacted to the wave of attacks inside Saudi Arabia in 2003 with an "iron fist" policy that further weakened al Qaeda there. Saudi clashes with local al Qaeda cells became a regular occurrence as of May 2003. By June 2004 Saudi authorities had killed several top al Qaeda leaders, including Yousef Bin Salih Al-Ayiri (killed May 31, 2003), Khaled Ali Haj (killed March 16, 2004), and Abdel Aziz al-Muqrin (Abu Hajer, killed June 18, 2004). By that December Saudi security services had killed seventeen of the twenty-six most-wanted al Qaeda militants. By 2006 all but one on the list of thirty-six most-wanted terrorists in Saudi Arabia had been captured or killed. Interestingly, as al Qaeda was faltering in Saudi Arabia, twenty-six Saudi religious scholars signed a religious ruling declaring it a duty for Muslims to fight the occupation in Iraq.[16]

Leaders of al Qaeda in the Arabian Peninsula (Saudi Arabia) initially were not willing to send their militants to Iraq or call on Saudis to go fight there, despite their vociferous calls to support Muslim jihads all over the world. They appear to have been concerned about maintaining their capabilities in Saudi Arabia. However, publicly they said that the best way to support the jihad in Iraq was to open another front against the Americans in Saudi Arabia to take the pressure off jihadists in Iraq. Al Qaeda's leaders in Saudi Arabia issued tapes supporting Zarqawi and al Qaeda action against U.S. rear-guard positions in Saudi Arabia. Such declarations fell short of urging Saudis to go fight in Iraq. Leaders such as Abdullah Rashid al-Rushud (killed in Al-Qaim, Iraq, June 26, 2005), Saud al-Utaybi (killed April 2005), Faris al-Zahrani (arrested August 5, 2005), and Salih al-Awfi (killed August 18, 2005) initially rejected offers to fight in Iraq. Al-Muqrin and al-Awfi, in particular, issued tapes and wrote articles in *Sawt al-Jihad* (*The Voice of Jihad*, al Qaeda's online magazine in Saudi Arabia) urging Saudis to fight in the kingdom, not in Iraq. They wanted to harness anti-U.S. anger to win new recruits in Saudi Arabia.[17]

However, things began to change when Zarqawi declared allegiance to bin Laden in 2004 and changed the name of his organization to al Qaeda in the Land of the Two Rivers (Iraq). Zarqawi also formed two brigades, one bearing the name of al-Muqrin and the other of Ayiri (both dead leaders of al Qaeda in Saudi Arabia). Bin Laden reciprocated by praising Zarqawi and naming him al Qaeda's representative in Iraq. This move encouraged Saudis and al Qaeda in the Arabian Peninsula, which also began to appear under the name al Qaeda in the Two Holy Places (echoing Zarqawi's al Qaeda in the Land of the Two Rivers), to throw their support behind jihadists in Iraq. For instance, Saud al-Utaybi issued a statement calling on people to join the jihad in Saudi Arabia, but if they could not, to join in Iraq, Afghanistan, or Chechnya.[18] Similarly, al-Awfi issued a declaration of support for Zarqawi: "We will not hesitate to support you with everything we own, our lives, our possessions...."[19]

But the main reason the leaders changed their minds is because the fight in Saudi Arabia appeared to be going nowhere. Only then did they begin calling on Saudis to go to Iraq. Perhaps they calculated that those who went to Iraq would constitute the future generations of recruits in Saudi Arabia, gaining new skills and experiences in jihad. This, of course, does not apply to the suicide bombers. But even Saudi suicide bombers in Iraq could create the conditions for future jihad in Saudi Arabia by setting up a jihadist base bordering the Saudi kingdom.

Plenty of evidence shows wanted Saudi militants ending up in Iraq. Muhammad Abdel Rahman al-Dhayt (ranked twenty-sixth on the Saudi most-wanted terrorist list) is reported to have died in a clash in Baquba. Similarly, Abdullah Salih al-Rimyan, ranked seventeenth on the list, spent time in Iraq before being arrested. His brother (al-Uwami) is reported to have carried out a suicide operation there. Abdullah Muhammad Salih al-Rumayan and Muhammad Salih Sulieman al-Rushudi, two Saudis on the list of thirty-six most-wanted terrorists in the kingdom, were captured in the Kurdistan region of Iraq. It is reported that they had escaped to Iraq via Jordan, Syria, and then Turkey.[20]

On May 13, 2006, the MSC issued a video of Abu Hassan al-Makki and Abu Nasser al-Tashady, both wanted by the Saudi authorities. They had journeyed across the border "to help and support our brothers in Iraq." One of them added, "We can't see how our sisters are being dishonored, and our brothers in Fallujah are being killed day and night, and no one is helping them, or standing beside them." In September 2006 the MSC issued a video of attacks dedicated to Sheikh Mohammed bin Abdul Rahman al-Utaybi (Abu Hafs al-Hijazi). The latter was a member of al Qaeda in Saudi Arabia and "went through the deserts" to join the holy warriors in Iraq. The MSC also issued a seven-minute video in November 2006 of Abdel Aziz al-Massoud and Addel Aziz al-Fallaj, two Saudi dissidents killed in Iraq after they had escaped from al-Malaz prison in Riyadh.

However, not all Saudis who volunteered to go to Iraq are connected directly to al Qaeda. Some appear to have been recruited in groups. According to one report, two recruiters tried to solicit an entire soccer team to go fight in Iraq. The players were between seventeen and twenty-five years old and included high school and university students. They were preached to and given leaflets and cassettes concerning the need for jihad and rewards of martyrdom. Many ended up traveling to Iraq and their fate is unknown (at least two are reported to have been killed there). Majid al-Sawwat, one of the team stars, appeared on Iraqi satellite television confessing his involvement in the insurgency. His father said al-Sawwat had become religious before going to Iraq. His family reports that he repeatedly discussed the need to engage in jihad in Iraq. However, it is unlikely that all those who made the trip to Iraq were equally committed. It is plausible to suspect that some joined because of their commitment to their friends.[21]

As for the Kuwaitis, some of Zarqawi's commanders who were killed in Iraq came from Kuwait. They included Abu Ahmad al-Kuwaiti (Abdul Aziz al-Shamari), Abu al-Bara al-Kuwaiti (Faysal Zaid al-Mutayri), and Abu Bakr al-Kuwaiti (Faysal Ali Musa al-Rashidi). Abu Ahmad was in Afghanistan and became a commander of one of the groups in Fallujah. Abu al-Bara fought in Chechnya and spent time in Afghanistan. After the fall of the Taliban regime, he returned to Kuwait and was immediately arrested. In November 2003 he made his way to Fallujah, Iraq, and subsequently was killed in a nonsuicide operation near Baghdad. Abu Bakr wanted to go to Afghanistan after the 9/11 attacks but was stranded at the

Iranian border until he eventually returned to Kuwait. The Kuwaiti authorities repeatedly arrested him. After the fall of Baghdad, he went to Iraq with two others, Abu Salih al-Kuwaiti (Nayif Salih al-Subayi) and Abu Wadha al-Kuwaiti (Mansoor al-Hajari), both of whom carried out suicide attacks there.

Both Abu al-Bara and Abu Bakr are linked to several other recruits from Kuwait, five of whom became suicide bombers. Of the eight Kuwaitis in chart 12, four were arrested or wanted in Kuwait for Islamist activism. All these Kuwaitis had an affiliation with an unidentified Salafi cleric in Kuwait who was their mentor. Some went to Iraq on their own, but the rest went in groups of two or three: Abu Salih was accompanied by Abu Bakr and Abu Wadha, and Abu Hamza was joined by Abu Awf.

Saudis and Kuwaitis together comprised 51 of the 102 known suicide bombers in Iraq. The overwhelming majority came from Saudi Arabia. Little is known about their personal motivations and recruitment. In all likelihood they had varying motives for joining the jihad in Iraq. Some undoubtedly volunteered out of a sense of religious duty and a sincere desire to defend fellow Muslims from non-Muslim invaders. Others probably went because their friends or family were on their way to Iraq. Still others, perhaps most, were escaping repression in their home countries or were escapees from Afghanistan following the fall of the Taliban regime. They knew that returning or staying in their home countries was not an attractive option.

THE SYRIAN AND LEBANESE NETWORKS

Like Jordan and Saudi Arabia, Syria has a long border with Iraq's Al Anbar province that facilitates the movement of volunteers into Iraq. Of the 102 known suicide bombers in Iraq (appendix 2), six come from Syria. More-over, the communiqués of AQI and other jihadi groups, as well as forums that disseminate jihadi videos and audio recordings, appear on the Al-Sham al-Islami (Islamic Syria) Web site. Syria has been charged by the new Iraqi regime, the United States, and other countries in the region with providing a passage or transit point to foreign insurgents and a base for former regime elements to organize and fund the insurgency, as well as sending its own militants to fight in Iraq. Foreign volunteers often use Syria as the final launch point into Iraq. Specifically, they use the towns of Al-Qamishi, a Syrian Kurdish town on Iraq's northwestern border, and

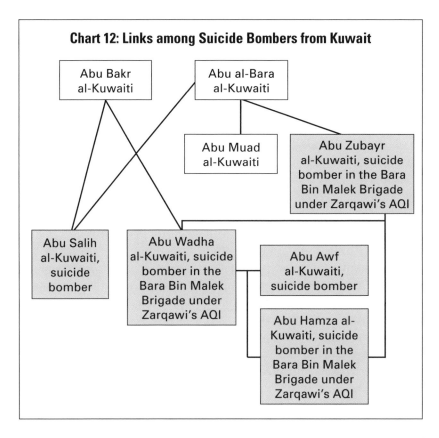

Chart 12: Links among Suicide Bombers from Kuwait

Abu Bakr al-Kuwaiti

Abu al-Bara al-Kuwaiti

Abu Muad al-Kuwaiti

Abu Zubayr al-Kuwaiti, suicide bomber in the Bara Bin Malek Brigade under Zarqawi's AQI

Abu Salih al-Kuwaiti, suicide bomber

Abu Wadha al-Kuwaiti, suicide bomber in the Bara Bin Malek Brigade under Zarqawi's AQI

Abu Awf al-Kuwaiti, suicide bomber

Abu Hamza al-Kuwaiti, suicide bomber in the Bara Bin Malek Brigade under Zarqawi's AQI

Abu Kamal, on the southern Syrian border adjacent to the Iraqi town of Al-Qaim. These two towns serve as entry points to Iraqi Sunni towns such as Al-Qaim, Ramadi, Fallujah, Tal Afar, and Mosul. Syrian volunteers in Iraq come from Hums, Dayr al-Zayr, al-Ladhikiyah, and Damascus.

Syria is an ideal transit point, not just because of its long border with the predominantly Sunni Al Anbar province, but also because during the years of sanctions Syrian and Iraqi smugglers developed elaborate routes through the desert to move goods in and out of Iraq. Fallujah was an important town for smuggling oil during the embargo years. Many of the tribes there engaged in this lucrative business, and the Saddam regime turned a blind eye to it. Since 2003 these routes have been used to smuggle fighters, weapons, and money for the insurgent groups. In the opening days of the war authorities waved buses filled with volunteers through open gates into Iraq. However, as pressure on Syria mounted, volunteers had to rely on more discreet means to enter the country.[22]

The flow of volunteers from and through Syria into Iraq is not merely an outcome of a policy of acquiescence by the Syrian state. Like many Muslim countries in the region, Syria witnessed the rise of Islamic revivalism during the 1990s. The state had some effect on this development. After crushing the Muslim Brotherhood's uprising in the early 1980s, Syria's Baathist regime launched a campaign to bolster its religious legitimacy in society and check the Islamists by promoting "official" Islam. It opened many mosques and Quranic recitation centers, among other institutions of Islamic teaching, to counter charges of atheism.[23]

Like other countries in the region, Syria experienced the phenomenon of "returnees" from Afghanistan, as well as the movement of second-generation jihadists to training camps in Afghanistan. On the list of 413 known foreigners captured in Afghanistan and detained in Guantanamo, nine come from Syria. Many who trained with Zarqawi in the Herat camp were Syrians from the Jund al-Sham (Soldiers of the Levant) faction. Syrians, Jordanians, and Palestinians formed this group in the 1990s in Afghanistan. Jund al-Sham also is associated with the suicide bombing of a British school in Doha, Qatar, in March 2005; the Lebanese camp of Palestinian refugees in Ayn al-Hilwa, which produced many volunteers to Iraq; and the June 2005 arrest of a cell belonging to Jund al-Sham lil-Tawhid wal-Jihad in Syria.[24] In October 2005 Syria arrested ten individuals belonging to a jihadi Salafi group, some of whom had gone to Afghanistan via Iran in 2001 to fight with al Qaeda and the Taliban regime against U.S. forces.[25]

Zarqawi himself spent time in Syria between May and September 2002, possibly setting up a jihadi network to strike in Jordan, which borders on Syria. According to a confidential report of the federal office of the Swiss police, an investigation in 2002 revealed that Islamists connected to al Qaeda in Syria had purchased a large number of Suisscom prepaid cellphone cards. A detailed log of the calls made with those cards reveals that Zarqawi called not only from Iraq but also from Syria, notably the Husseibah region. These calls continued even after the fall of the Saddam regime.[26]

Among Zarqawi's top aides killed in Iraq were Abu-Bakr al-Suri, a Syrian who served as a commander of a jihadi group in Qandahar, and Suleiman Khaled Darwish (Abu al-Ghadiya). The latter was a Syrian dentist married to a Jordanian woman. He was touted as Zarqawi's second in command and sentenced in absentia by a Jordanian court for his role in the failed plot to detonate chemical weapons in Amman, Jordan. He was killed during a raid June 26, 2005, in Al-Qaim, bordering on Syria, while in the company of Abdullah Rashid al-Rashud, one of the leaders of al Qaeda in Saudi Arabia.

Lebanon, on the other hand, does not have a border with Iraq. However, because Syria largely controlled the security services of Lebanon until 2005, the movement of Lebanese volunteers to Iraq through Syria was not difficult. Unlike volunteers from Saudi Arabia and Kuwait, who tend to be wealthier, volunteers from Lebanon come from marginal Sunni regions that have not benefited much from post–civil war reconstruction. Most are from the Ayn al-Hilwa Palestinian refugee camp, the western Bekka valley towns of al-Qaroun, Majdal Anjar, and al-Manara, and the predominantly Sunni towns of Sayda and Tarablous. What these groups have in common is their affiliation with the Salafi movement in Lebanon.[27]

A number of jihadists have gone from Lebanon to Iraq, and some have died in regular or suicide operations. The jihadi Salafi group Usbat al-Ansar (literally, League of the Prophet Muhammad's Supporters), based in the Ayn al-Hilwa Palestinian refugee camp, has dispatched recruits to Iraq.[28] Created by Hisham Shardi, it has been led by Ahmed Abdel Karim al-Saadi (Abu Muhjin, sentenced to death in absentia and, as of August 2006, in hiding), Wafiq Aqal (Abu Sharif), Abu Ubaydah, and Abu Tariq (brother of Abu Muhjin). Members of the group killed in Iraq include Salih al-Shayib (Palestinian), Ahmed Mahmoud al-Kurdi (Lebanese), Imad al-Hayak (Abu Bakr), Nidal Hassan al-Mustafa (brother of Abu Ubaydah, the spokesman for Usbat al-Ansar and wanted by the Lebanese security services), Omar Deeb al-Saeed, Ahmed Yassin, and Muhammad Khalifa (suicide bomber in Al-Qaim). It is not clear if they went to Iraq as individual volunteers or in coordination with Usbat al-Ansar and handlers from Iraq.

In January 2006, according to a Lebanese official, the authorities discovered in Beirut a cell of thirteen members recruiting from Ayn al-Hilwa.[29] The cell consisted of Syrians, Lebanese, Palestinians, Saudis, and Jordanians. All came to Lebanon through Syria after being pursued by Syrian authorities in 2004. One of the captured Lebanese is Hassan Muhammad Nabah (Abu Talhah), believed to be a high-level al Qaeda representative in the Lebanon-Syria *(bilad al-sham)* region. His two brothers were also part of the cell.[30] Yet despite this evidence of direct recruitment from regional networks associated with al Qaeda, according to one of the Lebanese who returned from Iraq, more than one group receives volunteers in Iraq, and each has had ties to groups that send the volunteers, suggesting coordination among the groups as opposed to "cold-calling" individuals into action.[31]

Other volunteers belong to Ansar Allah, which is close to Hezbollah and led by Jamal Suleiman. His son, Hassan, was killed in Iraq along with Muhammad Abdullah Zeidan. Other Lebanese killed in Iraq include Ahmed al-Furan, close to the Palestinian group Hamas in Lebanon, and Ibrahim al-Khalil, who belonged to the Arab Liberation Front, close to the Baathist party. AQI regularly issues communiqués announcing operations by Usud al-Sham fi Bilad al-Rafidayn (Lions of Levant in the Land of the Two Rivers), which includes Syria, Lebanon, Palestine, and Jordan. On June 29, 2006, the jihadi al-Meer Web forum posted a thirteen-minute video recorded in August 2005, showing Abu Jafar al-Maqdisi reading his last will and testament. He was from Lebanon's Ayn al-Hilwa camp and was killed with Zarqawi during the U.S. air strike of June 8, 2006. The message accompanying the video introduced al-Maqdisi as one of Zarqawi's closest aides.[32]

Another source of recruits for Iraq is the town of Majdal Anjar on the border with Syria. One of the personalities there is Mustafa Ramadan (Abu Muhammad al-Lubnani). He arrived from Denmark in 2003 and formed a small group based on his teaching of Salafi Islam. Ramadan was one of the first volunteers to Iraq and took his sixteen-year-old son with him. He became a close associate of Zarqawi and died in clashes with American forces in September 2004, a few months after his son was killed in unknown circumstances in al-Faruq camp in Iraq. Mustafa Ramadan was influenced by Kurdish fundamentalists in Denmark close to Ansar al-Islam, led by Mullah Krekar in Norway.[33]

As early as 2000, Lebanese forces clashed with radical Islamists led by Bassam Kanj (Abu Aisha) in Al-Dhuniyyah, north Lebanon, resulting in the death of eleven members of the security services and sixteen Islamists, including Kanj. The latter is believed to have fought in Afghanistan and Chechnya and is said to have had personal ties with bin Laden. He set up a training camp in Lebanon in the hope of producing a fighting group for future confrontations with the Lebanese regime.[34] Six days of clashes resulted when the state security forces tried to dismantle this training camp. Sixty-seven other Islamists were sought, some of whom are said to have joined the Usbat al-Ansar group in Ayn al-Hilwa.

Also in 2000 Lebanese security services captured Ayman Kamal al-Din, an Egyptian, along with eight others carrying weapons and explosives. They confessed to be associated with bin Laden and said they were transporting these weapons for operations against U.S. and Israeli targets in Jordan. In 2002 a twenty-seven-year-old Yemeni named Muamar Abdullah al-Awami (Ibn al-Shahid) and a Lebanese named Ahmad Salim al-Miqati were responsible for what came to be known as the McDonald's operation. They set off a series of bombs in foreign restaurants, including a McDonald's, injuring four people. Ibn al-Shahid was arrested in Ayn al-Hilwa camp, where he was hiding. He had fought in Bosnia and moved to Lebanon in 1996 with the help of Khaled al-Siayan (Abu Sarah al-Yemeni), said to be responsible for al Qaeda in Yemen. Ibn al-Shahid set up camp in Ayn al-Hilwa, where he met al-Miqati. Together they recruited forty-four members said to be responsible for the restaurant bombings.

In 2004 Lebanese security services foiled attempts by al Qaeda–inspired networks to carry out a number of operations against foreign targets, such as the Italian, Ukrainian, and American embassies; restaurants where foreigners gather; and Western diplomats. They also were planning to target Lebanese courts and some buildings belonging to the internal security services.[35]

These earlier attempts to organize an al Qaeda group in Lebanon and carry out operations in and from Lebanese territory suggest that radical Islamists with a Salafi bent found a potential ground for recruitment in Lebanon. Undoubtedly some of these networks aided some of the volunteers, including future suicide bombers, in making their way to Iraq.

CONCLUSION

The war in Iraq focused the attention of Islamic militants around the world. Its unpopularity, the moral shock generated by images of Muslim suffering in that country, the legitimacy given to martyrdom by earlier support for Palestinian suicide attacks against Israelis, and the diffusion of jihadi ideology and tactics via the Internet all contributed to a singular opportunity to mobilize experienced and novice cadres for a new jihad. Fighting against the unpopular Americans and their local allies gave the jihadists a chance to reconnect with the Muslim masses and gain the elusive legitimacy they have been seeking since the liberation of Afghanistan from Soviet invaders during the 1980s.

Disparate networks interlinked by ties to the Afghani training camps that emerged during the 1990s served as the mobilization structures of transnational martyrdom. Without these ties, angry Muslims and willing martyrs would not have been able to join the fray in Iraq in such a relatively short time. The prowess of these networks in mobilization suggests that they have the capacity to wreak havoc on neighboring and Western states if they can establish a solid base in Iraq after the withdrawal of multinational forces from that country.

NOTES

1. Fatih Krekar, "The Zarqawian Vision and its Heavy Load" (Arabic), Al Jazeera (www.aljazeera.net), June 15, 2006.

2. Al Jazeera estimated the number of Arab volunteers in Iraq before the invasion from 5,000 to 8,000. OSC, "Al-Jazirah Program Examines Issue of Arab Volunteers in Iraq," April 24, 2003. For an analysis of the first wave of volunteers to Iraq, see Muhammad Sulieman, "An Invitation to Reflect on and Discuss 'The Phenomenon of Arab Volunteers'" (Arabic), *Al-Asr* (Amman, Jordan), October 4–5, 2003 (three-part series).

3. The Pew Global Attitudes Project, "Views of a Changing World: How Global Publics View War in Iraq, Democracy, Islam and Governance, Globalization," June 2003, www.pewglobal.org. A substantial majority of Lebanese (73 percent), Palestinians (91 percent), Kuwaitis (63 percent), Pakistanis (64 percent), and Indonesians (59 percent) surveyed perceived a rising threat to Islam. A substantial majority of Moroccans (53 percent), Palestinians (85 percent), and Turks (45 percent) surveyed agreed that Iraq is worse off since the invasion, but only a minority of surveyed Kuwaitis (10 percent) and Lebanese (37 percent) agreed. Large majorities in Morocco (93 percent), Lebanon (92 percent), Indonesia (82 percent), Turkey (82 percent), and Palestine (81 percent) were disappointed by the lack of resistance in Iraq in 2003. Only in Kuwait did the majority (61 percent) express happiness at the lack of Iraqi resistance. More than 50 percent of those surveyed in seven out of eight Muslim countries felt more solidarity with Muslims; Turkey was the only exception.

4. The Pew Global Attitudes Project, "A Year After Iraq War: Mistrust of America in Europe Ever Higher, Muslim Anger Persists," March 16, 2004, www. Pewglobal.org. Regarding the view that the U.S. invasion of Iraq was motivated by oil and protection of Israel, the majority of surveyed Pakistanis (54 percent and 44 percent), Turks (64 percent and 45 percent), Moroccans (63 percent and

54 percent), and Jordanians (71 percent and 70 percent) expressed this view. The majority of surveyed Pakistanis (57 percent), Turks (73 percent), Moroccans (66 percent), and Jordanians (56 percent) expressed a lack of confidence in U.S. intentions to promote democracy in the Middle East. Substantial numbers of Pakistanis (46 percent), Moroccans (66 percent), and Jordanians (70 percent) felt suicide attacks against coalition forces in Iraq were justified.

5. Susan Sachs, "Internal Rift Dooms Arab League Plan to Help Avert a War by Pressing Iraq," *New York Times*, March 14, 2003.

6. Al-Takrouri, *Martyrdom Operations*, cites at least thirty-two religious rulings (*fatwas*) by Islamic scholars around the Muslim world supporting martyrdom operations in Palestine.

7. See, for instance, his declarations during his December 23, 2001, show addressing "Martyrdom Operations in Palestine" (Arabic) and his May 31, 2004, show addressing "Muslims and Political Violence" (Arabic). His religious rulings and publications can be found on his Web site, www.qaradawi.net.

8. OSC, "Website Publishes Training Guide for Jihad Participants," October 30, 2001; OSC, "Captured Afghanistan Videos Reveal Al-Qa`ida Training for Hotel Attack," November 17, 2002; OSC, "Young British Muslims Access Al-Qa`ida Terrorist Manuals on Internet," July 8, 2005; Steve Coll and Susan B. Glasser, "Terrorists Turn to the Web as Base of Operations," *Washington Post*, August 7, 2005; Graig Whitlock, "Briton Used Internet as His Bully Pulpit," *Washington Post*, August 8, 2005; Susan B. Glasser and Steve Coll, "The Web as Weapon: Zarqawi Intertwines Acts on Ground in Iraq with Propaganda Campaign on the Internet," *Washington Post*, August 9, 2005; OSC, "Jihadist Website Explains How to Sneak Explosives into Markets, Target Civilians," July 3, 2006; Gabriel Weimann, *Terror on the Internet: The New Arena, the New Challenges* (Washington, D.C.: United States Institute of Peace Press, 2006); Hassan M. Fattah, "Al Qaeda Increasingly Reliant on Media," *New York Times*, September 30, 2006.

9. Daniel McGrory, "Would-Be Martyrs Log on and Slip across the Border," *Times* (London) June 22, 2005. Similar advice was given to Egyptians seeking to travel to Iraq via Syria. Members of the mohajroon.net, password-protected Web site posted some thoughts on how to get to Iraq on May 8, 2006: "I think that the way through Syria is the best. Just enter Syria and the people there will guide you. But do not stay in Damascus because all of the hotels and apartments there are monitored.... You have to go to the areas in the north or south and stay there.... Do not tell anyone in your family that you are going to Iraq...." The forum member recommends going to a European country, such as Cyprus or Armenia, to get a tourist visa to Syria.

10. The following narrative is based on details gathered from Camille al-Tawil, "2000 Arab Jihadists in Iraq and Their Numbers are Rising" (Arabic),

Al-Hayat (London), August 11, 2004; Basel Rifayah, "The Migration of Jordanian Jihadists to Iraq Preceded the Fall of Saddam by Three Years" (Arabic), *Al-Hayat*, August 11, 2004; Hazem al-Amin, "Jordanian 'Zarqawis' Visit Their Clerics in Jail and Await the Opportunity to Join Abu Musab [al-Zarqawi] in Iraq" (Arabic), *Al-Hayat* (London), December 14, 2004; Hazem al-Amin, "Zarqa Gave Rise to [Ahmad Fadil] al-Khalaylah and [Abu Mohammed] al-Maqdisi; Returnees from Kuwait Revolved around Them" (Arabic), *Al-Hayat* (London), December 15, 2004; Hazem al-Amin, "Salt Salafis Hold Wedding Ceremonies for their Dead in Iraq and Call on Others to Fight" (Arabic), *Al-Hayat* (London), December 16, 2004; OSC, "Ansar al-Jihad Group Rejects Elections, Promise to Escalate Attacks; Names of Al-Zarqawi's Aides Killed Posted," February 16, 2005; Fuad Husayn, "Al-Zarqawi: The Second Generation of Al-Qaeda" (Arabic), *Al-Quds al-Arabi* (London), May 13–30, 2005, parts 1–15; James Glanz, "In Jordanian Case, Hints of Iraq Jihad Networks," *New York Times*, July 29, 2005; Jean-Charles Brisard, *Zarqawi: The New Face of Al-Qaeda* (New York: Other Press, 2005); Mashari al-Zaydi, "Jordanian Papers Concerning Fundamentalism and Politics" (Arabic), *Asharq al-Awsat* (London), October 13, 2005, part 4 of 5; International Crisis Group, "Jordan's 9/11: Dealing with Jihadi Islamism," *ICG Middle East Report* 47, November 23, 2005; Fatih Krekar, "The Zarqawian Vision and Its Heavy Load" (Arabic), Al Jazeera (www.aljazeera.net), June 15, 2006.

11. Krekar, "The Zarqawian Vision and Its Heavy Load"; Ahmad Kurayshan, "The General Intelligence Department Uncovers New al Qaeda and Ansar al-Islam Group that Planned Terrorist Operations against Tourists, U.S. Interests in Jordan, and Intelligence Officers" (Arabic), *Al-Rai* (Amman), September 13, 2003. Jordanian authorities revealed the names of thirteen wanted Jordanians and two Iraqis believed to have fled Afghanistan with Zarqawi in late 2001 and early 2002 and to be residing in Kurdistan in northern Iraq or Iran.

12. OSC, "Syria Reportedly Gives U.S. List of 1,200 Terrorists, 85 Percent of Them Saudis," August 20, 2005; Paz, "Arab Volunteers Killed in Iraq," found that of 154 Arabs killed in Iraq, 61 percent were from Saudi Arabia.

13. On April 19, 2006, the U.S. authorities at Guantanamo released the names of 558 detainees captured in Afghanistan. Of these, 123 Afghani nationals (obviously not foreigners in Afghanistan) and 22 Chinese detainees are recognized to be outside the al Qaeda network. The remaining 413 comprise 144 Saudis and Kuwaitis combined; 107 Yemenis (26 percent); 25 Algerians (6 percent); 11 Tunisians (2 percent); 10 Libyans (2 percent); 9 Moroccans, Syrians, and Sudanese (2 percent each); 6 Iraqis, 5 Britons, 5 Jordanians, and 4 Egyptians (1 percent each).

14. Natana J. Delong-Bas, *Wahhabi Islam: From Revival and Reform to Global Jihad* (New York: Oxford University Press, 2004).

15. Ghaith Abdul-Ahad, "Outside Iraq but Deep in the Fight: A Smuggler of Insurgents Reveals Syria's Influential, Changing Role," *Washington Post*, June 8, 2005.

16. Craig Whitlock, "Al-Qaeda Shifts Its Strategy in Saudi Arabia: Focus Placed on U.S. and Other Western Targets in Bid to Bolster Network, Officials Say," *Washington Post*, December 19, 2004; Hussein al-Uwami, "The Search for Foreign Elements to Aid in Activating the Organization: A Complex Task for al Qaeda in Saudi Arabia" (Arabic), *Al-Hayat* (London), April 12, 2006.

17. Interview with Abdel Aziz al-Muqrin, "One of the 19 [Most] Wanted," *Sawt al-Jihad*, issue 1, no author (October 2003): 22-25, www.e-prism.org/images/mag-w1.doc; interview with the Warrior Salih Bin Muhammad al-Awfi: "One of the 26 [Most] Wanted," ibid., issue 8, no author (January 2004): 23-28, www.e-prism.org/images/magalah8.pdf; Saud al-Sarhan, "Al Qaeda in Saudi Arabia" (Arabic), *Asharq al-Awsat* (London), May 20, 2005.

18. OSC, "Ramadan Statement by Al-Utaybi and Al-Qa`ida of Jihad in the Arabian Peninsula," November 5, 2004.

19. OSC, "Terrorism: Al-Qa`ida Saudi Leader Praises Al-Zarqawi, Offers Support," March 17, 2005.

20. Muhammad al-Shafi`i, "Two Saudis on the List of 36 in a Kurdish Prison" (Arabic), *Asharq al-Awsat* (London), May 30, 2006.

21. OSC, "Saudi Daily Reports Soccer Team in Al-Ta'if Recruited to Fight in Iraq," August 22, 2005.

22. James Risen and David E. Sanger, "G.I.'s and Syrians in Tense Clashes on Iraqi Border," *New York Times*, October 15, 2005. Abdul-Ahad, "Outside Iraq but Deep in the Fight."

23. Ibrahim Hamaydi, "Thousands of Mosques Present Four Hundred Thousand Weekly Lessons" (Arabic), *Al-Hayat*, January 5, 2006.

24. Ibrahim Hamaydi, "Islamic Trends Advance in Syria and the Authorities Wage 'Preemptive Operations' Against the Takfiris" (Arabic), *Al-Hayat*, January 4, 2006.

25. The ten individuals come from the northeastern part of Syria; they are Mahmud Arab Ahmad, Musab Husayn Ali, Mahmud Bin Muhammad al-Shafi`i, Habil Abd-al-Ghani al-Hamad, Muhammad Tawfiq Bin-Ahmad Murad, Muhammad Bin-Jumah Khalil, Usamah Bin-Mahmud al-Shafi`i, Ismail Bin-Said Mustafa, Umar Bin-Sharif Dawud, and Abd-al-Qadir Bin-Sulayman Murad. "The Road from Al-Qamishli to Damascus and from Tehran to Dost to Infiltrate Into Afghanistan" (Arabic), *Al-Hayat*, January 4, 2006.

26. OSC, "European Islamist Networks Flourish Despite Crackdown," July 16, 2005.

27. Hazem al-Amin, "Lebanese 'Jihadists' in Iraq: 'Salafis' from Peripheral Regions and Cities" (Arabic), *Al-Hayat* (London), August 11, 2004.

28. In April 2006 the Islamic Renewal Organization Web site posted a video by Usbat al-Ansar profiling five members of the organization killed in fighting in Iraq: Abu-Mahmud al-Kurdi (Muhammad Mahmud al-Kurdi), Nidal Mustafa (Abu-Hadithah), Ahmad Ali Awad (Abu-Ali), Salih al-Shayib (Abu-Mua`adh), and Shaykh Ahmad Yasin (Harun). OSC, "Lebanese 'Islamic Usbat al-Ansar' Posts Video of 'Martyrs' in Iraq," April 4, 2006.

29. The thirteen suspects, as reported in the Lebanese and Saudi press, are Ali Abdallah Hallaq, Hani Hashim al-Shatti (or al-Shanti), Muhammad Abid Wafai, Fahd Muhammad Khadim al-Yamani, Muhammad Kujah, Tariq Raja Jabir, Ali Jihad Sharaf al-Din, Khadir Muhammad al-Yamani (real name Faysal As`ad Akbar), Malik Muhammad Nab`ah, Hasan Muhammad Nab`ah, Baraa Muhammad Fuad, Mu`az Abdel Ghani Shushah, and Muhammad Ali al-Ammar.

30. OSC, "Saudi Paper Al-Watan Gives Details on Al-Qa`ida Members Arrested in Lebanon," January 15, 2006; OSC, "Lebanon: Investigations Note Possible Al-Qa`ida Link to Al-Hariri Assassination," February 11, 2006.

31. Nicholas Blanford, "Skeptics Look for Motives behind Arrest of Terror Suspects," *Daily Star* (Beirut), September 24, 2004; "Leaders ask how fugitives can so easily conduct activities from Ayn al-Hilwah," *Daily Star* (Beirut), September 24, 2004; Hazem al-Amin, "Strangers Come during 'Al Qaeda Season' to Recruit Suicide Bombers to Iraq" (Arabic), *Al-Hayat* (London), January 26–27, 2006, parts 1 and 2; Hazem al-Amin, "Beirut Is a Transit Point, not a Target, for Al-Qaeda" (Arabic), *Al-Hayat* (London), August 27, 2006.

32. OSC, "Al-Anfal Net Issues Video of Will of Al-Zarqawi's Companion Al-Maqdisi," June 30, 2006.

33. Al-Amin, "Strangers Come during 'Al Qaeda Season' to Recruit Suicide Bombers to Iraq."

34. "The Road of the Lebanese Afghans to Peshawar" (Arabic), *Al-Hayat* (London), September 18–19, 2001, parts 1 and 2.

35. Yousef Diyab, "Lebanon's Direct Confrontation with Terrorism Began in 2000, Resulting in Arrest of Six al Qaeda Networks" (Arabic), *Asharq al-Awsat* (London), October 8, 2004.

CHAPTER 7

EUROPEAN MUSLIMS
IN IRAQ

Of the 102 known suicide bombers in Iraq, 15 came from Europe. Many more volunteered to fight in Iraq; some were intercepted in Europe or Syria; others are missing and their whereabouts unknown. All the European suicide bombers, except one female from Belgium, were of North African origin. The presence of North African Muslim volunteers from Europe in international conflicts is not surprising. Many North African Islamic dissidents went into exile in Europe during the 1980s and 1990s because they were either denied opportunities to engage in the political process at home or wanted by the authorities for involvement in illegal Islamist organizations. This was particularly the case in Algeria, Tunisia, and Morocco. Many ended up in London (the "dissident capital of the world" before 9/11) or French-speaking societies. (Most North Africans speak French because of the legacy of French colonialism in the Maghreb region.) Of 413 known foreigners captured in Afghanistan following the collapse of the Taliban regime, ten (2 percent) came from Britain, France, and Belgium combined. They were of North African origin (from Egypt, Tunisia, Libya, Algeria, and Morocco). North Africans captured in Afghanistan number fifty-nine (14 percent).

European Muslims usually make their way to Iraq, through either Syria or Turkey.[1] The volunteers usually fly to Syria directly or make a stopover in another country such as Turkey as a transit point. In Syria they stay in safe houses or with persons connected to specific mosques known for facilitating the movement of volunteers to Iraq. Some have their personal documents replaced by false identity papers. According to a recruiter named Faruq, "All that is needed is a passport, a little money to meet Abu Barra, [an Iraqi] smuggler, and the doors to Iraq open up to you."[2] Abu Barra works through contacts in some Damascus mosques. The handlers in Syria clear the potential volunteers, making sure they come from a reliable source that can vouch for them. The volunteers then pay cash for their passage into Iraq, usually in a car to a Fallujah neighborhood or border towns such as Al-Qaim, Tal Afar, or al-Karabilah. Movement through Syria, in all likelihood, is facilitated by bribery more than by state acquiescence. In Iraq a handler receives the volunteers and assigns them to one of the groups.[3] According to a captured Kurdish Iraqi recruiter named Said Mahmud Abdel Aziz Haraz (Abu Umar al-Kurdi), the volunteers live in a house run by one of the groups. In one of the rooms, dubbed the "martyr's room," a list is posted and volunteers for suicide missions enter their names and dates of arrival. This system enables recruiters to establish a queue for suicide attacks.[4]

Why would European Muslims living in relatively affluent and democratic societies volunteer to fight and die in Iraq? This question is perhaps the most difficult one to answer. Some 15 to 20 million Muslims live in Europe. Yet only a few thousand have participated in jihads around the world, and even fewer have become suicide bombers. Therefore, one cannot rely on structural explanations such as societal racism, economic disenfranchisement, political exclusion, lack of cultural integration, or Western hegemony in the Muslim world to explain volunteerism for suicide attacks in Iraq. All these factors affect millions of European Muslims, but only a few have become violent militants. We must seek more proximate causes of Muslim radicalization in Europe.

Militant networks are crucial in facilitating volunteerism in Iraq. Although Muslims in Europe have important grievances that distinguish them from their counterparts in the Arab world, these grievances merely create what Wiktorowicz terms "cognitive opening," a process of questioning established beliefs, which facilitates the adoption of radical religious identities and extremist worldviews.[5] European Muslims also appear to have been radicalized by the new security environment that emerged after 9/11. Like their Arab counterparts, many European Muslims see the war on terrorism as a war on Islam. Finally, as seen earlier, radicalization may have been stimulated by jihadists outside Europe, who made concerted efforts to create moral shock among their coreligionists around the world by highlighting the suffering of Muslims at the hands of the United States and its Western allies.

I draw on the notion of cognitive opening to explain why the children of settled Muslim immigrants and some converts to Islam have embraced global jihad. However, it is important to make clear that cognitive opening does not automatically produce foot soldiers. Not every Muslim who has a cognitive opening turns to fundamentalism or radical activism. Those who do, however, are often connected to preexisting radical networks through friendship or kinship ties. At a minimum, the availability of radical networks in Europe is an important prerequisite for violent activism among European Muslims.

EUROPEAN MUSLIMS BECOMING RADICAL

Muslims in Europe are not monolithic. Not all of them encounter the same challenges, share the same identity, or seek the same objectives. Their Islamic heritage intersects with other identities, such as ethnicity, language, and nationality. Some European Muslims are secular integrationists, while others are religious fundamentalists.[6] The vast majority could be considered "cultural Muslims" who wish to maintain aspects of their Islamic identity while living harmoniously in Europe. They are not interested in proselytizing non-Muslims or applying Islamic law in European parliaments; they just want to be accepted as Muslims in Europe.

Even aggrieved Muslims do not always share the same grievances. Some are concerned about a lack of economic opportunity; others are resentful of the racial and religious discrimination directed at their communities; still others point to Western involvement in conflicts in their home countries as the source of their anger and may feel guilty living in the same Western countries that "oppress" their people.[7] Therefore, although the following analysis generalizes, this author recognizes the tremendous diversity in perspectives and interests within Europe's Muslim communities.

Muslims have been in Europe for centuries, but the vast majority arrived after World War II. They came as guest workers seeking employment opportunities in Europe's ravaged cities. Many came from Turkey, Africa, the Maghreb countries, Asia, and the Caribbean with the help of European governments seeking inexpensive labor. These Muslim workers expected to leave their host societies after they saved enough money to live decent lives in their home countries. However, economic uncertainty at home and family reunification schemes in Europe encouraged many to stay. North Africans became concentrated in France, Turks in Germany, and South Asians in Britain.

As immigrant communities expanded into the second and third generations, they inhabited ethnically homogenous and often dilapidated neighborhoods. The children of settled Muslim immigrants suffered disproportionately high levels of unemployment. Low socioeconomic status and residential discrimination or de facto segregation fostered criminality and other antisocial behavior among many second- and third-generation immigrants. Unemployment, poverty, and crime have produced the usual stereotypes concerning the "uncivilized foreigners," even when they are actually citizens.[8]

In addition, Muslim immigrants encountered a culturally rigid, hypersecular Europe that insisted on complete assimilation to norms and habits not always compatible with traditional Islamic values. Demands for acculturation were partly driven by what sociologist Tariq Modood called "compound racism": the conflation of cultural heritage with racial biases against people of color.[9] Opportunistic politicians and sensationalistic media personalities accentuated this problem by engaging in provocative anti-immigrant, anti-Muslim discourse, which further offended second- and third-generation Muslims who were born and raised in Europe and spoke European languages better than their ancestors' native tongue. As a result, European-born Muslims began asserting a "communalist identity" in defiance of the hegemonic culture.[10] In other words, the ambivalence of Europeans in accepting Muslims as a distinct cultural community encourages some Muslims to accentuate their religious identity, which in turn reinforces European inclinations to perceive them as different or subversive.

Muslim dissatisfaction with their host societies often combines with the impracticality of returning to their home countries. Many of the second-generation immigrants have lost their roots in their native countries and no longer share a cultural affinity with the motherland. They may speak French or German better than Arabic or Turkish, but they feel neither Moroccan nor French, neither Turkish nor German. Stuck in between, some develop an idealized vision of Islam, a "global Muslim *umma*" (nation) unadulterated by culture and unshaped by a specific ethno-national heritage.[11] Salafi doctrines that seek to purify Islam of any innovations or cultural accretions (see chapter 2) can take root in this cultural setting. Just as important, dislodging Islam from specific cultural reference points enables its adherents to identify with Muslims around the world regardless of national or ethnic boundaries.

In this context some second-generation Muslims have found a home in the global jihadist movement. Not every European Muslim with grievances turns to radical worldviews. However, grievances of some Muslims in Europe create a cognitive opening. Individuals begin to question accepted beliefs and become more willing than before to entertain new ideas about the world and their role in it. Some of those experiencing cognitive openings might adopt benign worldviews. Others might seek religious identities that are not necessarily radical. However, some might be susceptible to extreme fundamentalist doctrines and transformative ideologies.

Those who turn to radicalism do so not merely because of the power of ideas, but also because of their links to preexisting radical networks through friendship and kinship ties. As Wiktorowicz explained, individuals with cognitive opening "do not typically seek religious meaning in a vacuum. They turn to friends and family for direction and possible sources of religious learning. If social contacts are in a movement, the seeker is likely to be drawn to that movement's activities since social ties are trusted pathways of information."[12] Once they join the movement, the possibility for further radicalization emerges and the leap to violence becomes thinkable. It may well be that individuals become politically radicalized and religion is merely the discursive template through which they express their radicalism. Put simply, radical Islam in Europe has its roots in sociology, not theology.

RADICAL NETWORKS IN EUROPE

If radical networks are the key to turning aggrieved Muslims into militants, how and why did these networks take root in Europe? During the 1980s and 1990s, repression of Islamic dissidents in the Middle East and North Africa (MENA) forced them to seek new homes. Europe's liberal asylum laws and its geographic proximity to MENA made it hospitable to Islamic exiles. However, embittered Islamists were not content with simply having a new home; they used their safe haven to criticize the regimes that exiled them, publicize their radical worldviews in print and online, solicit financing for their fighting brethren back home and in conflict zones, and plan operations against their own governments. Radicals established organizations and informal networks in mosques and other public arenas. These organizations include Hizb al-Tahrir, al-Muhajirun, Ansar al-Islam, and other groups of Saudi, Algerian, Egyptian, Moroccan, and Syrian dissidents. Such organizations and networks became conveyer belts that sent ordinary Muslims to Afghanistan and Pakistan for training and indoctrination. Paradoxically, radical Islamists took advantage of Europe's liberal asylum laws, freedom of expression, and human rights to promote illiberal and anti-Western worldviews.[13]

These dissidents generally avoided direct terrorism in Europe for fear of losing their new safe haven.[14] France was a notable exception. There Algerian militants connected to the Armed Islamic Group (GIA) waged a campaign of subway bombings and one airline hijacking to pressure the French government to withdraw aid to the military regime in Algeria. It was only in the late 1990s, when al Qaeda declared war on the United States, that some of the networks began to use Europe as a staging ground for operations such as the foiled millennium plot by the Algerian operative Ahmed Ressam, who planned to detonate explosives in the Los Angeles International Airport, and, of course, the attacks of 9/11.

Radical European Muslims are recent immigrants who have taken advantage of asylum laws; second-generation, "born-again" Muslims; and converts to Islam.[15] The converts often have led a life of crime and converted in prison. The story of Richard Reid, the "shoe bomber" foiled as he tried to blow up American Airlines flight 63 over the Atlantic Ocean, exemplifies the third category. These converts come from a rebellious subculture that combines antisocial behavior such as drug taking or petty criminality with support for anti-mainstream rebels such as gangster rappers, bin Laden, or the 9/11 suicide bombers. These three categories of militants do not operate separately, however. Converts and born-again European Muslims rely heavily on radical networks of Muslim dissidents in Europe.[16] These networks exploit the willingness of young soldiers to join their jihad.

What drew the dissidents, the born-again immigrants, and the converts to Iraq? The hospitable environment for radical Islamic networks that existed in Europe before 9/11 began to disappear. New security and legal measures, surveillance, arrests, and public distrust of Islamists created new pressures on the radical dissidents.[17] Many dissidents knew they could not return to their home countries, but their radical commitments could not be subdued easily, especially in light of the wars in Afghanistan and Iraq. The dissidents who formed the radical networks during the late 1980s and 1990s began to seek recruits from their ranks, as well as from the disgruntled second-generation Muslims and recent converts. It was not difficult to find Muslim youths who were enraged by the fact that their communities were increasingly the objects of security concern and their loyalty was under suspicion. At the same time, conflicts in Muslim lands led them to ask questions about their identity, their fealty to suffering Muslims, and their governments, which sided with the United States against Iraq.

The volunteers in Iraq were largely connected to radical Islamic dissidents from Morocco, Algeria, and Tunisia. Like their Middle Eastern counterparts, many were motivated by images of Muslim suffering and humiliation in Iraq, just as earlier images of Muslim suffering in Bosnia, Chechnya, Palestine, and Kashmir had inspired some to volunteer to go to those troubled spots. Some were feeling hunted for prior Islamic militancy and perhaps wanted an honorable way out. Others were lost individuals leading a criminal life or drifting on the margins of society. Perhaps they were seeking opportunities for redemption after leading an un-Islamic life of vice and sin.

Salient among these European volunteers, however, are their preexisting ties to radical Islamist networks that facilitated, and perhaps encouraged, their journey to fight and die in Iraq. The convergence of marginality, criminality, and connections to radical networks under threat is part of the reason European Muslims have volunteered in Iraq. Unsafe in Europe and unwanted in their home lands, many may have sought to forge a new identity based on the brotherhood of arms and the security of tight bonds of friendship.

THE BELGIAN–SPANISH NETWORK

Belgium has been linked to several suicide bombers in Iraq, including the first European female suicide bomber, Muriel Degauque. However, Belgium contributed suicide bombers before the war in Iraq. As early as summer 2001, two men of North African origin, Abdelsatar Dahmane and Rashid El Ouar, traveled from Belgium to Afghanistan with forged Belgian passports. The two disguised themselves as journalists on assignment to interview Shah Masud, the Afghan leader opposed to the Taliban regime. In reality they were suicide bombers who killed Masud during the interview, which took place two days before the 9/11 attacks on the United States. As shown below, a Belgian connection to radical Islamic terrorism appeared again with the March 11, 2004, Madrid train bombings, in which 191 people perished.

At the center of this deadly network is the Moroccan Islamic Combatant Group (known by its French acronym, GICM), which spans several other European countries including Spain, Italy, France, and the Netherlands. GICM is a jihadi Salafi group that seeks to overthrow the monarchy in Morocco and establish an Islamic state in its stead. State repression in Morocco forced the group to seek a safe haven elsewhere. It ran several training camps in Afghanistan and dispersed across Europe following the U.S. invasion of Afghanistan in 2001.[18]

The stories of five individuals who volunteered for Iraq—Maymoun Belhadj, Abdelhy Asas, Mohammed Afalah (suicide bomber), Muriel Degauque (suicide bomber), and Issam Goris (failed suicide bomber)—help illustrate the connections among marginality, criminality, and radical networks in Belgium. Chart 13 illustrates the links among individuals over a wide geographic area, ranging from Belgium and Spain to Morocco, Syria, and Iraq. Each of the individuals in the white boxes has either played a direct role in sending the volunteers to Iraq or served as a social link to dispatchers.

MAYMOUN BELHADJ

Maymoun Belhadj was arrested in Syria as he tried to make his way into Iraq in 2004.[19] After capture by the Syrian authorities, he confessed his intention to join the ranks of the jihadists in Iraq. Belhadj was deported to Morocco, where he was previously wanted for involvement in terrorist activities in Tanja, northern Morocco. Before going to Syria, he had lived in Spain, where his sister lives, and eventually settled in Belgium.

In Spain Belhadj, a tailor by profession, contacted Abdelmajid Bouchar in Leganes, one of the immigrant suburbs of Madrid. Bouchar was a member of the GICM and one of five individuals on the run for their involvement in the March 11, 2004, Madrid bombings. There they talked with other Muslims in the Al-Aziz and Al-Khalil mosques in Malpique about the need to do something in Afghanistan. However, nothing came of these discussions. Belhadj traveled to Belgium and kept in touch with Bouchar.

The U.S.-led invasion of Iraq and the subsequent occupation of that country gave Belhadj the idea of fighting there. He attended the Tawhid mosque in Brussels, where he was influenced by a preacher named Abdel

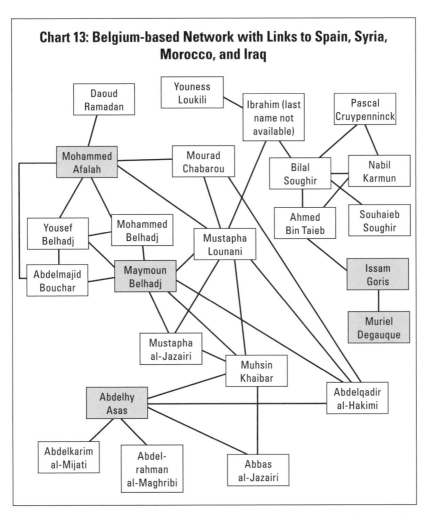

Chart 13: Belgium-based Network with Links to Spain, Syria, Morocco, and Iraq

Salam al-Kharaz, who promoted jihad in Iraq. Belhadj contacted Mustapha Lounani, a member of the GICM residing in Schaarbeek, Belgium. According to the Moroccan security services, Lounani frequented al Qaeda camps in Afghanistan, Chechnya, and Pakistan, among other places. He is one of eighteen Belgian-Moroccans charged in connection with the Madrid bombings. Lounani is the brother-in-law of Serhane Ben Abdelmajid Fakhet ("the Tunisian"), one of those responsible for the Madrid attacks. Fakhet subsequently killed himself along with others in a suicidal explosion to avoid capture by the Spanish authorities. Lounani is currently serving a six-year prison term in Vorst, Belgium, on charges that he "specializes in the networks that brought potential martyrs to Iraq." Previously he was charged with forging passports and possessing a manual for mobile-phone-controlled, remote detonation devices. Under interrogation he declared that "every good Muslim has the obligation to go and fight in Iraq. Me too." Police found his will at his sister's house, along with 5,000 euros for "those who are fighting on our borders."

Lounani rented an apartment in Brussels for Maymoun Belhadj and his brother, Yousef, currently in prison in Spain for involvement in the Madrid bombings. (Yousef is suspected of being the GICM military spokesman who claimed responsibility for the Madrid bombings.)

Lounani put Maymoun Belhadj in touch with an Algerian named Mustapha al-Jazairi. The latter helped Yousef Belhadj make his way to Belgium in exchange for 400 euros. Lounani put Maymoun Belhadj in touch with a Moroccan or Libyan named Muhsin Khaibar (Abdelrahim or Abdelmajid al-Libi or Abdelmajid al-Yasser). He also directed him to Abdelqadir al-Hakimi, who was sentenced to death in Morocco in 1985 and is believed to be the European leader of GICM. Al-Hakimi had spent time in Bosnia before settling in Belgium. Both Khaibar and al-Hakimi helped Belhadj go to Syria. In May 2004 Khaibar was arrested with Abdelhy Asas in Syria for communicating via the Internet with recruits in Europe, and both were deported to Morocco. Yousef Belhadj also wanted to go to Iraq, but Maymoun asked him to wait until he had arranged travel for himself.

Maymoun traveled to Syria on a KLM flight in March 2004. Muhsin Khaibar helped him stay in an apartment in Syria for a month. During his stay, Maymoun watched videos that encouraged jihad. He was arrested before making his way to Iraq.

The GICM connection to Syria is not entirely clear, but it appears that many of the Belgium-based GICM members spent time there under the pretext of studying Arabic and Islam. Of the eighteen GICM members in Belgium charged in connection with the Madrid bombings, five spent time in Syria: Abdelqadir al-Hakimi, Mustapha Lounani, Abdullah Ouabour, Khalid Bouloudo, and Khalid Oussaih. Another GICM name connected to Syria is Mohammed Reha, a Belgian arrested in Morocco in November 2005. Other sources report two additional GICM members in Syria to facilitate movement of fighters from Europe and North Africa into Iraq: Ameed al-Ulaybi and Ayoub al-Zaim.[20] Moreover, the close links between GICM members in Belgium and radical Islamists in Spain help explain connections to Syria. Spain in the 1980s and 1990s took in many Muslim Brotherhood dissidents from Syria after their movement was brutally crushed by the Syrian Baathist regime. Some of these dissidents constituted the radical "Abu Dahdah network," named after its central figure, Imad Eddin Yarkas (Abu Dahdah), who had close ties to al Qaeda in Afghanistan.[21]

ABDELHY ASAS (ABU ABDULLAH)

Abdelhy Asas was also arrested in Syria on his way to Iraq in 2004.[22] He admitted to the Syrian authorities that he intended to "join the Iraqi resistance to fight against American forces." However, he did not meet Maymoun Belhadj until his arrest in Syria. Asas came from Morocco, not Belgium; nonetheless, he came in contact with some of the same people who helped Belhadj make his way to Syria.

Asas had prior combat training experience in Afghanistan. However, his trip to Syria began in Tanja, Morocco, where Asas met with Abdelkarim al-Mijati (Abu al-Yas), who is wanted by the Moroccan authorities for his role in the May 16, 2002, suicide attacks in Casablanca and other attacks in Riyadh, Saudi Arabia. (It is important to note the connection with Tanja. One of the known Moroccan suicide bombers in Iraq, Abu Osama al-Maghribi, is also from Tanja, and Maymoun Belhadj was wanted on charges of terrorism in Tanja.) At this meeting was another, unnamed activist from the jihadi Salafi movement. In early 2004 both Asas and the unnamed militant went to Syria and, with the help of Muhsin Khaibar (Abdelrahim), contacted an Algerian named Abbas al-Jazairi and a Moroccan named Abdelrahman al-Maghribi. Recall that Khaibar is the person who arranged for Maymoun to stay in Syria on his way to Iraq.

Both Asas and the unnamed militant had contacts with Moroccan radicals in Spain and Belgium, including Abdelqadir al-Hakimi, who lives in Brussels. Abdelqadir al-Hakimi was one of the facilitators for Maymoun Belhadj.

MURIEL DEGAUQUE AND ISSAM GORIS

Muriel Degauque and Issam (or Hissam) Goris were husband and wife. Issam was a Muslim Moroccan living in Belgium; he married Muriel, seven years younger than he, and she converted to Islam. Both made their way to Iraq via Turkey and Syria in 2005, intending to participate in a suicide attack. On November 9, 2005, Muriel succeeded in her effort and earned the unenviable title of the first European female suicide bomber in Iraq; she detonated a car bomb in Baquba, killing five Iraqi policemen. Issam failed in his mission when he was shot down by U.S. forces a few hours later before detonating his explosives.

Muriel was born in Charleroi, Belgium, to a working-class family. She had a brother, Jean-Paul, who died at age twenty-four in a motorcycle accident. According to her family and teachers, Muriel was a difficult child who associated with other "problem children." As a teenager she took drugs and once ran away from home. Eventually she worked in a bakery, where she was accused of stealing from the cash register.[23] Muriel and Issam are said to have relied on unemployment benefits and lived in a rundown area around the Gare du Midi in Brussels.

Three years before her suicide operation, Muriel met Issam after two previous relationships, one with a Turkish and one with an Algerian man. She spent nearly three years in Morocco before returning to Belgium with a newfound religiosity that led her to don the chador. In her new family men and women sat separately, following the custom of religious Muslims. She also changed her name to Myriam.

According to Belgian authorities, Muriel and Issam were recruited with the help of Pascal Cruypenninck, Bilal Soughir, and Nabil Karmun. Cruypenninck, born in 1972, was an unemployed kitchen worker who converted to Islam. He came from a modest background and had a troubled childhood. His mother said he had been beaten by his father and served time in prison. He once married an African woman who had two children with him before they divorced. It was then, in 2002, that he converted to Islam. Cruypenninck grew a beard and his mother said he "looked like bin Laden."[24]

Bilal Soughir was born in 1973 and became a Belgian citizen in 2002 (it is not clear whether he was of Libyan or Tunisian origin). Along with two of his brothers, he had several encounters with the police in Belgium. In 1995 he was arrested for stealing; less than a year later his brother Souhaieb received a one-year sentence for a violent theft. The third brother was sentenced to one year in prison for theft and forgery. The third suspect, Nabil Karmun, was born in Morocco in 1975 and later became a Belgian citizen.

According to Belgian authorities, Youness Loukili, a Belgian citizen born in Morocco who lived in Syria, may have initiated the recruitment process. Loukili was a former fighter in Iraq and is said to have sent the following text message to an individual named Ibrahim: "Go to [Mustapha] Lounani in Molenbeek [Brussels district] and put him in touch with Bilal Sougir."[25] The link between Bilal Soughir and Nabil Karmun, on one hand, and Muriel Degauque and Issam Goris, on the other, was Ahmed Bin Taieb (Bentaieb), a Tunisian who lived illegally in France and traveled to Iraq. He was arrested by the French authorities at the same time the other suspects were arrested in Belgium. According to the Belgian authorities, Nabil Karmun served as Bin Taieb's driver from Italy to Belgium. Bin Taieb is said to have known Muriel's husband, Issam.

MOHAMMED AFALAH

In May 2005 Mohammed Afalah carried out a suicide attack in Iraq.[26] He drove a car packed with explosives into an Iraqi army checkpoint in Baghdad's Dora neighborhood, killing one soldier and injuring eight. Previously he had been indicted for his involvement in the Madrid bombings. Within hours of the Madrid bombings, Afalah retreated to a safe house in the Leganes district along with eight others involved in the plot. On April 3, 2004, as armed officers closed in, Afalah escaped, leaving the rest of the conspirators to blow themselves up rather than be captured. Three days later Afalah turned up in Maaseik, Belgium, with at least one other participant in the train bombing, Mohammed Belhadj (reportedly the cousin or brother of Yousef and Maymoun Belhadj). Police believe that Mohammed Belhadj, who rented the safe house in Leganes for the Madrid attackers, may have traveled to Iraq with Mohammed Afalah and Daoud Ramadan, also wanted in connection with the Madrid bombings.

Two days after the suicidal explosion in the Leganes safe house, Mohammed Afalah telephoned his brother Ibrahim from Barcelona and asked him to go to the house of Ibrahim Moussaten in Leganes to request Yousef Belhadj's telephone numbers in Belgium. Moussaten, arrested by the police on February 1, 2005, with three other family members, is the nephew of Yousef Belhadj. Ibrahim obtained the telephone numbers and gave them to his brother in a second call from Afalah. This was a clear indication that Afalah was planning to go to Belgium.

During his stay in Belgium, Afalah spent some time at the Brussels home of Mourad Chabarou, one of thirteen GICM militants tried for connections to the Madrid bombings. Chabarou also planned to blow himself up in Iraq or Europe. Investigators heard him declare his willingness to die as a martyr in a tapped telephone conversation with Rabi Uthman al-Sayyid ("the Egyptian"), who was investigated in connection with the Madrid bombings. They also found Afalah's last will and testament.[27]

According to the confession of Maymoun Belhadj, Afalah "insisted on me [sic] to help him go to Iraq to fight a jihad against the Americans. I promised him to do so if I succeeded in contacting one of the persons in charge of attracting the mujahidin."[28]

These connections between suicide bombers in Iraq and radical Islamists in Europe show how volunteerism is intricately connected to preexisting friendship and activist ties. Not everyone who wants to go to Iraq for jihad can do so. A person must be linked to individuals who have experience in the ways and means of jihad. Moreover, many of those who volunteered in Iraq or played a role in dispatching recruits appear to have been wanted or under surveillance by the authorities of their home or host countries. They may have seen jihad in Iraq as an opportunity to exit this world in an honorable way rather than be arrested or turned over to the authorities of their home countries. As shown below, the Belgian network was not at all unique.

THE FRENCH NETWORK

In 2003 and 2004, the French Territorial Surveillance Directorate (DST) arrested 117 individuals in connection with investigations of Islamist terrorism. According to French Interior Minister Nicolas Sarkozy, about a dozen French youth were preparing to become suicide bombers in Iraq. French intelligence services reported that seven French nationals had died in Iraq in combat or suicide attacks, and three were prisoners of the occupation forces.

The DST arrested four young Muslims planning to go to Iraq. They were of North African origin, possibly Tunisian and Algerian. These four were linked to others who died in Iraq, including three nineteen-year-olds, Redouane el-Hakim (of Tunisian origin), killed in Fallujah July 17, 2004; Tarek Ouinis, killed September 20, 2004, by a U.S. patrol; and Abdelhalim Badjoudj (of Algerian origin), killed October 20, 2004, in a suicide attack. Ouinis and Badjoudj left for Syria on their way to Iraq in August 2003. The two were not considered hard-core Islamists. According to one report, "They smoked marijuana, drank beer and listened to rap music, and wore jeans."[29] Badjoudj returned to France in January 2004 to marry a French woman of Moroccan origin. Two months later, however, he left again for Iraq, never to return.

Badjoudj and Redouane el-Hakim were unemployed and came from broken families. According to Badjoudj's uncle, "If he had work, this wouldn't have happened." Badjoudj's father left the family when the boy was three years old. Hakim, on the other hand, was raised by his mother. "He dropped out of an apprenticeship at a neighborhood bakery and later started a sandwich shop that failed."[30]

Two other French nationals killed in Iraq were Karim (Abou Salman) and the forty-one-year-old suicide bomber of Algerian origin, Bazis Idris, who died in February 2005. Like many of the other suicide bombers in Europe, Idris spent time in Bosnia-Herzegovina and Afghanistan in the 1990s. He returned to France in the mid-1990s but once again made his way back to Afghanistan in the late 1990s, only to return when the Taliban regime fell. Before leaving for Iraq, he spent some time in Manchester, England, but his purpose there is not clear. A few months earlier, a joint operation by French and British antiterrorist services led to the arrest of Mohamed Ali Abou Homam, a London-based Egyptian activist who forged documents for volunteers to Iraq.

Those recently arrested and those killed in Iraq had been recruited while attending the Al-Dawa mosque on rue Tanger in Paris's nineteenth district. Like the Moroccans in Belgium, they went to Syria in 2004 under the pretext of attending courses in Arabic and Islam at the al-Fateh al-Islami Institute. Redouane el-Hakim's brother, Boubaker, was already known to the intelligence services and was considered the group's most committed member. He was arrested in Syria in August 2004, having been apprehended on the Iraqi border. Those detained in Iraq since November 2004 include Chekou Diakhabi, aged nineteen, and Peter Cherif, twenty-two. Three were detained in France for attempting to go to Iraq: Farid Benyettou, twenty-three; Thamer Bouchnak, twenty-two; and Cherif Kouachi, twenty-two.[31]

In April 2005 French authorities arrested Said al-Maghrebi, a Moroccan Islamist wanted for several years. He and three associates were planning to go to Iraq via Syria. Al-Maghrebi was born in Morocco and involved in various Islamic movements. According to the French authorities, he was in contact with Laurent Mourad Djoumakh and Samir Korchi, two Islamists sentenced by a Parisian criminal court in December 2004 for involvement in the Frankfurt group, which was planning attacks in Strasbourg's Christmas market in December 2000. Before this association, al-Maghrebi spent time in Afghanistan during the 1990s. He left Afghanistan in 2001 and ultimately made his way to France.[32]

A possible link between recruits in France and handlers in Syria is Said Arif, an Algerian connected to Zarqawi. Syrian authorities arrested Arif in May 2003 and extradited him to France in June 2004. Arif had deserted the Algerian army and joined al Qaeda in Afghanistan during the second half of the 1990s, when the Islamist insurgency was raging in Algeria. He then moved to Germany, where he was reportedly in contact with the Frankfurt group led by Mohammed Bensakhria, who was arrested and extradited to France after the aborted attack on the Strasbourg Christmas market. Arif escaped to Pakistan to avoid arrest by German authorities. After the fall of the Taliban regime, he went to the Caucasus and tried to join Chechen guerrilla forces. There he came in contact with Adnan Muhammad al-Sadiq (Abu Atiya, currently imprisoned in Jordan), who served as the local commander of Zarqawi's al-Tawhid wal-Jihad. Arif decided to stay in training camps in the Pankisi Gorge region, where "he reportedly came in contact with other jihadists from France, including Menad Benchellali, alias 'the Chemist,' the brains of the 'Chechen networks' dismantled in France in December 2003."[33]

Arif is linked to another Algerian, Rashid Bukhalfa (Abu Doha). The latter was responsible for hosting Algerian dissidents in Jalalabad, Afghanistan, with Abu Qatada, currently in jail in England. Abu Doha was in charge of raising funds for the Algerian Salafist Group for Call and Combat and was arrested on several occasions in London. According to one source, Arif admitted to being in an al Qaeda meeting in Kabul in early 2000 with Abu Doha. "At this luncheon, Arif said, he talked with members of the Zarqawi group while Zarqawi himself was in the company of Abu Doha."[34]

Another possible link between France and Iraq is the now-defunct AI group. Although it lost its base in Iraq by late 2003 because of organizational splits and crushing blows by the coalition forces and the Kurdish Peshmerga militias, it still operated in a number of European states. In June 2005 the DST arrested seven Iraq-bound volunteers who allegedly were in contact with the Iraqi AI. This group is said to have forged travel documents and collected money for jihadists in Iraq. Although these connections are not sufficient to link French nationals to Iraq, they do suggest that it is plausible, indeed likely, that preexisting radical networks in France facilitated the movement of Muslim volunteers to Iraq.

THE ITALIAN NETWORK

Of the 102 known suicide bombers in Iraq, 8 came from Italy and were of North African, mostly Tunisian, origin.[35] In May 2004 Italian authorities uncovered a cell linked to AI based in a Sorgane mosque. The cell had plans to send suicide bombers to Iraq. One of the former clerics of the Sorgane mosque, Mohammed Rafik, was arrested in October 2003 for his involvement in the May 16, 2003, Casablanca bombings. He is also suspected of having ties to the Moroccan GICM. The cell consisted of Rachid Maamri, an Algerian, and four others from Tunisia in their mid-twenties. All four came from well-to-do families and had their own funds to travel to Iraq. The cell members were eager to gain exit visas from Italy, and hours of monitored phone conversations revealed a persistent desire to die as "martyrs" in Iraq.

The cell's leader, Rachid Maamri, was in his thirties and served as the head cleric of the Sorgane mosque until he was arrested in May 2004. He is suspected of having ties to the Algerian Armed Islamic Group and other Algerians in the Georgian valley of Pankisi. Recall that one of the key figures imprisoned in France was Said Arif, the Algerian terrorist arrested in Syria in 2003. Along with Abu Doha (also an Algerian), Arif spent time in al Qaeda training camps in the Pankisi Gorge region. The other recruits, however, do not appear to have had previous ties to earlier jihads, nor were they wanted by the authorities for criminal or terrorism offenses. Their volunteerism appears to have resulted from bloc recruitment by Maamri in his capacity as head of a local mosque.

Italy is home to other networks that send recruits to Iraq. These are linked to the AI movement. One of the key names to emerge in connection with AI in Italy and recruits to Iraq via Syria is Mohammed Majid, better known as Mullah Fouad. He was a member of the Islamic Movement in Kurdistan, from which some of the AI cadres emerged. It is reported that Mullah Fouad moved to Syria from Parma in 2002. Milan's Italian Division for General Investigations and Special Operations (DIGOS) monitored his phone conversations, which revealed his role in moving recruits from Europe to Syria on their way to Iraq. In one of the conversations with the Egyptian Islamist Al-Ayashi Radi (Merai), Mullah Fouad declared, "I want people trained in kidnapping and hijacking techniques" and expressed interest in enlisting suicide bombers.[36]

Another important person is the Algerian Shaykh Mahdjoub Abderrazak, who was living in Hamburg with his German wife. According to Italian authorities, he is one of the coordinators with AI in Italy. He sends recruits to Turkey before they make their way to Syria and, eventually, Iraq. Abderrazak arrived in Germany as a political asylum seeker in 1992, the year a military coup in Algeria erased the electoral victory of the Islamic Salvation Front. His asylum application was rejected, and so, like many second-generation jihadists, he went to train in Afghanistan and ended up fighting alongside the Muslim guerrillas in Chechnya. In 1999 he reentered Germany after marrying a German citizen. While in Hamburg, Abderrazak frequented the Al-Quds mosque led by Shaykh Al-Fazazi, an extremist cleric possibly connected to the Casablanca bombings.

Other people associated with recruitment for Iraq in Italy include the twenty-year-old Tunisian Jamal Housni (Jamal al-Maghrebi), a mechanic jailed for procuring forged documents and a cell phone for an AI member in Turkey. Others in the cell included Maher Bouyahia from Tunisia and Ali Ben Sassi (Ali the Tunisian).

According to an Italian intelligence analyst, the volunteers from Italy "are almost always … individuals trained ideologically and militarily in the training camps in Afghanistan, in Iraq, and in Somalia, and in the Horn of Africa, too."[37] Moreover, many were wanted on previous charges of terrorism or lesser crimes.

The story of Fadhal Saadi, a Tunisian suicide bomber from Italy, illustrates this point. Born in Haidra, Tunisia, on July 28, 1979, Saadi lived in Milan. In September 2001 he and his brother Nassim left Italy with a number of volunteers to fight in Afghanistan against the United States. At the end of the war in Afghanistan in late 2001, the Saadi brothers fled to Iran, where they were briefly arrested. Eventually they were allowed to return to Europe. In spring 2002 Italian authorities intercepted phone calls between the European cell and an individual in Malaysia named Umar Lhazazba (Abu Hani), who is connected to al Qaeda and implicated in the assassination of Shah Masud in Afghanistan in 2001. It was reported that while Fadhal Saadi was residing in France, he transferred two Italian driver's licenses, two residence permits, and two Tunisian passports forged in Naples to Abu Hani. In fall 2002 Saadi left France for Iraqi Kurdistan to join AI, apparently seeking to escape from Europe. U.S. air strikes forced Saadi and others to cross the border into Iran, where he was arrested once again. It is not clear how he managed to leave Iran the second time, but in July 2003 Saadi carried out a suicide attack in Iraq.

Two other suicide bombers from Italy exemplify the Afghanistan connection and the fear of being hunted down by European authorities. The first is Kamal Morchidi, a twenty-three-year-old Tunisian who lived legally in Italy. He died in a suicide attack on the al-Rashid Hotel in Baghdad, October 26, 2003, possibly targeting U.S. Deputy Defense Secretary Paul Wolfowitz. Like Saadi, Morchidi was seen in an al Qaeda training camp in Afghanistan in 2001 and was implicated in supplying forged documents to immigrants seeking access to Iraq. According to one report, "Italian documents including an 'identity card and a social security number,' as well as a photocopy of his Moroccan passport, were found in January 2004 in AI's Kurmal training camp in Iraqi Kurdistan."[38] Morchidi was wanted by the Italian authorities.

The second bomber was Habib Waddani (Said), also a Tunisian, who was living in Milan. He was wanted on charges of "trafficking weapons and explosives [for al Qaeda training camps] from Russia to Pakistan."[39] Monitored phone calls between his brother and his mother suggest that others in Milan knew of his operation and were proud of him. "Mother, here everyone admires and envies him. Everyone says they dream of him at night," his brother said. The caller went on to say that someone was offering the family 8,000 euros to compensate for "Said's martyrdom." [40]

CONCLUSION

These accounts of the European networks reveal that seemingly disparate individuals were connected by friendship, family, or activist ties. One cannot rely on press reports to derive the motivations of these volunteers in Iraq and their handlers, but it is apparent that many were connected to individuals who had prior experience in the ways and means of jihad. Not just any individual enraged by Muslim suffering can act on this rage. Connections to individuals who can mediate between those willing to die and those willing to dispatch suicide bombings are necessary.

Network ties are not sufficient, however, to explain why individuals volunteered to fight in Iraq. One can only speculate about what drove the young men and a woman to volunteer there. Perhaps some saw volunteerism in Iraq as an opportunity to engage in jihad when it was not possible to do so in their own countries. Images of Muslim suffering and humiliation, on one hand, and resistance and martyrdom, on the other, may have inspired some to join the Iraqi fray. Some may have felt hunted and no longer welcome in their home or host countries; others were marginal individuals drifting in life and associating with criminal elements, in need of a new path and an opportunity for redemption. Or perhaps these unwanted wanderers were seeking a world without borders, where their Muslim identity was the only passport they needed, and where their sacrifice would be the price for a new Islamic order that defends all Muslims, whoever they are and wherever they may be.

NOTES

1. OSC, "European Islamist Networks Flourish Despite Crackdown," July 16, 2005.

2. OSC, "Underground Network Feeds French, Other Islamic Fighters from Syria to Iraq," February 10, 2005.

3. Michael Evans, "How Britain and Iraq Are Linked by Death Route for Bombers," *Times* (London), June 22, 2005.

4. OSC, "Italian DNA Finding Identifies Al-Nasiriyah Bomber's Brother in Spanish Roundup," January 11, 2006.

5. Quintan Wiktorowicz, *Radical Islam Rising: Muslim Extremism in the West* (Lanham, Md.: Rowman and Littlefield, 2005), chapter 2.

6. Nezar Al Sayyad and Manuel Castells, eds., *Muslim Europe or Euro-Islam: Politics, Culture, and Citizenship in the Age of Globalization* (Lanham, Md.: Lexington Books, 2002); Jytte Klausen, *The Islamic Challenge: Politics and Religion in Western Europe* (New York: Oxford University Press, 2005).

7. Farhad Khosrokhavar, *Suicide Bombers: Allah's New Martyrs* (London: Pluto Press, 2005), 152–57.

8. Robert J. Pauly, Jr., *Islam in Europe: Integration or Marginalization?* (Burlington, Vt.: Ashgate Publishing, 2004).

9. Tariq Modood, *Multicultural Politics: Racism, Ethnicity, and Muslims in Britain* (Minneapolis: University of Minnesota Press, 2005), 7.

10. Gilles Kepel, *Allah in the West: Islamic Movements in America and Europe* (Oxford, U.K.: Polity, 1997), 233; see also Jocelyne Césari, *When Islam and*

Democracy Meet: Muslims in Europe and the United States (New York: Palgrave Macmillan, 2006).

11. Peter G. Mandaville, *Transnational Muslim Politics: Reimagining the Umma* (New York: Routledge, 2001); Olivier Roy, *Globalized Islam: The Search for a New Ummah* (New York: Columbia University Press, 2004).

12. Wiktorowicz, *Radical Islam Rising*, 22.

13. Peter Nesser, "Jihad in Europe: A Survey of the Motivations for Sunni Islamist Terrorism in Post-Millennium Europe," unclassified report FFI/RAPPORT-2004/01146, issued by Norwegian Defense Research Establishment, April 13, 2004; Javier Jordan and Luisa Boix, "Al-Qaeda and Western Islam," *Terrorism and Political Violence* 16 (Spring 2004): 1–17; Craig Whitlock, "Al-Qaeda's Far-Reaching New Partner: Salafist Group Finds Limited Appeal in Its Native Algeria," *Washington Post*, October 5, 2006.

14. Sageman, *Understanding Terror Networks*; Peter R. Neumann, "Europe's Jihadist Dilemma," *Survival* 48, no. 2 (Summer 2006): 71–84.

15. Olivier Roy, "Europe's Response to Radical Islam," *Current History* 104 (November 2005): 360–64; Neumann, "Europe's Jihadist Dilemma," 73.

16. Robert S. Leiken, "Europe's Angry Muslims," *Foreign Affairs* 84, no. 4 (July–August 2005): 120–26.

17. Mar Jimeno-Bulnes, "After September 11th: The Fight against Terrorism in National and European Law. Substantive and Procedural Rules: Some Examples," *European Law Journal* 10, no. 2 (2004): 235–53; Carl Levy, "The European Union after 9/11: The Demise of a Liberal Democratic Asylum Regime?" *Government and Opposition* 40, no. 1 (2005): 26–34.

18. Craig Whitlock, "How a Town Became a Terror Hub: Belgian Haven Seen at the Heart of Network," *Washington Post*, November 24, 2005; OSC, "Report Details Belgian Operations of Moroccan Islamic Group Terrorists," August 13, 2005; OSC, "Report Releases Details of Belgian Investigation into GICM Network," November 16, 2005.

19. His story is derived from Muhammed al-Ashhab, "European Networks for Smuggling Jihadists" (Arabic), *Al-Hayat* (London), February 11, 2005; Khaled al-Aayser, "The Dajlah Operation Breaks up a Network Connected to Zarqawi" (Arabic), *Azzaman* (London), June 19, 2005; Ahmed al-Arqam, "The Moroccan Judiciary Sentences to Prison Deportees from Syria on Their Way to Fight in Iraq" (Arabic), *Asharq al-Awsat* (London), July 2, 2005; Muhammed al-Ashhab, "Details Uncovered during Police Investigations in Rabat [Morocco] … European Cells Recruit Suicidal Moroccans and Send Them to Iraq" (Arabic), *Al-Hayat* (London), January 1, 2006.

20. OSC, "Report Details Belgium Operations of Moroccan Islamic Combatant Group Terrorists," August 13, 2005; OSC, "Belgium Trial Exposes Terror Suspects' Links with International Networks," November 22, 2005.

21. Javier Jordan and Nicola Horsburgh, "Mapping Jihadist Terrorism in Spain," *Studies in Conflict and Terrorism* 28 (2005): 169–91.

22. His story is derived from al-Ashhab, "European Networks for Smuggling Jihadists"; al-Aayser, "The Dajlah Operation Breaks up a Network Connected to Zarqawi"; al-Arqam, "The Moroccan Judiciary Sentences to Prison Deportees from Syria on Their Way to Fight in Iraq"; al-Ashhab, "Details Uncovered during Police Investigations in Rabat."

23. OSC, "Belgium Paper Identifies Woman Suicide Bomber Killed in Iraq," December 1, 2005.

24. OSC, "Belgium: Daily Provides Names, Contacts of Suicide Bomber Recruiter," December 2, 2005; OSC, "Belgium: Profile of Suspected Suicide Recruiter Bilal Soughir, Associates," March 10, 2006.

25. OSC, "Brussels Terror Trial Reveals Link between Moroccan GICM, Belgian Iraq Kamikazes," December 23, 2005.

26. The details of Mohammed Afalah's story are based on OSC, "Spanish Daily Details Role of Youssef Belhadj in Madrid Bomb Attack," February 28 2005; OSC, "Two Madrid Train Bombers Said to Have Died in Iraq," June 16, 2005; OSC, "UK Source Reports on Madrid Train Bomber Killed During Suicide Attack in Iraq," June 22, 2005.

27. OSC, "Belgian Terror Trial Suspect Reportedly Preparing Suicide Attack in Iraq," December 1, 2005.

28. Al-Ashhab, "European Networks for Smuggling Jihadists."

29. Scheherezade Faramarzi, "Leaving Slums of Paris, Two Muslim Teens Turn to Waging Jihad," *Associated Press*, November 27, 2004, www.ap.org.

30. Ibid.

31. OSC, "French Islamists Arrested Monday Linked to Iraqi Insurgency," January 26, 2005; OSC, "Members of French Islamist Group from Paris's 19th District Taken out of Action," February 4, 2005; OSC, "French Police Arrest Seven People Suspected of Sending Fighters to Iraq," June 24, 2005; OSC, "European Islamist Networks Flourish Despite Crackdown," July 16, 2005.

32. OSC, "French Intelligence Arrests Suspected Members of Cell Sending Jihadists to Iraq," May 4, 2005.

33. OSC, "European Islamist Networks Flourish Despite Crackdown."

34. See also OSC, "Islamist Cell Planned to Blow up Spanish-US Naval Base," March 23, 2005.

35. The following narrative on the Italian network is based on OSC, "Italy: Key Figure Arrested in Hamburg after Ansar al-Islam Cell Bust in Italy," November 30, 2003; OSC, "Italian Daily Reports on Mullah Fouad's Purported Involvement in Istanbul Attacks," December 8, 2003; OSC, "Norwegian Official on Report Ansar-al-Islam Recruiting Fighters for Iraq," December 18, 2003; OSC, "Italian Commentary Details Islamic Community in Milan, Cell Linked to Al-Qa`ida," June 16, 2004; OSC, "Florence's Sorgane Mosque Identified as Site of Recruitment Cell for Iraq-Bound Suicide Bombers," August 29, 2005.

36. OSC, "Italian Daily Reports on Mullah Fouad's Purported Involvement."

37. OSC, "Italian Intelligence Reveals 3 Suicide Terrorists in Iraq Came from Italy," July 16, 2005.

38. OSC, "Profile of Tunisian Extremist Fadhal Saadi, Associates," March 1, 2006.

39. OSC, "Italian Intelligence Reveals 3 Suicide Terrorists in Iraq Came from Italy."

40. OSC, "Profile of Tunisian Extremist Fadhal Saadi, Associates."

CHAPTER 8

IMPLICATIONS FOR THEORY AND POLICY

HOW TO EXPLAIN SUICIDE TERRORISM IN IRAQ?

What is the explanation for the rapid rise and pace of suicide terrorism in the Iraqi insurgency? How can we shed light on the number of non-Iraqis fighting and dying in Iraq? Why do some groups in the insurgency carry out suicide attacks while others do not?

Previous campaigns of suicide bombings in Lebanon, Sri Lanka, Israel, and elsewhere resulted in numerous studies that tried to explain why organizations deploy suicide bombers and why normal men and women are willing to strap explosives around their bodies and kill themselves to kill others. In the introduction I briefly discussed some of these studies. It is useful to assess to what extent they help explain suicide attacks in Iraq.

Four interpretations of this deadly phenomenon have been proffered: strategic logic, group competition, psychological trauma, and religious fanaticism. These theories fall short of convincingly explaining what is happening in Iraq. Although they explicate some aspects of the phenomenon, they fail to provide necessary and sufficient conditions for suicide terrorism at three levels of analysis: individual motivations to become martyrs, organizational motives to send suicide bombers, and societal motives to support suicide attacks.

SUICIDE TERRORISM AS A STRATEGY TO END OCCUPATION?

Professor Robert Pape of the University of Chicago contends in *Dying to Win* that suicide terrorism is a strategy. It is often part of a violent campaign against democracies with a military presence in territories claimed by the insurgents. Religion is a secondary factor in suicide attacks, Pape argues. He supports his claim by pointing out that secular nationalists, not religious fundamentalists, have carried out most suicide attacks, at least until the Iraqi campaign. Even the religious groups that employ human bombs, such as Hamas and al Qaeda, do so not because of religion but because of the presence of foreign militaries in their land.

Suicide terrorism is particularly effective against democracies, which are sensitive to high casualty rates. Terrorists may calculate that a wave of suicide attacks will raise the costs for the affected populace and force it to push its government to shift policies to end the violence directed at them. Hezbollah's attacks on American and French personnel in Lebanon in 1983, which resulted in the withdrawal of multinational forces from the region, are a classic example of how this tactic can work. Pape aptly expresses his view, "Modern suicide terrorism is best understood as an extreme strategy for national liberation against democracies with troops that pose an imminent threat to control of territory the terrorists view as their homeland."[1]

As for why individuals agree to become human bombs, Pape draws upon Emile Durkheim's sociological theory of "altruistic suicide."[2] Individuals who are highly integrated in their communities or societies will assume personal risks and even sacrifice their lives to end perceived injustices by outsiders. These communities provide the support network and social approval for martyrdom. If these highly integrated individuals were not in a situation of actual or perceived occupation, they would not commit suicide to kill their enemies.

Pape's argument about the strategic logic of suicide attacks appears, at first glance, to conform to the facts in Iraq. Suicide terrorism did not exist in Iraq before the U.S.-led coalition invaded. The correlation between suicide attacks and occupation is valid in Iraq, but correlation is not causation. The link between occupation and suicide attacks in Iraq is an apparent one. As my analysis shows, most suicide attacks in Iraq are directed not at foreign forces but at the security forces or civilian gathering places. Moreover, most of the attacks on Shia civilians are intended to spark a sectarian civil war and collapse an emerging political system, not to end the occupation.

Most damaging for Pape's argument is the fact that a large percentage, if not most, of the suicide bombers are not Iraqis. Although the insurgents are overwhelmingly Iraqi, the suicide bombers come from many parts of the Muslim world. So the use of this strategy cannot be seen merely as a product of a nationalist struggle to liberate land occupied by foreigners. To the extent foreign jihadists view Iraq as their land, it is because their religious worldview rejects nationalist borders and deems Muslim unity as the sole legitimate basis for identification and jihad. In this respect, religion matters.

Furthermore, since many suicide bombers have come from outside Iraq and as far away as Europe, one wonders what to make of the thesis that suicide bombers are altruists highly integrated into their occupied communities. The majority of the Shia and Kurds in Iraq, who constitute approximately 75 to 85 percent of the Iraqi population, do not view insurgents as their saviors, even if many want the coalition forces to leave their country. Even the Sunni nationalists who have a stake in driving the coalition forces out of Iraq have used suicide attacks sparingly. To be sure, the acquiescence of Sunni insurgents to suicide attacks in Iraq facilitates the movement of volunteers into the country, but it does not explain why non-Iraqis would volunteer in the first place.

One could argue that suicide attacks on Iraqi security forces and the government serve to hasten the departure of coalition forces. The Iraqi military and police serve as frontline soldiers for the multinational troops while the government gives the foreign presence legitimacy. The chaos in Iraq puts pressure on the democratic countries with forces there to expend more resources to stabilize the country, and this effort is likely to test the public's patience and increase calls among their citizens to end foreign entanglement. This scenario is exactly what is occurring in Iraq.

This explanation comes closer to reality than the previous one, but it is still insufficient. First, it does not explain why foreigners have taken it upon themselves to liberate Iraq. Second, it does not show why the majority faction in the insurgency, composed of Iraqi nationalists and Islamists, has not taken the lead in suicide terrorism. Third, groups such as AQI and ASG have made it clear that they see the struggle in Iraq as much bigger than merely ending the occupation; their goal is to install a "true" Islamic government to replace the "apostate" one currently in power. AQI has an additional goal of creating a base for regional and global jihad. The attacks on the existing regime are not intended merely as a circuitous way to exert pressure on the coalition forces; they are an end in themselves.[3]

SUICIDE TERRORISM AS A PRODUCT OF COMPETITIVE OUTBIDDING?

In the same year Pape published *Dying to Win*, Mia Bloom published *Dying to Kill*. In this study, Bloom gives primacy to factional competition in explaining suicide terror campaigns. She maintains that in insurgencies where numerous factions exist, suicide attacks could be used to increase the popularity of the groups carrying them out. Factions seeking to satisfy their constituency and maintain their market share of public support in a highly competitive field will employ this tactic repeatedly to outbid competitors. Bloom writes, "Under conditions of group competition, there are incentives for further groups to jump on the 'suicide bandwagon' and ramp up the violence in order to distinguish themselves from the other organizations."[4] To her credit, Bloom recognizes the myriad other factors that go into producing a campaign of suicide attacks, but nonetheless she gives factional competition tremendous weight in her explanatory schema.

Like Pape's argument, Bloom's competitive outbidding thesis does not appear to hold in Iraq. To be sure, the jihadi Salafis and Baathists who have engaged in most suicide attacks in Iraq are politically marginal and therefore need extraordinary tactics to influence the insurgency. However, their primary motivation is not to compete with other political factions. Their goal is to cause chaos and spark a sectarian civil war to collapse the political system and create an environment conducive to their survival.

Despite the proliferation of hundreds of groups in Iraq, these groups rarely appear to compete with one another. They often operate on their own turf (at least at the level of brigades) and show tremendous respect for one another in public statements. Many have claimed joint operations with potential competitors. Unlike in previous campaigns, different groups rarely issue claims of responsibility for the same operation, the most tangible indication of competition. To be sure, conflicting claims of responsibility occurred in the beginning of the insurgency and in some of the major operations; but given the thousands of operations that have taken place in Iraq, these conflicting claims are more an anomaly than a trend. The fact that most suicide attacks in Iraq remain unclaimed suggests that suicide bombings against civilians are a liability, not a way to raise a group's stock in a factional contest.

More damaging to Bloom's thesis is the fact that other groups have not taken up the tactic of suicide attacks in a consistent way to compete with AQI and some of the other groups that deploy suicide terrorism. Key to Bloom's escalatory dynamic is the diffusion of the tactic from one group to another. In the case of the Palestinians, the initial wave of suicide bombings by Hamas and Islamic Jihad prompted other secular groups, such as Al Aqsa Martyrs Brigades and the PFLP, to adopt this tactic. This contagion effect, generally speaking, has not taken place among the groups in Iraq.

TRAUMA AS AN EXPLANATION OF SUICIDE ATTACKS IN IRAQ?

A number of writers claim that psychological trauma is at the root of volunteerism for suicide attacks. In societies undergoing violent conflicts, personal trauma and bereavement create psychic pain that demands a response. Images of lost friends or family, experiences of humiliation, and the overwhelming weight of daily risks associated with living under violent conditions result in emotional suffering, survivor guilt, and loss of hope for a normal future. All these feelings lead some to seek an outlet in violence aimed at real and perceived enemies. Radical ideologies appeal to individuals seeking vengeance against those who have inflicted pain on them, their families, and their communities. Suicide bombings offer victims of psychological trauma a heroic way out of their misery and powerlessness. Not only do trauma victims end their suffering through an act of suicide, they also reverse the pain by inflicting it on the offending powers.[5]

This interpretation may, at best, shed light on why individuals become suicide bombers, but it does not explain why groups engage in this activity. Are organizations acting out of a feeling of trauma, or are they motivated by other factors, such as tactical effectiveness or strategic calculation? Chapter 2 on the jihadi Salafis showed that Zarqawi had a strategy in mind when he deployed suicide attacks in Iraq. The strategy may have arisen from deep-seated psychic pain, but that does not explain why so many other leaders around him went along with it.

Even at the level of individual volunteerism, the trauma theory is not completely convincing. Since most suicide bombers in Iraq are non-Iraqis, one is hard-pressed to see how they could have been traumatized by the conflict in Iraq. To the extent that images of Muslim suffering inspired them—which I believe to be largely the case—their trauma is based on cultural and religious identity, not direct physical oppression. This suggests that the notion of trauma must be broadened if we are to explain transnational martyrdom.

The fact that many of the known bombers participated in earlier jihads, had connections to experienced jihadists, or were escaping from their home or host countries suggests that trauma may not have been their primary motive to join the jihad in Iraq. It could well be that they were driven by ideological or friendship commitments more than psychic pain. Even if these individuals were traumatized by ongoing or earlier societal conflicts, they could have expressed their rage through other violent means. Yet they chose to carry out suicide attacks. Personal suffering does not naturally turn into terrorism. Individuals tend to attribute their pain to external causes or enemies. This process of attribution, however, does not usually take place in isolation from groups. Valued peers must identify personal suffering as a byproduct of "unjust authority" or some other deleterious condition to mobilize aggrieved individuals, especially when those individuals are far from the conflict zone.[6]

Moreover, many of the victims of suicide attacks in Iraq are not members of the coalition forces but defenseless Shia who could not have engaged in overt oppression of these suicidal warriors. To the extent that Shia militias engage in abductions, torture, and extrajudicial killings against ordinary Sunnis, this development is largely in response to earlier waves of suicide attacks and other forms of violence on Shia communities, not the cause of suicide terrorism against the Shia.

RELIGIOUS FANATICISM AND THE CULTURE OF MARTYRDOM AS AN EXPLANATION?

A popular Western view is that the Muslim world has a fatal enchantment with martyrdom. Religious fanaticism is one of the most common explanations of why individuals volunteer to become human bombs.[7] Basically this argument maintains that fundamentalist ideology and charismatic religious figures such as Hezbollah's Hassan Nasrallah or al Qaeda's Osama bin Laden sanction suicide attacks and promise volunteers eternal salvation in heaven, where they will reap many rewards, including heavenly maidens. These seemingly authoritative religious personalities selectively highlight texts and traditions that demand violent struggle against real and perceived enemies. In doing so, they present suicide attacks as a fulfillment of God's imperative and a vehicle to salvation and paradise.

Proponents of this perspective point out that many of the recent bombers—in Israel, Iraq, Chechnya, Pakistan, Afghanistan, and Europe— are religious fundamentalists with deep faith and Manichaean worldviews. Indeed, many justify their attacks by referring to Quranic passages and traditions that call for jihad and martyrdom in the path of God. Their religious framings have the dual effect of demonizing others to facilitate mass murder and motivating people to sacrifice themselves in the process. These fanatical groups use text, ritual, and ceremony to foster a cult of martyrdom that generates volunteers for suicide missions. Religious authorities legitimize their mayhem by issuing rulings (*fatwas*) that validate their murderous ideology.

In the case of Iraq, this theory appears to hold. Many of the known suicide bombers are said to be deeply religious people from jihadi Salafi networks. There are exceptions in Europe, but even there some of the bombers appear to have experienced a religious awakening before they became suicide bombers. The groups that deploy suicide attackers espouse the most virulent rhetoric rooted in religious discourse and mythologies. The attacks on the "heretical" Shia also can be explained by the fanaticism of the Salafi suicide bombers raised on Wahhabi doctrines. Even attacks on the Iraqi security forces and the foreign coalition are described as attacks on "apostates" and "crusaders." Finally, the fact that many of the suicide bombers are not Iraqis waging a strictly nationalist struggle, but foreigners coming from disparate locations to liberate a Muslim land, indicates that religion is a primary motivation.

Chapters 4 and 5 have shown that religious fanaticism is an important part of the motivation for suicide attacks. Yet, religious fanaticism is only part of the explanation in Iraq. First, many of the groups in Iraq espouse Islamist and even Salafi worldviews, yet only some of the Islamist factions engage in suicide attacks. Therefore, additional factors must help explain why some jihadists engage in suicide attacks while others do not. Moreover, although they are fewer in number, there have been Baathist suicide attackers. To be sure, their attacks were framed in religious terms, but it strains credulity to argue that these Baathists were genuine religious fanatics fighting in the path of God.

Second, even though the perpetrators appear to be overwhelmingly jihadi Salafis, it is not necessarily true that at the group level suicide attacks are carried out for religious reasons. Zarqawi's primary reason for engaging in suicide attacks in Iraq (as expressed in the captured document cited in chapter 2) was a desire to spark sectarian strife to drag the hesitant Sunni populations to the battlefield. His goal was worldly: to create conditions that would allow foreign jihadists to thrive in the heart of the Arab Muslim world after losing a valuable base in Afghanistan. Moreover, as chart 6 in chapter 3 shows, suicide attacks are timed to spoil political developments and exhibit resolve in the face of counterinsurgency operations. These are strategic choices that have little to do with religion.

Third, and perhaps most important, jihadi Salafis do not rely solely on religious rhetoric to appeal to the wider public or to justify their Muslim-on-Muslim violence. As previously shown, religious arguments tend to reach a narrow base of jihadists who may question the legitimacy of certain tactics or insurgent targets. The more salient appeals in Iraq interweave nationalistic and worldly discourse with religious notions and traditions. They also contain a large dose of shame to pique the masculine honor of fellow Arabs who fail to protect their women. The narratives concerning humiliation suffered by Muslims at the hands of foreigners, the collusion of Arab and Muslim governments with the West, and redemption through revenge and sacrifice are not strictly religious appeals. They are more nationalistic and chauvinistic.

Fourth, this theory does not explain why radical religious authorities gain a following in the first place. Since notions of jihad and martyrdom are contested concepts subject to competing interpretations, why have radical appeals been successful in mobilizing people to fight and die in Iraq? Is the charisma of fanatical leaders sufficient to convince young people to make the ultimate sacrifice, or must additional factors operate, such as links to radical networks, opportunities and resources for mobilization, and external state support? Is the success of the religious fanatics strictly related to their persuasive capacity, or is the political environment a crucial determinant of the credibility of their appeals? I have tried to show throughout this book that the resonance of the jihadi message is intricately linked to new political environments and ties to activist networks. Fanatical religious ideologies alone are not sufficient to move people from inaction to martyrdom.

There can be little doubt that religious appeals play an important part in inspiring many of the suicide bombers in Iraq, but the causal link between religious inspiration and suicide attacks is not a direct one. The weight of religious appeals in the explanatory schema can be assessed only by placing those appeals in the broader context of societal conflicts, social networks, and security environments.

A SOCIAL MOVEMENT THEORY OF SUICIDE TERRORISM IN IRAQ

In previous investigations of Palestinian suicide bombers, I argued that suicide terrorism is a complex phenomenon that must be studied at three levels of analysis: individual motivations, organizational strategies, and societal conflicts.[8] It is not possible to understand the rise, pace, and scope of suicide attacks in any conflict without looking at how these three levels interact. Furthermore, in the introduction I presented several concepts that came out of research on social movements: political opportunity structures, strategic framing, mobilization structures, and repertoires of action, modularity, and diffusion. These concepts have reappeared explicitly or implicitly throughout the book, but it is worthwhile to stress their importance in explaining suicide terrorism in Iraq as they relate to each level of analysis.

SOCIETAL CONFLICTS AS POLITICAL OPPORTUNITIES FOR MOBILIZING TRANSNATIONAL MARTYRS

Although non-Iraqis carry out most suicide attacks in Iraq, the new political opportunity structure in the Iraqi polity in 2003 created conditions for the rise of transnational martyrs. Suicide terrorism in Iraq emerged in the context of major external shocks and internal crises associated with rapid regime change, mass disenfranchisement and dislocation, and collective resentment associated with sectarian grievances.

Reversal of centuries of Shia-Kurdish marginalization virtually overnight guaranteed that Sunni Arab communities would harbor grievances against the new Iraqi regime, even in the best of circumstances. The dismissal of the Iraqi army and de-Baathification following the occupation of Iraq created fertile soil for insurgent recruitment. Rapid political change and a relatively weak security structure created political opportunities for transnational mobilization and rebellion. The lack of sufficient coalition troops and the delay in raising a new Iraqi security force meant that insurgents could move across Iraq's open borders and gain access to the arms caches left behind by the former regime. This mix of Sunni grievances, weak security structures, and available resources for insurgents made insurgency possible. In turn, insurgency created space for global jihadists to mobilize their cadres. Although many of the dismissed soldiers and former Baathists might not have engaged in suicide attacks, they certainly were not going to stand in the way of those who did against a government they deemed illegitimate and threatening to their interests. All indications suggest that they benefit from having an extremist flank that can preoccupy the coalition forces and new Iraqi government while the nationalist insurgency thrives.

But why would foreign jihadists make their way to Iraq in the first place? Second-generation global jihadists were threatened by the new security environment created by the war on terrorism. They lost their bases in Afghanistan, their state ally in Pakistan, and a hospitable environment in Europe. The one-two punch of tightening security and removal of a safe haven for transnational Islamic militants could have destroyed al Qaeda as an organization, but then came the invasion of Iraq: *deus ex machina.*

Islamists who were feeling hunted and in urgent need of a new haven found in Iraq the ideal situation. Not only was the country accessible through several bordering states, but some of them, such as Syria and Iran, had an interest in spoiling America's agenda in Iraq. At least initially, these states allowed the migration of fleeing militants and new volunteers into Iraq. Moreover, in the eyes of much of the Muslim world, the invasion of Iraq was an unjustifiable aggression to serve Israel and plunder Iraq's oil resources. Jihad in Iraq was seen as defensive and not much different from the jihad waged two decades earlier in Afghanistan. Jihadists before 9/11 might have quarreled over whether to attack the near enemy (their own governments) or the far enemy (the United States). In Iraq, the far enemy became the near enemy; the issue was no longer debatable.

The political and security situation in Iraq presented an opportunity for Islamic nationalists, ideological Baathists, and jihadi Salafis, who stepped into the fray to promote their own political agendas. My major finding is that groups that cannot compete in Iraq's new coalition politics are the ones carrying out suicide attacks. Suicide terrorism is intended to produce system collapse, sectarian warfare, and a failed state. For former Baathists who sponsor or engage in suicide attacks, their widespread unpopularity guarantees marginality in the political process. Jihadi Salafis' rigid ideological outlook, which resembles that of the Taliban regime in Afghanistan, is not likely to win over a historically secular Iraq with a Shia majority.

Both these factions have an interest in creating a failed state in Iraq. The jihadi Salafis in particular are counting on armed lawlessness and ethnosectarian schisms similar to those in Afghanistan after the departure of Soviet troops in 1989. Political chaos allows the jihadi Salafis to position themselves as the protectors of Sunni Iraq. A victory in Iraq not only would ensure their survival, it would provide them with a new base in the heart of the Arab world and coveted strategic presence near the oil-rich Gulf region and religiously significant Saudi Arabia. Above all, they would have the symbolic victory over the only remaining superpower in the world after overcoming the second superpower more than a decade earlier in Afghanistan.

The jihadist informal networks were instrumental in mobilizing the transnational martyrs. Many of the countries that contributed suicide bombers to Iraq had activists who were part of the jihadi Salafi movement and had participated in the training camps of Afghanistan during the 1990s. Even those who appear to have been newcomers to jihad were connected to experienced jihadists. Without these preexisting networks, mobilization would have been difficult and would have taken some time to develop.

THE STRATEGIC FRAMING OF MARTYRDOM

Beyond the activist cadres, what explains the phenomenon of volunteers going to fight and die in Iraq? Jihadists in Iraq strategically exploit social, religious, cultural, and political symbols to appeal to wider audiences beyond their core constituencies. They make conscious efforts to legitimate and motivate collective action. They use religion and culture as tool kits, selecting narratives, traditions, and symbols to infuse risky activism and self-sacrifice with morality.

Jihadists in Iraq use a variety of instrumental, ideological, and theological claims to demonize their targets, heighten the sense of threat among Sunnis in Iraq and Muslims around the world, and deactivate self-inhibiting norms against killing civilians and fellow Muslims. However, it is their emotional appeals that reach the hearts and minds of ordinary Muslims around the world and cut across ideological lines. In particular, the jihadists tell a grand narrative of humiliation at the hands of foreigners and unbelievers and betrayal by governments that repeatedly let Muslims down. Such masterful framing of the conflict in Iraq is intended to shame the passive bystander and call into question his masculinity and honor. The only way to erase the shame is by redeeming himself and the nation through sacrifice on the battlefield.

Jihadists in Iraq are aware of the symbolic universe that shapes the imagination of Arabs and Muslims. They know which chords to strike to incite ordinary people to righteous indignation. The uninterrupted series of defeats against Israel, Iraq's humiliation in the Gulf War, the rapid fall of Baghdad in 2003, the suffering of the Palestinian people in the Aqsa uprising, and the humiliating torture of prisoners in Abu Ghraib are just some of the symbols in their ideological arsenal. They marshal these images and sentiments effectively to show that the war on terrorism is a war on Islam, and that victory in Iraq would be a victory for all Muslims.

Jihadists in Iraq interweave these themes, texts, and symbols to present martyrdom as an act of redemption, empowerment, and defiance against unjust authorities. This is an opportunity to fulfill an obligation to God, sacrifice for the nation, and avenge a humiliated people. These religious and emotional appeals have led some Muslims around the world to accept the urgings of recruiters or make a personal effort to join the struggle in Iraq through preexisting group ties. At a minimum, these religious and emotional pleas have provided the rationale for individuals with other conscious or subconscious motivations to engage in violent activism.

CONTENTION, MODULARITY, AND THE DIFFUSION OF SUICIDE ATTACKS

Why did the transnational jihadists adopt the tactic of suicide terrorism? Why did they not rely on the use of conventional warfare like many of their nationalist counterparts? First-generation jihadists in Afghanistan did not adopt suicide attacks, so why did second-generation militants embrace this form of self-sacrifice? Suicide attacks have become a form of resistance that is both effective and culturally venerated. In other words, the appeal of martyrdom lies not just in its efficacy, but also in its perceived normative value. The conflicts in Lebanon and Palestine and the use of suicide attacks in those arenas gave martyrdom special legitimacy in the Muslim world. Religious scholars have insisted that these actions are genuine forms of jihad and devotion to the faith. The Muslim public supported them because they served as an "equalizing weapon" in the face of "arrogant" powers and demonstrated Muslim loyalty and sacrifice when governments were viewed as impotent collaborators. Jihadists in Iraq took advantage of this normative environment and drew on the texts, arguments, and symbolism of earlier suicide attackers.

More important, the notion of martyrdom in the Muslim world has proven to be exceptionally ductile; it can be reshaped and applied in different contexts without losing its underlying legitimacy in the public's eye. Initially suicide attacks were deemed legitimate only against powerful armies occupying Muslim lands. This justification served militants interested in attacking Israeli and multinational forces in Lebanon during the 1980s and 1990s. The Palestinians later expanded the category of "legitimate martyrdom" to include attacks on Israeli civilians. Next bin Laden's al Qaeda expanded the use of this form of martyrdom to attack American and Jewish civilians all over the world, setting the stage for the 9/11 attacks. It did not take long for affiliates of al Qaeda to legitimate suicide attacks against tourists (in Egypt and Indonesia), "apostate regimes" (in Saudi Arabia, Iraq, Bangladesh, and Afghanistan), "Shia heretics" (in Pakistan and Iraq), "Sunni collaborators" (in Iraq and Afghanistan), and even ordinary Muslims who might be victims of collateral damage (in all those countries).[9]

The diffusion of this tactic is linked not only to the normative context, but also to relational and nonrelational ties. Second-generation jihadists who trained in Afghanistan picked it up from al Qaeda during the second half of the 1990s. In addition to teaching advanced courses in manufacturing explosives and building car bombs in its training camps, al Qaeda and its affiliates became known for simultaneous mass-casualty attacks using suicide bombers on 9/11, in the Bali bombings of 2002, and in the Casablanca bombings of 2003. Before 9/11 al Qaeda promoted suicide attacks, including the Kenya and Tanzania embassy bombings in 1998 and the attack on the USS *Cole* in Yemen in 2000, in its literature and multimedia productions. When al Qaeda and its affiliates lost their base in Afghanistan, they distributed their training manuals, including the infamous *Encyclopedia of Jihad*, online for all would-be jihadists to see.[10]

Therefore, by the time the insurgency developed in Iraq, suicide attacks had become modular, diffused, and normatively accepted. It did not require great imagination to apply this tactic in the Iraqi context. Although the tactic has remained the same, however, its strategic use has altered substantially. Deployed by nationalist insurgents in the 1980s and 1990s to coerce foreign powers to abandon territory they deemed important, since 2003 it has become jihadists' tool to spark sectarian violence and collapse an emerging democratic order. Suicide bombing may be jihadi Salafis' greatest innovation in Iraq.

THE LIMITS OF COUNTERING SUICIDE TERRORISM IN IRAQ

Coalition forces, along with the emerging Iraqi security services, have failed to contain the insurgency in general and suicide terrorism in particular. Suicide attacks do not appear to be abating. Counterinsurgency has gone through three phases. In phase 1 (from April 2003, when the Baathist regime fell, to mid-2004), coalition forces viewed the insurgents as illegitimate "dead-enders" and Saddam loyalists seeking to retain power by whatever means they could. The authorities did not perceive, or at least did not acknowledge, the widespread grievances gripping the dismissed military personnel, the tribes in central Iraq, and the nominal Baathists who were not loyal to the former regime.

Therefore, the first phase of counterinsurgency concentrated on the tactical elimination of insurgents in rebellious towns such as Fallujah and other "pockets of resistance." In this phase coalition forces and the war planners within the U.S. administration underestimated the insurgents. Critical mistakes, such as the failure to secure arms depots, resulted. Other mistakes stemmed from the lack of sufficient troops to control daily looting and crime, secure the abandoned bases and arsenals of the former regime, protect reconstruction projects, establish the new Iraqi security forces, and overwhelm the insurgents. These mistakes were rooted in the preconceived notion that Iraqis would welcome the invading coalition forces with open arms.[11]

In phase 1 the United States exerted pressure on neighboring countries, especially Syria, to monitor their borders with Iraq, halt the flow of volunteers into the country, and arrest and hand over former Baathist officials who were financing the insurgency from outside Iraq. These measures produced limited success, as Syria and Saudi Arabia did make efforts to stop the flow of volunteers into Iraq. But after a while it became obvious that the extensive border between Syria and Iraq could not be sealed, even with the best-intentioned efforts. Therefore, further pressure on neighboring states to halt the insurgency in Iraq is not likely to bear fruit.

Phase 2 (from mid-2004 to the second half of 2005) began with the recognition that the overwhelming majority of insurgents were not Saddam loyalists, but disgruntled Sunnis with some legitimate grievances. Coalition forces combined tactical military measures with strategic political initiatives to extend a hand to representatives of the Sunni communities and tribes in Iraq. The coalition forces hoped political inclusion might entice the Sunni insurgents to put down their arms and negotiate new political alignments.[12] Unfortunately, extending a hand to the Sunnis did not halt the insurgency, nor did it diminish the rate of suicide bombings. As indicated previously, major political and institutional developments caused a spike in suicide terrorism, not a drop in attacks.

Groups that might entertain the idea of participating in the political process—the Islamic nationalist factions—are not the ones that deploy suicide bombers. Rather, the politically marginalized use suicide attacks. Institutional inclusion is not attractive to them because they are not likely to garner mass political support. They are more likely to use suicide attacks to sabotage any potential rapprochement between Sunni and Shia factions in Iraq. As for the Islamic nationalists, they believe that time and the current balance of forces favor their strategy of continuing insurgency. They want recognition from the coalition forces that they are the sole legitimate representatives of the Iraqi people and any negotiations for the withdrawal of coalition forces must be conducted through them, not the current government.

In phase 2 practical measures of target hardening and situational awareness by U.S. personnel in the field helped shift suicide attacks away from U.S. forces. Intelligence tips by Iraqis and interrogation of captured insurgents also helped foil some attacks, eliminate "factories" producing car bombs, and capture potential suicide bombers. However, as the rate and pace of suicide attacks indicate, much more is needed to overcome suicide bombers in Iraq.

Defensive measures in phase 2 combined with major offensive counterinsurgency operations. However, they have not produced a long-term decrease in suicide attacks, either. On the contrary, counterinsurgency operations usually result in a spike in such attacks, followed by a return to previous levels of suicide bombings. Part of the difficulty is that counter-insurgency operations usually sweep into towns and subsequently move on to the next theater of battle, leaving the swept town open for insurgents to return. Under these circumstances, it becomes difficult to assure the Iraqi inhabitants that they will be protected if they cooperate with the coalition and Iraqi security forces.

Phase 3 of the insurgency (starting in late 2005) maintained all the elements of phase 2 but added five components. First, Iraqi forces have been given the responsibility of leading some counterinsurgency operations to test their mettle, but more are interspersed with coalition forces to give them side-by-side experience in counterinsurgency strategies and tactics.

Second, U.S. forces have given more emphasis to bridging the cultural gap with the Iraqi people to reduce unnecessary friction during counter-insurgency operations, remove some incentives to join the insurgency, and possibly gain the cooperation of ordinary Iraqis in providing tips about insurgent activities.[13]

Third, coalition forces have begun to pressure the interior ministry to bring the Shia militias in its apparatus under tighter control and stop them from engaging in abductions, torture, and extrajudicial killings.[14]

Fourth, the United States is making an extra effort to incorporate Sunnis into the new security services, placate the insurgents who might have joined the insurgency because they were dismissed from their jobs, and answer Sunni criticism that the new security services are an arm of Shia and Kurdish dominance. The presence of Sunnis in the security forces is intended to constrain the Shia and Kurdish militias from engaging in extrajudicial "justice."[15]

All these measures, unfortunately, have not ended the insurgency or halted sectarian killings. Observers note that internal displacement of Iraqis is on the rise because of sectarian violence. As of July 2006, approximately 162,000 refugees had registered with the Ministry of Migration since February 22, 2006, when Sunni insurgents affiliated with AQI blew up the Askari mosque, a revered Shia shrine in the town of Samarra.[16] Insurgents and militias increasingly are purging Baghdad neighborhoods along sectarian lines. Some inhabitants are killed, others are given notice to leave under the threat of death, and some have simply picked up and left. As a result, some neighborhoods in Baghdad are turning into sectarian enclaves, which may set the stage for future conflict and ethnic cleansing. This development helps explain the recent emphasis by the new Iraqi government and the United States on protecting the city in what Zalmay Khalilzad, the U.S. ambassador to Iraq, has labeled "the battle of Baghdad."[17]

Iraqis are turning increasingly to sectarian militias for protection because of the new Iraqi government's inability to offer its citizens basic security and protection from insurgents and death squads.[18] Many Iraqis are no longer praying in their mosques for fear of sectarian attacks.[19] And in a tragicomic turn of events, Iraqis are learning to hide their identity to avoid being killed in cold blood by insurgents, militias, or death squads of the opposite sect. Sunnis are learning the names of the twelve imams revered by the Shia. The Shia are adopting names such as Umar and Uthman (two of the three Islamic caliphs rejected by Shia as usurpers of power following the death of the Prophet Muhammad).[20]

The last component of the third counterinsurgency phase is perhaps the most strategic. Coalition forces have been seeking to exploit potential rifts between the Sunni nationalists and jihadi Salafis to divide and conquer.[21] As early as 2004 many Iraqi nationalists sympathetic to the insurgency were repulsed by the excesses of AQI.[22] Indiscriminate attacks have harmed not only Shia but also many Sunnis because of Shia retaliation. Furthermore, Zarqawi's faction killed many Sunnis seeking to integrate into the new Iraqi regime. In return, members from forty tribes formed the Anbar Salvation Council to resist the foreign fighters. They receive material and military support from the government to fight the "takfirs" in their province. A group calling itself the Anbar Revenge Brigade claimed responsibility for killing several AQI and ASG commanders in March 2006.[23]

At least three episodes turned nationalists and tribes against AQI. The first was the assassination of Sheikh Hikmat Mumtaz al-Bazi, head of the Samarra tribal council, after he met with Defense Minister Saadun al-Dulymi. The second was an attack by Zarqawi's group on a Ramadi police recruitment center that was recruiting Sunnis. The third was the assassination of the Sunni Sheikh Kamal al-Nazzal, the head of the local council in Fallujah. He opposed the new constitution and supported the insurgency but also opposed Zarqawi and fought against him. Zarqawi's formation of the Mujahidin Shura Council (MSC), headed by Abdullah Rashid al-Baghdadi (an Iraqi), was an attempt to deal with these growing rifts.[24]

Greater pressure on the jihadi Salafis by local tribes has not been sufficient to induce the Salafis to halt their suicide attacks against Iraqi citizens. So far some of the major groups within the Islamic nationalist faction, including the IAI, have not found it necessary to criticize their "brothers" in AQI or ASG for using suicide attacks. The nationalist faction does not consider it in its interest to stop attacks on Iraqi security forces and civilians. It denies the legitimacy of the new government that formed in June 2006 and declined its offer for national reconciliation and amnesty.[25] Moreover, Abu Hamza al-Muhajir, AQI's new leader after the death of Zarqawi, has threatened to attack the tribal chiefs who cooperate with the new Iraqi government.[26]

Keeping the existing government and the coalition forces preoccupied with extremists takes the military pressure off the nationalist insurgents. Furthermore, the nationalists could benefit from having a radical flank. It would establish them as the potential moderate interlocutors if they chose to negotiate with the government or coalition forces. The jihadi Salafis are politically marginal in Iraq, so they pose little threat or challenge to the legitimacy of the Islamic nationalist faction. Therefore, the nationalists have little incentive to constrain the extreme jihadists.

One strategy for countering suicide terrorism has yet to be fully explored. It entails addressing the mythology of martyrdom that is necessary to legitimate suicide attacks. The ideology and tactics of jihadi Salafis make them vulnerable to counter-appeals. First of all, jihadi Salafis kill more Muslims than foreign forces. This is the case not only in Iraq but also in Algeria, Saudi Arabia, Pakistan, Jordan, Morocco, and Indonesia. Furthermore, their anti-Shia rhetoric polarizes the Muslim nation and creates dissension (*fitna*) among the faithful, which could benefit potential enemies seeking to exploit Muslim divisions. Their anti-Shia violence also produces a violent backlash that endangers Sunni communities. The civil war in Iraq is killing thousands of Sunnis because of the provocations of the extreme Salafis. Suicide bombings against the Shia are forcing their communities to turn to militias and death squads for protection and retaliation against the Sunnis. Finally, when the jihadi Salafis come to power or control territory, they impose rules that alienate many Muslims. These include prohibitions on watching television, listening to music, or mixing the sexes. They force men to grow beards and women to wear the *hijab* (head cover). Many Muslims are willing to support the radicals because they strike at foreign enemies, but they are not likely to embrace their rigid ideology and oppressive form of Islam.

Strategies and tactics for countering the mythology of martyrdom cannot be fully explored here. I can say in this context that jihadists are astute cultural agents who know how to frame and segment their messages to appeal to multiple audiences. Their theological and ideological messages appeal to core activists in Islamic movements who may need additional encouragement and justification for joining the jihad in Iraq; their emotional messages target Muslim publics in general and are rooted in nationalistic and even chauvinistic themes that appeal to nonreligious activists. Countering their appeal, therefore, requires counterinsurgents to develop their cultural awareness of Muslim societies and understand the grievances that animate them. This cultural knowledge must go beyond understanding their languages and religions; it must also encompass knowledge of their history, politics, and conflicts that underpin the culture of martyrdom. Only then will counterinsurgents be able to create credible, moderate messages that resonate in the Muslim world. Multinational forces alone cannot achieve such an undertaking; Muslim governments and leaders must contribute to the effort to eradicate the pernicious ideology of jihadi Salafism.

THIRD-GENERATION JIHADISTS AND THE FUTURE OF TRANSNATIONAL MARTYRDOM

The devastating blow delivered to al Qaeda in Afghanistan in late 2001 destroyed the centralized and hierarchical aspects of its organization, but it did not eliminate its geographic reach through preexisting networks or damage the idea of al Qaeda as an ideological movement that represents the grievances of Muslims against their own governments, Israel, and U.S. foreign policy in the Middle East. To be sure, the global jihadist movement has to proceed without an overarching organization capable of extending a helping hand with leadership, resources, and operatives. Al Qaeda's ideologues are seeking to survive by forging a loosely structured social movement with diffused leadership, amorphous networks, and a unifying ideology that promotes the myth of a "crusader-Zionist conspiracy" to undermine Islam, divide Muslims, and control their resources. Their message is rooted more in popular anti-U.S. sentiment than in a positive strategy for advancing the well-being of Muslims around the world.

The transformation of al Qaeda into a fragmented and multiheaded social movement has its origins in its earlier efforts to develop a transnational strategy linking local struggles of Islamists against their own governments with a broader movement of global jihad against what they consider "the head of the snake" or the "crusader-Zionist alliance against Islam." This strategy involved ideologically co-opting disparate jihadist groups, sharing intelligence and encouraging regional networking among militants, and allocating resources to hot spots to fan the flames of revolutionary Islamism. In the age of globalization, al Qaeda sought to transcend the boundaries of the nation-state by globalizing terror.

Social movements, whether national or global, require political opportunities, resource mobilization structures, and ideological appeals to grow and persist. The insurgency in Iraq and its outcome might generate the necessary opportunities, networks, and ideological frameworks for the revival of al Qaeda as a movement of global jihad. The war in Iraq has already inspired groups and cells to take action far beyond the conflict zone, as witnessed in the March 11, 2004, train bombings in Madrid; the July 7, 2005, suicide bombings in London; and the November 9, 2005, suicide attacks in Amman.[27]

To understand how the war in Iraq is central to the future of al Qaeda and the creation of the third generation of jihadists, it is important to look at the historical developments that gave rise to al Qaeda in the first place. Understanding this history reveals how al Qaeda's second-generation jihadists coalesced during the 1990s by exploiting political opportunities, mobilization structures, and ideological frameworks. This history might be repeating itself before our eyes.

Al Qaeda emerged initially and grew into a major force through four developments that were never completely under its control. The first was the defeat of the Soviet Union in Afghanistan because of the resistance of the Afghan mujahidin, aided, in small part, by Arab volunteers from various parts of the Middle East and North Africa. This victory was the second major experiential milestone that confirmed to Muslims around the world that resistance and rebellion by weaker groups committed to their faith could topple powerful adversaries despite the apparent odds; the first was the 1979 Iranian revolution led by Ayatollah Khomeini against the

U.S.-backed shah. This victory gave jihadists the symbolic capital neces-sary for recruiting and motivating future cadres for jihad.

The second factor contributing to the rise of al Qaeda during the 1990s was the presence of U.S. forces in Saudi Arabia following the Iraqi invasion of Kuwait in 1990. The United States led a multinational coali-tion of both Western and Arab forces against Iraq. Following the libera-tion of Kuwait in 1991, the United States maintained forces in the Arabian Peninsula to deter Saddam Hussein from embarking on another attack on his neighbors. The presence of U.S. forces near the holiest sites of Islam (Mecca and Medina) angered many traditionally minded Saudis and gave rise to internal critiques of the Saudi monarchy and its close alliance with the United States. The Saudi ruling family dealt with this criticism as it does with all other political challenges: It repressed the opposition and threw many in jail.[28] Osama bin Laden was forced into permanent exile when the Saudi government revoked his citizenship after he refused to cease giving advice to the ruling monarchs. Failure to alter policies in Saudi Arabia through peaceful means gave bin Laden the *casus belli* to wage war on the Saudi regime. Additional pressure by the Saudis and the United States to drive bin Laden from the Sudan in the mid-1990s solidi-fied his anger against Saudi Arabia and its U.S. backer. Perhaps at this juncture bin Laden began to view war on the United States as a necessary prelude to toppling the Saudi regime; the road to Mecca goes through Washington, he must have thought.

Also contributing to the rise of al Qaeda during the 1990s was the failure of Islamist insurgencies around the Muslim world. The 1980s and 1990s witnessed Islamic rebellions and violence in many countries and almost every region, including Algeria, Chechnya, Egypt, Indonesia, Iraq, Kashmir, the occupied Palestinian territories, the southern Philippines, and Tajikistan. In many of these countries, armed Islamists went on the offensive after being excluded from the political process and violently per-secuted by secular governments. Others rebelled out of a sense of ethno-religious nationalism. Had some of these insurgencies succeeded, Islamist movements would have viewed the strategy of rebellion against the near enemy (as opposed to attacking the United States and other Western pow-ers) as effective, thus negating the need to turn against the far enemy that presumably props up these regimes.[29]

Osama bin Laden benefited from these failures in three ways. First, many of the experienced leaders and cadres of these insurgencies were driven into exile because they could no longer sustain insurgency in their home countries. Given their radicalism, not many countries were willing to welcome them; Europe, Pakistan, and Afghanistan were notable exceptions. Those who went to Afghanistan fell into the hands of bin Laden, who set up training camps for his impending global jihad.[30]

Second, many of those foiled insurgents were now open to new ideas and strategies for confronting their home governments. Dependent on their rich benefactor, they were amenable to engaging in global jihad against Western powers that had not opposed their persecution and might even have welcomed it.

Third, Osama bin Laden adopted the disparate causes of Muslim insurgents, from Algeria to the Philippines, by turning these causes into one big struggle against "apostate" regimes that do the bidding of their Western "masters." The rebel without a cause now had several he could champion in the name of Islam.

Also contributing to the consolidation of al Qaeda during the 1990s was the rise of the Taliban regime in Afghanistan. After years of factional fighting and lawlessness in Afghanistan, the Taliban, backed by Pakistani security services, swept to power and subdued many of the factions that had wreaked havoc in the impoverished Central Asian state. The ultra-traditional Taliban benefited from the largesse of bin Laden; the latter, in turn, benefited from their acquiescence in placing jihadi training camps in their territory.[31] Without such a haven, insurgents from around the world would not have been able to train, acquire expertise in explosives and other valuable skills for jihad, and plan operations against their home governments and Western states.

Victory over the Soviets in Afghanistan, the U.S. presence in Saudi Arabia, failed insurgencies in Muslim states, and the rise of the Taliban regime in Afghanistan presented second-generation jihadists with the political opportunity, mobilization networks, and ideological appeal necessary for their survival.

The insurgency in Iraq might well replicate the conditions necessary for the emergence of the third generation of global jihadists. First, the mere fact that the United States, the only remaining superpower in the world, is publicly discussing the need for an exit strategy from Iraq is palpable confirmation that jihad and martyrdom by a few committed jihadists can bring a powerful adversary to its knees. Just as the defeat of the Soviets empowered the second generation of jihadists during the 1990s,

U.S. travails in Iraq guarantee that third-generation jihadists will seek to inspire future recruits by pointing to this victory in the opening decade of the new millennium.

Second, the success of jihadists in Iraq could result in the replication of their martyrdom strategy in other struggles around the globe, not just those in the Middle East or the Muslim world. The successful use of this tactic by Hezbollah in Lebanon in the early 1980s served as a model of violence for secular nationalist factions in that country and as far away as Sri Lanka, where the Tamil Tigers have used it more than 200 times since 1987. Hezbollah's apparent success in driving Israel out of southern Lebanon in May 2000 through resistance and suicide attacks directly influenced the thinking of the Palestinian factions across the border, leading them to value militancy over negotiations during the Aqsa uprising that began in September 2000. In light of Hezbollah's "victory" in southern Lebanon in 2000 and the failure of the Palestinian Authority to extract the necessary concessions to establish a viable Palestinian state in the July 2000 final-status negotiations with Israel, Hamas presented violent insurgency as the optimal strategy to force the Israelis to leave Palestinian lands. The use of suicide attacks by Hamas and Islamic Jihad, and their initial success in terrorizing Israeli society, played an important role in encouraging secular factions such as Al Aqsa Martyrs Brigades and the PFLP to take up this tactic.

The success of IEDs, suicide bombings, and televised beheadings in Iraq has resulted in the diffusion of those tactics to Saudi Arabia and Afghanistan. Before the war in Iraq, Saudi Arabia had never witnessed televised beheadings of hostages (although the state regularly engages in public beheadings of criminals, deviants, and terrorists). After TWJ used this tactic in May 2004 on the twenty-six-year-old U.S. national Nicholas Berg, Saudi terrorists televised the beheading of Paul Johnson Jr., a forty-nine-year-old U.S. citizen employed by Lockheed Martin Corporation in Riyadh. Similarly, before the war in Iraq, suicide bombings and IED detonations were rare in Afghanistan. However, it did not take long for those tactics to become a regular occurrence there.[32]

Third, the cycle of violence against Shia civilians and Iraqi security forces has important strategic consequences for the U.S.-led coalition in Iraq. The tit-for-tat violence is likely to hinder rapprochement between Shia and Sunni political parties, and thus the goal of promoting stability and democracy in Iraq through an inclusive political process is in jeopardy.

The inability to foster a stable and democratic Iraq empowers authoritarian regimes in the Middle East region and allows them to argue that security and stability take priority over political inclusion, human rights, and good governance. Yet repression may quell Islamist violence in one place but push it into other vulnerable arenas. Many of the groups that constituted al Qaeda's network during the 1990s were defeated in their home countries and forced to seek other outlets for their violence. Many repressed Islamists reemerged in newly constituted transnational networks, such as the Jordanian and Belgian-Spanish networks, with more radical ideologies and tactical repertoires. Muslim regimes may defeat their own Islamist dissidents, but they have not been able to stop—indeed, their repression has facilitated—the spread of violence, as the world tragically witnessed on 9/11.

Fourth, the inability of coalition forces and the new Iraqi regime to quell the insurgency means that potential global jihadists and dissidents from near and far have an arena in which to fight their first jihad and acquire the skills necessary for future struggles or operations. Iraq could become the field of dreams for jihadists seeking training, expertise, and experience in the ways and means of terrorism and guerrilla warfare. These youngsters will carry the torch of global jihad from the hands of the second generation that developed in Afghanistan during the 1990s. The presence of true believers and opportunists in the insurgency guarantees that the novices will have access to leaders, networks, weapons, training camps, and safe havens where they can develop into professional terrorists, revolutionaries, and guerrilla fighters.

Fifth, the failure to establish democracy with stability in Iraq is likely to discourage future U.S. administrations from pushing their authoritarian allies in the Muslim world to liberalize their political systems and foster inclusion of the Islamist opposition. Moreover, the United States is likely to rely on these regimes for security cooperation and intelligence sharing concerning potential operatives and cells. And the United States is likely to support efforts by these governments to control the spillover effect from Iraq, including displaced refugees who may become recruits for terrorists seeking to attack U.S. targets in the Middle East. Having been bitten once by returnees from Afghanistan during the 1990s, governments in the Muslim world and Europe are likely to adopt repressive strategies against the returnees from Iraq. The persistent authoritarianism in many Muslim countries means that the legitimacy crisis that gave rise to Islamist extremism will continue to inspire future generations of malcontents.

Sixth, persistent violence against the Shia and the Iraqi security forces may encourage Iran to play the role of protector of its coreligionists in Iraq. This scenario resembles what happened in Lebanon during the 1970s and 1980s, when Syria and Israel fought their proxy wars by supporting local militias at the expense of thousands of Lebanese lives. Israel positioned itself as the protector of the Christian Maronites, while Syria and Iran acted as the protector of the Shia by sponsoring Hezbollah. Iran, which continues to support Hezbollah in Lebanon today, has further expanded its sphere of influence into Iraq through its military support to Shia militias. The July–August 2006 war between Hezbollah and Israel demonstrated how local militias are empowered by foreign support, which in turn produces military escalation and unnecessary destruction of civilian populations. Moreover, the uncertain future of Iran's nuclear program means that Iran has the option of utilizing Iraq-based terrorists to strike back at Western powers if the latter choose to further constrain Iran's nuclear ambitions.

The resurgence of Iranian influence is especially troubling for the Salafis because of their intrinsic rejection of Shia Islam as heresy. This situation may force the jihadi Salafis to concentrate their efforts on fighting Shia ascendancy, but it could also generate opportunities for anti-Western recruitment through the claim that the United States and its Western allies have given primacy to the Shia over true believers.

These are mere forecasts; they are by no means inevitable. However, if recent history is our guide, the conjunction of insurgency in Iraq, calls for U.S. disengagement from that country, and pressure on the U.S. administration to abandon its advocacy of democratization in the Muslim world are creating the conditions for the reemergence of al Qaeda as a global jihadist movement after the brief interruption following its demise in Afghanistan.

Paradoxically, the liberation of Iraq from the secular tyranny of Baathism has emboldened the would-be tyrants of al Qaeda. Jihadi Salafis have been using the insurgency in Iraq to argue that only through Islamic militancy will Muslims achieve victory over the United States and its local collaborators. By obstructing the plans of the only remaining superpower, global jihadists appear to be heroic, courageous, righteous, self-sacrificing, and the only source of resistance in the Muslim world. Just as the Afghan fighters humiliated the superior military of the Soviet Union by forcing it to retreat after nearly a decade of occupation, jihadists will use their impending victory in Iraq to deliver the message that Muslims can triumph if they exhibit determination and continue with the strategy of martyrdom. Iraq, therefore, will not only be a locale where jihadists can converge for training in the ways and means of jihad; it also will reinforce their mythology of victory achieved through patient struggle and faithful sacrifice.

NOTES

1. Pape, *Dying to Win*, 23.

2. Emile Durkheim, *Suicide: A Study in Sociology* (New York: The Free Press, 1951). The book was first published in 1897.

3. For additional criticisms of the occupation thesis, see Assaf Moghadam, "Suicide Terrorism, Occupation, and the Globalization of Martyrdom: A Critique of *Dying to Win*," *Studies in Conflict and Terrorism* 29: 707–29.

4. Bloom, *Dying to Kill*, 94.

5. Speckhard, Tarabrina, Krasnov, and Akhmedova, "Research Note: Observations of Suicidal Terrorist in Action"; Speckhard and Akhmedova, "The Making of a Martyr."

6. Gamson, Fireman, and Rytina, *Encounters with Unjust Authority*; Passy, "Social Networks Matter."

7. Israeli, *Islamikaze*; Shay, *The Shahids*; Habeck, *Knowing the Enemy.*

8. Hafez, *Manufacturing Human Bombs*; Hafez, "Rationality, Culture, and Structure in the Making of Suicide Bombers"; also see Moghadam, "Palestinian Suicide Terrorism in the Second Intifada."

9. On this point, I am indebted to discussions with Reuven Paz, a leading Israeli analyst of Islamic movements and the global jihadists, at the "Transnational Violence in the Persian Gulf" workshop at MIT's Center for International Studies, April 20–21, 2006.

10. The *Encyclopedia of Jihad*, written in Arabic, is a lengthy textbook for jihadists-in-training, with religious messages and information on, inter alia, building explosive devices, conducting assassinations, and communicating secretly. It contains the experiences of jihadists in Afghanistan as well as excerpts from military manuals from various countries.

11. Raymond Bonner, "The Struggle for Iraq: Weapons, Iraqi Arms Caches Cited in Attacks," *New York Times*, October 14, 2003; Michael Moss, "How Iraq Police Reform Became Casualty of War," *New York Times*, May 22, 2006;

Michael Moss and David Rohde, "Misjudgments Marred U.S. Plans for Iraqi Police," *New York Times*, May 21, 2006.

12. Dexter Filkins, "Votes Counted. Deals Made. Chaos Wins," *New York Times*, April 30, 2006.

13. Thomas E. Ricks, "Lessons Learned in Iraq Show up in Army Classes: Culture Shifts to Counterinsurgency," *Washington Post*, January 21, 2006; Thomas E. Ricks, "U.S. Counterinsurgency Academy Giving Officers a New Mind-Set: Course in Iraq Stresses the Cultural, Challenges the Conventional," *Washington Post*, February 21, 2006; Thom Shanker, "U.S. Changes Guidelines for Troops to Lessen Everyday Tensions with Iraqi Civilians," *New York Times*, May 2, 2006.

14. Louise Roug, "U.S. to Restrict Iraqi Police; Military oversight will be bolstered in response to reports of prisoner abuse, reasserting American authority over security forces," *Los Angeles Times*, December 30, 2005; Paul Richter, "U.S. Goals Adapt to New Iraq; Disappointed with vote results, Washington is now focused on keeping security forces out of the hands of religious or nationalist parties," *Los Angeles Times*, January 21, 2006.

15. Louise Roug, "Iraq Sunnis Seek Police Jobs after Attack," *Los Angeles Times*, January 13, 2006; Edward Wong, "U.S. Is Seeking Better Balance in Iraqi Police," *New York Times*, March 7, 2006; Michael R. Gordon, "Wary Iraqis Are Recruited as Policemen," *New York Times*, July 24, 2006.

16. Andy Mosher, "An Ebb Proves No Respite in Violent Summer in Iraq," *Washington Post*, July 21, 2006; Sudarsan Raghavan, "Distrust Breaks the Bonds of a Baghdad Neighborhood: In Mixed Area, Violence Defies Peace Efforts," *Washington Post*, September 27, 2006.

17. Muhammad Madhloum, "A Scary Scenario for Civil War in Iraq" (Arabic), *Al-Hayat* (London), June 21, 2006.

18. Solomon Moore, "Killings Linked to Shiite Squads in Iraqi Police Force; With loyalties to banned paramilitary groups, the fighters have kidnapped, tortured and slain Sunnis, officials and witnesses say," *Los Angeles Times*, November 29, 2005; Megan K. Stack, "Neighborhood Militias Add Another Armed Layer; Fearing Shiite attacks, Sunni Arabs in Iraq are organizing fighters and storing guns in mosques," *Los Angeles Times*, April 1, 2006; Dan Murphy and Awadh al-Taiee, "Seeking Safety, Iraqis Turn to Militias," *Christian Science Monitor*, July 24, 2006.

19. Edward Wong, "Fearful Iraqis Avoid Mosques as Attacks Rise," *New York Times*, August 19, 2006.

20. Sudarsan Raghavan, "At Checkpoints in Baghdad, Disguise Is a Lifesaving Ritual," *Washington Post*, September 29, 2006.

21. Thomas E. Ricks, "Military Plays up Role of Zarqawi: Jordanian Painted as Foreign Threat to Iraq's Stability," *Washington Post*, April 10, 2006.

22. Ian Fisher and Edward Wong, "Iraq's Rebellion Develops Signs of Internal Rift," *New York Times*, July 11, 2004; Thanassis Cambanis, "Sunni Leaders Press Insurgents to Fight U.S. Forces, Not Iraqis," *Boston Globe*, July 24, 2004; Karl Vick, "Insurgent Alliance Is Fraying in Fallujah; Locals, Fearing Invasion, Turn against Foreign Arabs," *Washington Post*, October 13, 2004; Ellen Knickmeyer, "Zarqawi Followers Clash with Local Sunnis," *Washington Post*, May 29, 2005.

23. *Al-Hayat*, "Six Armed Groups Form 'Popular Cells' for Defense of Anbar" (Arabic), January 23, 2006; OSC, "Anbar Revenge Brigade Claims Killing Five Elements of al-Qa`ida Organization in the Land of the Two Rivers," March 14, 2006; OSC, "Iraq: Killings Spur Al-Anbar Tribes into Action Against al-Qa`ida," September 18, 2006.

24. *Al-Hayat*, "American Officials Hold Secret Talks with Tribal Leaders" (Arabic), February 10, 2006; *Al-Hayat*, "Killing of [Tribal Head Hikmat] Mumtaz Precipitated Open War on al Qaeda" (Arabic), February 18, 2006.

25. OSC, "Ansar al-Sunnah Group Rejects Iraqi National Reconciliation Plan," June 28, 2006; OSC, "Mujahidin Shura Council Responds to National Reconciliation Plan," June 27, 2006; OSC, "Islamic Resistance Movement Renounces Iraqi National Reconciliation Initiative," June 27, 2006; OSC, "'National, Pan-Arab, and Islamic Front' Rejects Reconciliation Plan," June 28, 2006; OSC, "Iraqi Ba'th Party Issues Statement Criticizing Call for National Reconciliation," June 28, 2006; OSC, "Al-Mujahidin Army Explains Stand on National Reconciliation Initiative," June 28, 2006; OSC, "Salah al-Din al-Ayyubi Brigades Reject Al-Maliki's Plan for National Reconciliation," June 29, 2006; OSC, "Islamic Army in Iraq Issues Statement on Future of Iraqi Coalition Government," June 30, 2006.

26. The veiled threat was delivered on September 28, 2006, in a twenty-minute audio recording entitled "Come to an agreement between us and you," in which al-Muhajir offered to forgive tribal leaders who had turned against the MSC and declared, "We will not harm you provided that you declare your repentance among your tribes" (audio translated by the author).

27. In April 2006 a classified National Intelligence Estimate report, which contains the consensus view of sixteen U.S. intelligence agencies, confirmed earlier speculation by critics of the war on Iraq that the ongoing conflict has given life to a new generation of global Islamic insurgents. The report was leaked to the *New York Times* in September 2006.

28. For an excellent analysis of the contemporary Islamist movement in Saudi Arabia and its suppression by the Saudi regime during the early 1990s, see International Crisis Group, "Saudi Arabia Backgrounder: Who Are the Islamists," *ICG Middle East Report* 31, September 21, 2004.

29. Hafez, *Why Muslims Rebel*; Gerges, *The Far Enemy*.

30. Muhammad Salah, *The Facts of the Jihad Years: The Journey of the Arab Afghans* (Arabic. Cairo: Kulud lil-Nashr, 2001); Muhammad Muqadam, "The Journey of 'Algerian Afghans' from the [Armed Islamic] Group to the 'al Qaeda' Organization" (Arabic), *Al-Hayat*, November 23–29, 2001, seven parts; Doug Struck, Howard Schneider, Karl Vick, and Peter Baker, "Borderless Network of Terror," *Washington Post*, March 26, 2002.

31. Ahmed Rashid, *Taliban: Militant Islam, Oil, and Fundamentalism in Central Asia* (New Haven, Conn.: Yale University Press, 2000); Bergen, *The Osama bin Laden I Know*.

32. Griff Witte, "Afghans Confront Surge in Violence: Foreign Support Seen Behind Attacks That Mimic Those in Iraq," *Washington Post*, November 28, 2005; Ron Synovitz, "Afghanistan: Are Militants Copying Iraqi Insurgents' Suicide Tactics?" *Radio Free Europe/Radio Liberty*, January 17, 2006.

LIST OF SUNNI INSURGENT GROUPS IN IRAQ, 2003–2006

The names below appeared at one time or another in communiqués issued by insurgents claiming responsibility for attacks on a variety of targets. The names of some brigades appear under different groupings, suggesting two plausible scenarios: Multiple insurgent groups are claiming responsibility for attacks by a single brigade, or brigades that operated under the name of one group shifted allegiance to another group. A third explanation could be that some groups unintentionally adopted the same title.

Indentation of the group name implies that the brigade or squadron has taken responsibility for attacks under the entity above it or in the same communiqué. It does not necessarily mean that these groups constitute a unified movement or organization.

1. Ansar al-Islam

2. Leaders of the Resistance and Liberation (or the General Command of the Iraqi Armed Forces, Resistance and Liberation, Baathist)

   The following groups sometimes appear separately and sometimes under the title of the Leaders of the Resistance and Liberation, or the General Command of the Armed Forces. The lack of consistency in how they appear suggests that they began as separate groups with little real coordination across groups.

   • Al-Faruq Brigades (or the Command of the Jihadi Faruq Brigades), the suicide brigade of the Islamic Movement of Iraq (Baathist)
   • Al-Hussein Brigades (or Al-Hussein Groups)
   • Iraqi Armed Forces General Command
   • Liberation Brigades
   • Republican Guards

- Fedayeen Saddam
- Fedayeen Iraq

3. Front for the Liberation of Iraq

4. The Iraqi Resistance Battalions

5. Al-Khalil Battalions

6. Al-Awdah Brigades

7. The Iraqi Patriotic Fedayeen Front

8. The Iraqi Jihad Movement

9. Muhammad's Army (Baathists)
   - Awdah Brigade (Returnees Brigade)
   - Fedayeen Brigade
   - Armed Forces General Command
   - Mujahidin Brigade

10. General Command of the Mujahidin of the Armed Forces (Baathists)
    - Azzat Al-Duri Mujahidin Operation Division—Diyala
    - Al-Rashid Operations Command
      Al-Imam Al-Shafii Brigade
    - Diyala Organization's Al-Mujahidin Branch Command
      The Martyr Harun Company
      Balad Ruz Branch
    - Amuriyah Forces Mujahidin Command (or Amuriyah Operations Command)
      Abdullah Bin Masud Brigade
      Imam Al-Husayn Bin Ali Brigade
      Al-Shaykh Abdel Qadir Al-Kaylani Brigade
      Muhammad Al-Qasim Brigade
    - Al-Yarmuk Operations Command
    - Al-Qaqa Brigade
    - Saddam's Fedayeen Brigades

11. Mujahidin Shura Council (merged into the Islamic State of Iraq, October 2006)
    - Al Qaeda fi Bilad Al-Rafidayyn (al Qaeda in the Land of Two Rivers, or al Qaeda in Iraq; previously Al-Tawhid Wal-Jihad, or Monotheism and Holy War)
      Abu Ans Al-Shami Brigades

Umar Brigade
Abu Hafs Al-Masri Brigades
Al-Qaid Abu-Sufyan Al-Zaydi Brigade
Khalid Ibn Al-Walid Brigade
Abi Al-Yaman Al-Madaini Brigade
Al Qaeda Brigade
Al-Bara Bin Malik Battalion (or Al-Bara Bin Malik
Martyrdom Brigade)
Martyrs Brigade (or Martyrdom Brigade)
Sayf Al-Haq Battalion
Al-Miqdad Ibn Al-Aswad Brigade (or Al-Miqdad Platoon)
Islamic Wrath Brigade
Abu Basir Brigade
Al-Furqan Brigade
Al-Fatah Brigade or Battalions
Al-Zubair Bin Al-Awam Brigade
Abu-Ubaydah Ibn Al-Jarrah Brigade
Al-Faruq Battalions
Abu Mariyah Brigade
Uthman Bin Afan Brigade
Al-Mujahidin Brigade
Shaykh Al-Ayiri Brigade
Abdel Aziz Al-Muqrin Brigade
Al-Qiqa Brigade
Jamaat Al-Bara Al-Mujahida
Al-Rayat Al-Sud (The Black Banners)
Rayat Al-Haq (The Banners of Truth)
- Victorious Sect
Ibn Taymiyya Brigades
- The Monotheism Supporters Brigades (Saraya Ansar Al-Tawhid)
- The Islamic Jihad Brigades (Saraya Al-Jihad Al-Islami)
- The Al-Ghuraba (Foreigners) Brigades
- The Al-Ahwal (Fear) Brigades
- Ahl Al-Sunna Wal Jamaah Army
Al-Falluja Brigades
Yathrib Brigade
Al-Duluiyah Brigade
Sayf Al-Haq Brigade

- Al-Murabitun Brigades
12. Ansar Al-Sunna Group (previously Ansar Al-Sunna Army)
    - Al-Firqa Al-Mansoura
        Siryat Hamza
    - Zi Al-Nurayn Brigade of Ansar Al-Sunna (or Dhi Al-Nurayn Brigade)
        Shahid Muhammad Unit
        Abdallah Bin Zubayr Brigade
    - Martyrs Brigade of Ansar Al-Sunna
    - Umar Ibn Al-Khattab Brigade
    - Al-Mustafa Brigade
        Al-Asnad
    - Zayd Bin Al-Khattab Brigade
    - Khalid Ibn Al-Walid Brigade
    - Amr Bin Al-As Brigade
    - Al-Qaqa Brigade
13. The Islamic Army in Iraq
    - Islamic Army Brigades
    - Jund Allah Brigade (God's Soldiers Brigade)
14. The Mujahidin Army in Iraq
15. The Islamic Resistance Movement (or National Islamic Resistance Movement)—1920 Revolution Brigades
    - Al-Jihad Battalions
    - Saad Bin Abi Waqqas Brigades
    - Saad Bin Muath Battalion
    - Al-Hasan Bin Ali Brigades
    - Abdallah Bin Mubarak Unit
    - Khalid Ibn Al-Walid Brigades
    - Al-Zubayr Bin Al-Awam Brigade
    - Al-Zilazal Brigade
    - Kirkuk Brigades
    - Suqur Al-Islam Brigades (or Battalion)
    - Badr Al-Kubra Company
    - Hamat Al-Islam Company
    - Ayn Jalut fi Haditha Company
    - Abu Basir Brigade (or Abi Basir Battalion)
    - Ali Bin Abi Talib Battalion

- Al-Fardus Battalion
- Al-Shahid Ahmad Yasin Battalion
- Muslim Bin Uqayl Battalion
- Al-Fath Battalion
- Mahmud Shayt Khattab Battalion
- Nur Al-Din Battalion
- Salah Al-Din Al-Ayubi Battalion
- Sayf Al-Haq Battalion
- Al-Hazm Battalion
- Al-Faruq Umar Bin Al-Khattab Battalion
- Jafar Al-Tayar Brigade

16. The Islamic Front for Iraqi Resistance—Salah Al-Din Al-Ayoubi Brigades

17. Conquest Army or Conqueror Army (Jaish Al-Fatihin)

18. Mujahidin Central Command

19. Ali Bin Abi Talib Brigades

20. Iraq Liberation Army
    - Al-Imam Muslim Bin Aqil Brigade

21. Katib Al Al-Bayt Al-Salafiyya
    - Jamaat Jaysh Al-Mujahidin

22. Iraq Mujahidin Organization
    - Al-Rafah Brigade
    - Al-Madinah Al-Munawarah Brigade

23. Sunnah Lions Army
    - Abu Bakr Al-Siddiq Brigade (or Abu Bakr Al-Siddiq Salafi Army)

24. Iraqi Jihadist Leagues
    - Al-Zubayr Bin Al-Awam Brigade
    - Al-Faruq Brigade
    - Al-Tawhid Wal-Jihad Brigade

25. Iraqi National Alliance

26. Islamic Jihad Army
    - Iraqi Islamic Army
    - Islamic Jihad Brigades

27. Iraqi Response Brigades

28. Jamaat Jund Al-Sahaba (The Soldiers of the Prophet's Companions Groups)

29. Sarayya Suyuf Al-Haq (The Swords of Truth Brigades)

30. The Islamic Badr Brigades

31. Al-Imam Hassan Al-Basri Brigades

32. Ansar Al-Jihad Group

33. Imam Al-Mujahidin Brigades

34. Al-Rashidin Army
    - Ali Al-Hadi Brigade
    - Dhu (or Dhi) Al-Nurayn Brigade
    - Khalid Ibn Al-Walid Brigade
    - Uways Al-Qirani Brigade
    - Imam Zain Al-Abidin Ibn Ali Brigade (joined in May 2006)
    - Muslim Bin Aqil Brigades (joined in May 2006)
    - Sayf Allah Al-Maslul Brigade
    - Muhammadiyyah Brigades

35. The Islamic Movement of Iraqi Mujahidin

36. Al-Fuhud Al-Sawda (The Black Panthers)

37. Al-Sawda (Black) Brigades

38. Al-Sirat Al-Mustaqim (The Straight Path)

39. Al-Fedayeen Al-Ahrar (The Free Fedayeen)

40. Fedayeen Muhammad

41. Muslim Youth

42. Jihad for the Liberation of Iraq

43. The Unification Front for the Liberation of Iraq

44. Armed Iraqi National Resistance Front

45. The Command Committee for the Nasirite Organization in Iraq
    - The Liberation Group

46. Mujahidin Battalions of the Salafi Group in Iraq

47. Saddam's Knights

48. The Jihadi Salafi Group

49. The National Organization for the Liberation of Iraq

50. Armed Vanguards of Muhammad's Second Army

51. The Just Punishment Brigades

52. Dhu Al-Fiqar Brigade

53. Islamic Vanguards Movement of Iraq

54. Jamaat Jund Al-Sahahbah

55. Al-Durah Operations Command

56. The Lions of Justice Battalion

NAMES AND NATIONALITIES OF KNOWN SUICIDE BOMBERS IN IRAQ

This list contains the names and countries of origin of 102 known suicide bombers in Iraq. Many more are not yet known and may never be known. Three of the known bombers are females. The bombers came from the following countries: Saudi Arabia (44), Italy (8), Kuwait (7), Iraq (7), Syria (6), Libya (3), Jordan (3), Belgium (2), France (2), Spain (2), Egypt (2), Lebanon (1), Tunisia (1), Morocco (1), Britain (1), Turkey (1), and Unknown (11).

Name	Country
1 Adnan, Muhammad Zayd Muhammad (Abu Umayer al-Shami)	Unknown
2 Afalah, Mohammed	Spain (Moroccan)
3 al-Abdo, Uruha (Abu Abdel Karim)	Syria
4 al-Ajami, Khaled (Abu Al-Zubayr al-Kuwaiti)	Kuwait
5 al-Anizi, Ahmed (Abu Ma`az)	Iraq
6 al-Anizi, Rawaf	Kuwait
7 al-Ansari, Abu-Basir	Unknown
8 al-Ashqari, Ans Jamal (Abu al-Bara al-Urduni)	Jordan
9 al-Bahili, Naser Bin Fahd (Abu Fahd)	Saudi Arabia
10 al-Banna, Raed Mansoor (Abu Radwan al-Urduni)	Jordan
11 al-Baqmi, Abu Zayad	Saudi Arabia
12 al-Dhaleai, Wail	Britain (Yemeni)
13 al-Dousari, Abu Abdullah (brother of Abu Harith)	Saudi Arabia
14 al-Dousari, Abu Harith	Saudi Arabia

	Name	Country
15	al-Dulaymi, Widad Jamil Jasim (female suicide bomber)	Iraq
16	al-Fahmi, Suluh Salih	Saudi Arabia
17	al-Falaj, Adel Bin Ali	Saudi Arabia
18	al-Ghamidi, Ahmed Said Ahmed	Saudi Arabia
19	al-Ghuninam, Sami Bin Sulieman	Saudi Arabia
20	al-Hajari, Mansoor (Abu-Wadha al-Kuwaiti)	Kuwait
21	al-Halil, Mohammed	Saudi Arabia
22	al-Harbi, Faris Abdullah	Saudi Arabia
23	al-Hijazi, Abi Amama	Saudi Arabia
24	al-Hijazi, Abu Hurayrah	Unknown
25	al-Iraqi, Abu Ayoub	Iraq
26	al-Iraqi, Yassin Jarrad	Iraq
27	al-Jumayli, Abu Amar	Iraq
28	al-Libi, Abu Abdullal	Libya
29	al-Libi, Abu Bara	Libya
30	al-Maghribi, Abu Osama	Morocco
31	al-Misri, Abu Farid	Italy (Egyptian)
32	al-Misri, Abu Omar	Egypt
33	al-Muhajir, Abu Abdullah	Egypt
34	al-Muhajir, Abu-Zubayr	Unknown
35	al-Mutayri, Abu al-Walid	Saudi Arabia
36	al-Mutayri, Haydarah	Saudi Arabia
37	al-Mutayri, Majid Bin Sahnt	Saudi Arabia
38	al-Najdi, Abu Abdel Malik	Saudi Arabia
39	al-Najdi, Abu Naim	Saudi Arabia
40	al-Najdi, Abu Nur	Saudi Arabia
41	al-Najdi, Abu Ubayda (Abdullah)	Saudi Arabia
42	al-Nufayi, Abu al-Zubayr	Unknown
43	al-Qahtani, Abu Ans al-Tahami	Saudi Arabia
44	al-Qarnamri, Hamoud `Ayad	Unknown
45	al-Qarni, Abdullah al-Buhayri	Saudi Arabia
46	al-Qurayshi, Abdul Rahman Saad (Abu Saad al-Makki)	Saudi Arabia

Name	Country
47 al-Rahimi, Ahmed (or Ahmed al-Fawal Abu Hassan)	Saudi Arabia
48 al-Rashid, Abdel Aziz Hamd	Saudi Arabia
49 al-Rashid, Yazid Bin Qayid (Abu Juhayman)	Saudi Arabia
50 al-Rumi, Fahd (Abu Amshi)	Unknown
51 al-Ruwayli, Farhan Mayes	Unknown
52 al-Ruwayli, Jamil Battah	Unknown
53 al-Sa`ayri, Abu Mashari	Saudi Arabia
54 al-Saraqibi, Warid al-Qudur	Syria
55 al-Sarmini, Muhammad Sha`aban Abu Abdullah	Saudi Arabia
56 al-Shamali, Abu-Muawiyah	Saudi Arabia
57 al-Shamari, Abd-al-Aziz (Abu-Ahmad al-Kuwaiti)	Kuwait
58 al-Shamari, Abdullah al-Zubai	Unknown
59 al-Shamari, Abu Abd	Unknown
60 al-Shamari, Abu Musab	Saudi Arabia
61 al-Shamari, Fahd Nayef al-Shulaqi (Abu Amshi al-Shamari)	Saudi Arabia
62 al-Shamari, Khaled Bin Khalaf al-Sulayti (Abu Mutib)	Saudi Arabia
63 al-Shamari, Majid Salamah al-Haqs	Saudi Arabia
64 al-Shamari, Muhammad Bin Rahayman al-Tawmi (Abu Salih)	Saudi Arabia
65 al-Shamari, Nawaf bin Mishl Al Khalil	Saudi Arabia
66 al-Shamari, Nusha Mujalli Munayfir (female suicide bomber)	Iraq
67 al-Shamari, Walid al-Asmar	Saudi Arabia
68 al-Shayi`a, Ahmed Bin Abdullah Bin Abdel Rahman	Saudi Arabia
69 al-Shukri, Salih (Abu Ibrahim al-Makki)	Saudi Arabia
70 al-Subay'i, Nayif Salih (Abu-Salih al-Kuwaiti)	Kuwait
71 al-Suri, Abu Khaled or Abu Khaled al-Falastini	Syria
72 al-Suri, Abu Muhammad	Syria

Name	Country
73 al-Suri, Abu Ubayda	Syria
74 al-Suri, Abu Umayr	Syria
75 al-Tamimi, Abdelaziz Bin Saud Bin Mahmoud al-Gharbi al-Mufidi	Saudi Arabia
76 al-Tunisi, Abu Samir	Tunisia
77 al-Turki, Abu Abdullah (Azzad Akanji)	Turkey
78 al-Urduni, Abu Sulaiman	Jordan
79 al-Usaymi, Nawaf	Saudi Arabia
80 al-Usaymi, Safr bin Matr	Saudi Arabia
81 al-Utaybi, Abdel Rahman Bin-Shuja (Abu-Awf al-Kuwaiti)	Kuwait
82 al-Utaybi, Azzam Turki al-Muraybadh	Saudi Arabia
83 al-Utaybi, Muqrin Majid Shayb	Saudi Arabia
84 al-Utaybi, Nashi Dhayb	Saudi Arabia
85 al-Zahrani, Fawaz Hussein	Saudi Arabia
86 al-Zayidi, Khaled	Libya
87 Badjoudj, Abdelhalim	France (Algerian)
88 Bazis, Idris	France (Algerian)
89 Belgacem, Bellil	Spain (Algerian)
90 Ben Amor, Muhammad	Italy (Tunisian)
91 Degauque, Muriel (female suicide bomber)	Belgium
92 Goris, Issam (foiled bomber killed by U.S. forces)	Belgium (Moroccan)
93 Khalifa, Mohammed	Italy (Tunisian)
94 Khalifa, Muhammad	Lebanon
95 Marwan, Abu Ubeida	Iraq
96 Morchidi, Kamal	Italy (Moroccan)
97 Nassim, Fahdal	Italy (Algerian)
98 Rihani, Lotfi (Abdel Rahman)	Italy (Tunisian)
99 Saadi, Fadhal	Italy (Tunisian)
100 Sa'id al-Hajari (Abu-Hamza al-Kuwaiti)	Kuwait
101 Sayf al-Umma al-Mankuba (not the actual name; real name unknown)	Saudi Arabia
102 Waddani, Habib (Said)	Italy (Tunisian)

ZARQAWI'S MEN

These individuals were with Abu Musab al-Zarqawi in the Herat, Afghanistan, military training camp during 1999–2001. All played a role in the Iraqi insurgency.

Name	Association with Abu Musab al-Zarqawi
Khaled Mustafa al-Aruri (Abu Qassam or Abu Ashraf)	Zarqawi's brother-in-law and one of his closest associates in Afghanistan between 1989 and 1993 and in the Herat camp between 2000 and 2001. He was also from Zarqa and in a Jordanian prison with Zarqawi between 1993 and 1999. He was a key liaison between Zarqawi in Afghanistan and Ansar al-Islam in northern Iraq in 2001 and became Zarqawi's lieutenant in Iraq before being arrested in Iran.
Abdel Hadi Ahmad Mahmoud Daghlas (Abu Ubaydah; Abu Muhammad al-Sham)	Spent time in a Jordanian prison with Zarqawi. Along with al-Aruri, he liaised between Zarqawi and Ansar al-Islam in 2001. He was also one of Zarqawi's commanders in Iraq and was killed there.
Raed Khuraysat (Abu Abdel Rahman Al-Shami); Mutasim Musa Abdallah Muhammad al-Darikah; Mahmoud Muhammad Al-Nusur; and Ibrahim Khuraysat	All four took part in the creation of an Islamist group known as Jund al-Islam in September 2001 in Kurdistan (northern Iraq). Jund al-Islam was later renamed Ansar al-Islam.

Name	Association with Abu Musab al-Zarqawi
Nidal Arabiyat	Specialized in car bombs and was killed in Baghdad in February 2004.
Nidal Mohammed al-Arabi (Abu Hamza Mohammed)	A Jordanian who specialized in car bombs and was killed in Iraq by coalition forces in 2003.
Muammar al-Jaghbir (Moammar Ahmed Yussef al-Jaghbir); Ali Mustafa Yousef Siam; Salim Bin Suwaid; and Yasir Farayhat	Al-Jaghbir was from Salt, Jordan. He and Siam were arrested in Iraq and sent back to Jordan in 2004 in connection with the October 2002 assassination of Lawrence Foley, head of USAID in Amman. In 2002 Suwaid (Libyan) and Farayhat (Jordanian) confessed to killing Foley and said they had come from Iraq after planning the operation with Zarqawi in the Kurdistan region. Both were executed in 2006.
Abu-Khbab al-Falastini	Born and raised in Jordan, he joined the fight against the Soviets in Afghanistan and spent a great deal of time in Jalalabad. He returned to Jordan but later left for Turkey because he was wanted by the Jordanian authorities. He was arrested in Azerbaijan, presumably on his way to fight in Chechnya. He went back to Afghanistan after being released from jail. Among the first to join the jihad in Iraq, he was killed there in a raid by coalition forces.
Yassin Jerad	An Iraqi and the father of Zarqawi's second wife, he is believed to have carried out the suicide operation that killed the Shia leader Muhammad Baqir al-Hakim in Najaf in late 2003.

AL QAEDA'S EVOLUTION IN IRAQ

1999–2001	**Tawhid wal-Jihad in Afghanistan** Jordanian-born Abu Musab al-Zarqawi and his associates set up the Tawhid wal-Jihad military camp in Herat, Afghanistan, for training radical militants from the Middle East.
2001–2003	**Ansar al-Islam** Mullah Fatih Krekar, leader of the Ansar al-Islam movement in the Kurdish region of northern Iraq, agrees to host militants fleeing from Afghanistan following the collapse of the Taliban regime. Zarqawi and his Tawhid wal-Jihad group seek refuge in the Ansar al-Islam camps.
2003–2004	**Tawhid wal-Jihad in Iraq** Zarqawi emerges as an insurgent leader of the Tawhid wal-Jihad group in Iraq after the rapid demise of the Ansar al-Islam movement. Tawhid wal-Jihad captures the spotlight through gruesome suicide attacks and beheadings.
October 2004	**Al Qaeda in Iraq** Zarqawi changes the name of his Tawhid wal-Jihad group to al Qaeda in the Land of the Two Rivers (al Qaeda in Iraq). Two months later, Osama bin Laden publicly gives Zarqawi his blessings.

January 2006	**Mujahidin Shura Council** Al Qaeda in Iraq merges with several smaller groups to form the Mujahidin Shura Council. Zarqawi maintains leadership of al Qaeda in Iraq, but the official leader of the new Council is Abdallah Ibn-Rashid al-Baghdadi.
October 2006	**Islamic State of Iraq** After Zarqawi's death, the Mujahidin Shura Council announces the formation of the Islamic State of Iraq under the leadership of Abu Umar al-Baghdadi. The Mujahidin Shura Council ceases to exist as a separate entity.

B

Baathists. *See also* Ideological Baathists;
   Islamic nationalists
   de-Baathification policies and, 37,
      41, 42, 50–51, 221
   main groups of, 63
   number of members, 49
   suicide attack responsibility claims,
      93
Badjoudj, Abdelhalim, 202–203
Badr, Battle of, 153–154
Badr Corps
   infiltration of the interior ministry,
      42
   Islamic Army in Iraq view of, 80
   justification for violence against,
      122, 136 *n*11
   Shia militias of, 122
   view of as collaborators with the
      coalition, 122, 135 *n*9
Baghdad
   counterinsurgency operations, 95
   suicide bomb attacks, 94–95, 96,
      110, 207, ix
al-Baghdad, Abu Hamza
   leadership of, 54
al-Baghdadi, Abu Umar, 258
Bakr, Abu, 181
Bali
   suicide bombings, 225
Bandura, Albert
   moral disengagement concept,
      119–121
al-Banna, Raed Mansoor, 171
Baquba
   counterinsurgency operations, 95
Bara, Abu
   biography of, 151
al-Bara Bin-Malik Brigade
   description, 64
   leadership of, 121

al-Barqawi, Issam Muhammad Tahir,
   172
Barra, Abu, 189
Barzani, Massoud, 173
Baz, Sheikh Abdel Aziz bin, 65, 129
al-Bazi, Sheikh Hikmat Mumtaz, 229
Belgian-Spanish network
   background of, 195
   Belgium-based network with links
      to Spain, Syria, Morocco, and
      Iraq (chart), 197
   biographical information on suicide
      bombers, 196–202, 209 *n*19,
      210 *n*22, 210 *n*26
   Moroccan Islamic Combatant
      Group and, 198–199
Belgium. *See also* Belgian-Spanish
   network
   percentage of suicide bombers from,
      189
Belhadj, Maymoun
   biographical information, 196–199,
      201, 202, 209 *n*19
Benchellali, Menad, 204
Bensakhria, Mohammed, 204
Bentaieb, 201
Benyettou, Farid, 203
Berg, Nicholas, 235
Beslan, Russia, hostage crisis, 12, 28
   *n*22
bin Laden, Sheikh Osama
   benefits from the failure of Islamist
      insurgencies, 233–234
   exile of, 233
   interest in fighting the "far enemy"
      represented by the United
      States, 78
   original home of, 74
   sanctioning of suicide attacks, 218
   suicide attack directions, 121
   support for Zarqawi, 176, 257
   training camps in Afghanistan and,
      234

system reintegration strategy,
36–46, 55–56, 92–93
toppling of Saddam Hussein's
regime and, 39
ultimate goal of, 36, 38
Islamic State of Iraq
formation of, 258
Italian network
Ansar al-Islam links, 205–207, 210
*n*35
Division for General Investigations
and Operations and, 205–206
key figures, 210 *n*35
Tunisian origin of bombers, 205
Italy. *See also* Italian network
Ansar al-Islam cell based in Sorgane,
205
Division for General Investigations
and Operations, 205–206
number of suicide bombers from,
205

J

al-Jaafari, Ibrahim, 145
Japanese kamikaze pilots
compared with suicide bombers, 6–7
al-Jazairi, Abbas, 199
al-Jazairi, Mustapha, 198
JCB. *See* Joint Coordination Bureau for
Jihad Groups
Jemaah Islamiah
al Qaeda training camps and, 24
"Jihad in Iraq: Hopes and Dangers," 74
Jihadi Salafis
anti-Shia views, x, 70, 73, 75, 78–79,
86 *n*26
compared with ideological Baathists
and Islamic nationalists, 72,
78–82, 223

coordination and cooperation with
Islamic nationalists and
Ideological Baathists, 52–55
dehumanization of targets of
violence, 120
differences between Islamic Army in
Iraq and, 79–82
foreign members, 36, 71
"humiliations" and "crusades"
against Islam and, 75, 122–123,
134, 219
ideological commitment to
establishing an Islamic state,
36, 90, 237
ideological justifications for suicide
attacks, 117
importance of Iraq for the global
jihad, 74–75, 237
Islamic prohibition against suicide
and, 129–131
justification for killing human
shields, 133–134
justifications for killing civilians,
131–132, 134
justifications for suicide attacks
compared with justifications by
Hamas and Hezbollah, 117
labeling of suicide attacks as
"martyrdom operations," 129
major groups, 64
martyrdom and, 109–110, 123–125
moral disengagement and, 118–121
presence in Jordan, 171–172
pressure by local tribes to halt
suicide attacks, 230
prohibitions against Muslims killing
themselves or other Muslims
and, 125, 134, 136 *n*16
reasons for suicide attacks, 109–110
reasons for the strength of, x
refusal to support Hezbollah, 79
religious justifications for suicide
attacks, 123–125

ABOUT THE AUTHOR

Mohammed M. Hafez is a visiting professor of political science at the University of Missouri in Kansas City. He is the author of *Manufacturing Human Bombs: The Making of Palestinian Suicide Bombers* (United States Institute of Peace Press, 2006) and *Why Muslims Rebel: Repression and Resistance in the Islamic World* (Lynne Rienner, 2003).

SUICIDE BOMBERS IN IRAQ: THE STRATEGY AND IDEOLOGY OF MARTYRDOM

This book was set in the typeface Adobe Garamond Pro; the display type is Michelangelo and Univers. Cover design by Creative Shop. Interior design by Katharine Moore; page makeup, copyediting, and proofreading by EEI Communications, Inc., Alexandria, Va. Production supervised by Marie Marr Jackson. Linda Rabben was the book's editor.